T0347895

Probabilistic Nodes Combination (PNC) for Object Modeling and Contour Reconstruction

Dariusz Jacek Jakóbczak
Technical University of Koszalin, Poland

A volume in the Advances in
Systems Analysis, Software
Engineering, and High Performance
Computing (ASASEHPC) Book Series

www.igi-global.com

Published in the United States of America by
IGI Global
Information Science Reference (an imprint of IGI Global)
701 E. Chocolate Avenue
Hershey PA, USA 17033
Tel: 717-533-8845
Fax: 717-533-8661
E-mail: cust@igi-global.com
Web site: http://www.igi-global.com

Library of Congress Cataloging-in-Publication Data

Names: Jakobczak, Dariusz Jacek, 1965-
Title: Probabilistic nodes combination (PNC) for object modeling and contour
  reconstruction / by Dariusz Jacek Jakobczak.
Description: Hershey PA : Information Science Reference, [2017] | Includes
  bibliographical references.
Identifiers: LCCN 2017005141| ISBN 9781522525318 (hardcover) | ISBN
  9781522525325 (ebook)
Subjects: LCSH: Curves, Algebraic. | Surfaces, Algebraic. | Geometry,
  Differential. | Geometrical constructions.
Classification: LCC QA643 .J35 2017 | DDC 516.3/52--dc23 LC record available at https://lccn.
loc.gov/2017005141

This book is published in the IGI Global book series Advances in Systems Analysis, Software Engineering, and High Performance Computing (ASASEHPC) (ISSN: 2327-3453; eISSN: 2327-3461)

Advances in Systems Analysis, Software Engineering, and High Performance Computing (ASASEHPC) Book Series

ISSN:2327-3453
EISSN:2327-3461

Editor-in-Chief: Vijayan Sugumaran, Oakland University, USA

MISSION

The theory and practice of computing applications and distributed systems has emerged as one of the key areas of research driving innovations in business, engineering, and science. The fields of software engineering, systems analysis, and high performance computing offer a wide range of applications and solutions in solving computational problems for any modern organization.

The **Advances in Systems Analysis, Software Engineering, and High Performance Computing (ASASEHPC) Book Series** brings together research in the areas of distributed computing, systems and software engineering, high performance computing, and service science. This collection of publications is useful for academics, researchers, and practitioners seeking the latest practices and knowledge in this field.

COVERAGE

- Computer graphics
- Software Engineering
- Human-Computer Interaction
- Metadata and Semantic Web
- Computer System Analysis
- Network Management
- Storage Systems
- Engineering Environments
- Performance Modelling
- Distributed Cloud Computing

IGI Global is currently accepting manuscripts for publication within this series. To submit a proposal for a volume in this series, please contact our Acquisition Editors at Acquisitions@igi-global.com or visit: http://www.igi-global.com/publish/.

Titles in this Series

For a list of additional titles in this series, please visit:
http://www.igi-global.com/book-series/advances-systems-analysis-software-engineering

Model-Based Design for Effective Control System Development
Wei Wu (Independent Researcher, USA)
Information Science Reference ● ©2017 ● 299pp ● H/C (ISBN: 9781522523031) ● US $185.00

Comparative Approaches to Using R and Python for Statistical Data Analysis
Rui Sarmento (University of Porto, Portugal) and Vera Costa (University of Porto, Portugal)
Information Science Reference ● ©2017 ● 197pp ● H/C (ISBN: 9781683180166) ● US $180.00

Developing Service-Oriented Applications Using the Windows Communication Foundation (WCF) Framework
Chirag Patel (Charotar University of Science and Technology, India)
Information Science Reference ● ©2017 ● 487pp ● H/C (ISBN: 9781522519973) ● US $200.00

Resource Management and Efficiency in Cloud Computing Environments
Ashok Kumar Turuk (National Institute of Technology Rourkela, India) Bibhudatta Sahoo (National Institute of Technology Rourkela, India) and Sourav Kanti Addya (National Institute of Technology Rourkela, India)
Information Science Reference ● ©2017 ● 352pp ● H/C (ISBN: 9781522517214) ● US $205.00

Handbook of Research on End-to-End Cloud Computing Architecture Design
Jianwen "Wendy" Chen (IBM, Australia) Yan Zhang (Western Sydney University, Australia) and Ron Gottschalk (IBM, Australia)
Information Science Reference ● ©2017 ● 507pp ● H/C (ISBN: 9781522507598) ● US $325.00

Innovative Research and Applications in Next-Generation High Performance Computing
Qusay F. Hassan (Mansoura University, Egypt)
Information Science Reference ● ©2016 ● 488pp ● H/C (ISBN: 9781522502876) ● US $205.00

For an enitre list of titles in this series, please visit:
http://www.igi-global.com/book-series/advances-systems-analysis-software-engineering

www.igi-global.com

701 East Chocolate Avenue, Hershey, PA 17033, USA
Tel: 717-533-8845 x100 ● Fax: 717-533-8661
E-Mail: cust@igi-global.com ● www.igi-global.com

Table of Contents

Preface.. vi

Chapter 1
Introduction: MHR Method 1

Chapter 2
Probabilistic Nodes Combination (PNC): Formulas and Examples 44

Chapter 3
PNC in 2D Curve Modeling: Interpolation and Extrapolation 87

Chapter 4
Contour Reconstruction: 2D Object Modeling 132

Chapter 5
PNC in 3D Surface Modeling 178

Chapter 6
PNC in 4D Object and Multi-Dimensional Data Modeling.............................209

Chapter 7
Applications of PNC in Numerical Methods 235

Chapter 8
Applications of PNC in Artificial Intelligence..269

About the Author 309

Index.. 310

Preface

Providing relevant and current research, this book and its author's individual publications would be useful for academics, researchers, scholars, and practitioners interested in improving decision making models and business functions.

Probabilistic modeling represents a subject arising in many branches of mathematics, economics and computer science. Such modeling connects pure mathematics with applied sciences. Operations research similarly is situated on the border between pure mathematics and applied sciences. So when probabilistic modeling meets operations research, it is very interesting occasion. Our life and work are impossible without planning, time-tabling, scheduling, decision making, optimization, simulation, data analysis, risk analysis and process modeling. Thus, it is a part of management science or decision science.

This book looks to discuss and address the difficulties and challenges that occur during the process of planning or decision making. The editors have found the chapters that address different aspects of probabilistic modeling, stochastic methods, probabilistic distributions, data analysis, optimization methods, probabilistic methods in risk analysis, and related topics. Additionally, the book explores the impact of such probabilistic modeling with other approaches.

This comprehensive and timely publication aims to be an essential reference source, building on the available literature in the field of probabilistic modeling, operational research, planning and scheduling, data extrapolation in decision making, probabilistic interpolation and extrapolation in simulation, stochastic processes, and decision analysis. It is hoped that this text will provide the resources necessary for economics and management sciences, also for mathematics and computer sciences.

Decision makers, academicians, researchers, advanced-level students, technology developers, and government officials will find this text useful in furthering their research exposure to pertinent topics in operations research and assisting in furthering their own research efforts in this field. Proposed method, called Probabilistic Features Combination (PFC), is the method of 2D curve interpolation and extrapolation using the set of key points (knots or nodes). Nodes can be treated as characteristic points of data for modeling and analyzing. The model of data can be built by choice of probability distribution function and nodes combination. PFC modeling via nodes combination and parameter γ as probability distribution function enables value anticipation in risk analysis and decision making. Two-dimensional curve is extrapolated and interpolated via nodes combination and different functions as discrete or continuous probability distribution functions: polynomial, sine, cosine, tangent, cotangent, logarithm, exponent, arc sin, arc cos, arc tan, arc cot or power function.

Book topics include the following:

- Probabilistic Modeling,
- Operations Research,
- Stochastic Methods,
- Probabilistic Methods in Planning,
- Decision Making,
- Data Analysis,
- Optimization Methods,
- Probabilistic Methods in Risk Analysis,
- Probabilistic Interpolation and Extrapolation,
- Process Modeling,
- Data Simulation,
- Decision Analysis,
- Stochastic Processes,
- Probabilistic Optimization,
- Data Mining,
- Mathematical Modeling,
- Probabilistic Models in Scheduling,
- Time-Tabling,
- Data Extrapolation in Planning and Decision Making.

The chapters are as follows:

1. Introduction: MHR Method,
2. Probabilistic Nodes Combination (PNC): Formulas and Examples,
3. PNC in 2D Curve Modeling: Interpolation and Extrapolation,
4. Contour Reconstruction: 2D Object Modeling,
5. PNC in 3D Surface Modeling,
6. PNC in 4D Object and Multi-Dimensional Data Modeling,
7. Applications of PNC in Numerical Methods,
8. Applications of PNC in Artificial Intelligence.

Risk analysis needs suitable methods of data extrapolation and decision making. Proposed method of Hurwitz-Radon Matrices (MHR) can be used in extrapolation and interpolation of curves in the plane. For example quotations from the Stock Exchange, the market prices or rate of a currency form a curve. This chapter contains the way of data anticipation and extrapolation via MHR method and decision making: to buy or not, to sell or not. Proposed method is based on a family of Hurwitz-Radon (HR) matrices. The matrices are skew-symmetric and possess columns composed of orthogonal vectors. The operator of Hurwitz-Radon (OHR), built from these matrices, is described. Two-dimensional data are represented by the set of curve points. It is shown how to create the orthogonal and discrete OHR and how to use it in a process of data foreseeing and extrapolation. MHR method is interpolating and extrapolating the curve point by point without using any formula or function.

Proposed method, called Probabilistic Nodes Combination (PNC), is the method of 2D curve interpolation and extrapolation using the set of key points (knots or nodes). Nodes can be treated as characteristic points of data for modeling and analyzing. The model of data can be built by choice of probability distribution function and nodes combination. PNC modeling via nodes combination and parameter γ as probability distribution function enables value anticipation in risk analysis and decision making. Two-dimensional curve is extrapolated and interpolated via nodes combination and different functions as discrete or continuous probability distribution functions: polynomial, sine, cosine, tangent, cotangent, logarithm, exponent, arc sin, arc cos, arc tan, arc cot or power function. Novelty of this book consists of two generalizations: generalization of previous MHR method with various nodes combinations and generalization of linear interpolation with different (no basic) probability distribution functions and nodes combinations.

Computer vision needs suitable methods of shape representation and contour reconstruction. One of them, invented by the author and called method of Hurwitz-Radon Matrices (MHR), can be used in representation and reconstruction of shapes of the objects in the plane. Proposed method is based on a family of Hurwitz-Radon (HR) matrices. The matrices are skew-symmetric and possess columns composed of orthogonal vectors. 2D shape is represented by the set of successive nodes. It is shown how to create the orthogonal and discrete OHR operator and how to use it in a process of shape representation and reconstruction. Then MHR method is generalized to Probabilistic Nodes Combination (PNC) method.

This work clarifies the significance and novelty of the proposed method compared to existing methods (for example polynomial interpolations and Bézier curves). Previous published papers of the author were dealing with the method of Hurwitz-Radon Matrices (MHR method). Novelty of this monograph and proposed method consists in the fact that calculations are free from the family of Hurwitz-Radon Matrices. Problem statement of this monograph is: how to reconstruct (interpolate) missing points of 2D curve having the set of interpolation nodes (key points) and using the information about probabilistic distribution of unknown points. For example the simplest basic distribution leads to the easiest interpolation – linear interpolation. Apart from probability distribution, additionally there is the second factor of proposed interpolation method: nodes combination. The simplest nodes combination is zero. Thus proposed curve modeling is based on two agents: probability distribution and nodes combination. Significance of this book consists in generalization for MHR method: the computations are done without matrices in curve fitting and shape modeling, with clear point interpolation formula based on probability distribution function (continuous or discrete) and nodes combination. This book also consists of generalization for linear interpolation with different (no basic) probability distribution functions and nodes combinations. So this book answers the question: "Why and when should we use PNC method?".

Curve interpolation represents one of the most important problems in mathematics and computer science: how to model the curve via discrete set of two-dimensional points? Also the matter of shape representation (as closed curve - contour) and curve parameterization is still opened. For example pattern recognition, signature verification or handwriting identification problems are based on curve modeling via the choice of key points. So interpolation is not only a pure mathematical problem but important task in computer vision and artificial intelligence. The monograph wants to approach a problem of curve modeling by characteristic points. Proposed method relies on nodes combination and functional modeling of curve points situated between the basic set of key points. The functions that are used in calculations represent whole family of elementary functions with inverse functions: polynomials, trigonometric, cyclometric, logarithmic, exponential and power function. These functions are treated as probability distribution functions in the range [0;1].

Significant problem in machine vision and computer vision is that of appropriate 2D shape representation and reconstruction. Classical discussion about shape representation is based on the problem: contour versus skeleton. This monograph is voting for contour which forms boundary of the object. Contour of the object, represented by successive contour points, consists of information which allows us to describe many important features of the object as shape coefficients. 2D curve modeling and generation is a basic subject in many branches of industry and computer science, for example in the cad/cam software. The representation of shape can have a great impact on the accuracy and effectiveness of object recognition. In the literature, shape has been represented by many options including curves, graph-based algorithms and medial axis to enable shape-based object recognition. Digital 2D curve (open or closed) can be represented by chain code (Freeman's code). Chain code depends on selection of the started point and transformations of the object. So Freeman's code is one of the method how to describe and to find contour of the object. Analog (continuous) version of Freeman's code is the curve α - s. Another contour representation and reconstruction is based on Fourier coefficients calculated in discrete Fourier transformation (DFT). These coefficients are used to fix similarity of the contours with different sizes or directions. If we assume that contour is built from segments of a line and fragments of circles or ellipses, hough transformation is applied to detect contour lines. Also geometrical moments of the object are used during the process of object shape representation. Contour is also applied in shape decomposition. Many branches of medicine, industry and manufacturing are looking for methods connected with geometry of the contour. Why and when should we use MHR and PNC methods? Interpolation methods and curve fitting represent so huge problem that each individual interpolation is exceptional and requires specific solutions. PNC method is such a novel tool with its all pros and cons. The user has to decide which interpolation method is the best in a single situation. The choice is yours if you have any choice. Presented method is such a new possibility for curve fitting and interpolation when specific data (for example handwritten symbol or character) starts up with no rules for polynomial interpolation. This book consists of two generalizations: generalization of previous MHR method with various nodes combinations and generalization of linear interpolation with different (no basic) probability distribution functions and nodes combinations.

The method of Probabilistic Nodes Combination (PNC) enables interpolation and modeling of two-dimensional curves using nodes combinations and different coefficients γ: polynomial, sinusoidal, cosinusoidal, tangent, cotangent, logarithmic, exponential, arc sin, arc cos, arc tan, arc cot or power function, also inverse functions. This probabilistic view is novel approach a problem of modeling and interpolation. Computer vision and pattern recognition are interested in appropriate methods of shape representation and curve modeling. PNC method represents the possibilities of shape reconstruction and curve interpolation via the choice of nodes combination and probability distribution function for interpolated points. It seems to be quite new look at the problem of contour representation and curve modeling in artificial intelligence and computer vision.

Function for γ calculations is chosen individually at each curve modeling and it is treated as probability distribution function: γ depends on initial requirements and curve specifications. PNC method leads to curve interpolation as handwriting modeling via discrete set of fixed knots. So PNC makes possible the combination of two important problems: interpolation and modeling. Main features of PNC method are:

1. The smaller distance between knots the better;
2. Calculations for coordinates close to zero and near by extremum require more attention because of importance of these points;
3. PNC interpolation develops a linear interpolation into other functions as probability distribution functions;
4. PNC is a generalization of MHR method via different nodes combinations;
5. Interpolation of L points is connected with the computational cost of rank $O(L)$ as in MHR method;
6. Nodes combination and coefficient γ are crucial in the process of curve probabilistic parameterization and interpolation: they are computed individually for a single curve.

Why and when should we use MHR and PNC methods? Interpolation methods and curve fitting represent so huge problem that each individual interpolation is exceptional and requires specific solutions. PNC method is such a novel tool with its all pros and cons. The user has to decide which interpolation method is the best in a single situation. The choice is yours if you have any choice. Presented method is such a new possibility for curve fitting and interpolation when specific data (for example handwritten symbol or character) starts up with no rules for polynomial interpolation.

The method of Probabilistic Nodes Combination (PNC) enables interpolation and modeling of two-dimensional curves using nodes combinations and different coefficients γ: polynomial, sinusoidal, cosinusoidal, tangent, cotangent, logarithmic, exponential, arc sin, arc cos, arc tan, arc cot or power function, also inverse functions. This probabilistic view is novel approach a problem of modeling and interpolation. Computer vision and pattern recognition are interested in appropriate methods of shape representation and curve modeling. PNC method represents the possibilities of shape reconstruction and curve interpolation via the choice of nodes combination and probability distribution function for interpolated points. It seems to be quite new look at the problem of contour representation and curve modeling in artificial intelligence and computer vision. Function for γ calculations is chosen individually at each curve modeling and it is treated as probability distribution function: γ depends on initial requirements and curve specifications. PNC method leads to curve interpolation as handwriting modeling via discrete set of fixed knots. So PNC makes possible the combination of two important problems: interpolation and modeling. The method of Probabilistic Features Combination (PFC) enables interpolation and modeling of high-dimensional N data using features' combinations and different coefficients γ: polynomial, sinusoidal, cosinusoidal, tangent, cotangent, logarithmic, exponential, arc sin, arc cos, arc tan, arc cot or power function. Functions for γ calculations are chosen individually at each data modeling and it is treated as N-dimensional probability distribution function: γ depends on initial requirements and features' specifications. PFC method leads to data interpolation as handwriting or signature identification and image retrieval via discrete set of feature vectors in N-dimensional feature space. So PFC method makes possible the combination of two important problems: interpolation and modeling in a matter of image retrieval or writer identification. Main features of PFC method are: PFC interpolation develops a linear interpolation in multidimensional feature spaces into other functions as N-dimensional probability distribution functions; PFC is a generalization of MHR method and PNC method via different nodes combinations; interpolation of L points is connected with the computational cost of rank $O(L)$ as in MHR and PNC method; nodes combination and coefficients γ are crucial in the process of data probabilistic parameterization and interpolation: they are computed individually for a single feature. Proposed method, called Probabilistic Features Combination (PFC), is the method of N-dimensional data interpolation and extrapolation using the set of key points (knots or nodes). Nodes can be treated as characteristic points of data for modeling and analyzing. The model of data can be built by choice of probability distribution function and nodes combination. PFC modeling via nodes combination and parameter γ as probability distribution function enables value anticipation in risk analysis and decision making. N-dimensional object is extrapolated and interpolated via nodes combination and different functions as discrete or continuous probability distribution functions: polynomial, sine, cosine, tangent, cotangent, logarithm, exponent, arc sin, arc cos, arc tan, arc cot or power function.

The method of Probabilistic Features Combination (PFC) enables interpolation and modeling of high-dimensional data using features' combinations and different coefficients γ as modeling function. Functions for γ calculations are chosen individually at each data modeling and it is treated as N-dimensional probability distribution function: γ depends on initial requirements and features' specifications. PFC method leads to data interpolation as handwriting or signature identification and image retrieval via discrete set of feature vectors in N-dimensional feature space. So PFC method makes possible the combination of two important problems: interpolation and modeling in a matter of image retrieval or writer identification. PFC interpolation develops a linear interpolation in multidimensional feature spaces into other functions as N-dimensional probability distribution functions. Future works are going to applications of PFC method in biometric recognition, computer vision and artificial intelligence.

Nodes are treated as characteristic points of data for modeling and analyzing. The model of data can be built by choice of probability distribution function and nodes combination. PFC modeling via nodes combination and parameter γ as probability distribution function enables value anticipation in risk analysis and decision making. Two-dimensional object is extrapolated and interpolated via nodes combination and different functions as discrete or continuous probability distribution functions: polynomial, sine, cosine, tangent, cotangent, logarithm, exponent, arc sin, arc cos, arc tan, arc cot or power function.

Functions for γ calculations are chosen individually at each data modeling and it is treated as 2-dimensional probability distribution function: γ depends on initial requirements and features' specifications. PFC method leads to data interpolation as handwriting or signature identification and image retrieval via discrete set of feature vectors in 2-dimensional feature space. So PFC method makes possible the combination of two important problems: interpolation and modeling in a matter of image retrieval or writer identification. PFC interpolation develops a linear interpolation in multidimensional feature spaces into other functions as two-dimensional probability distribution functions. Future works are going to applications of PFC method in biometric recognition, computer vision and artificial intelligence.

The editor, the publisher, and the authors hope that this book, *Probabilistic Nodes Combination (PNC) for Object Modeling and Contour Reconstruction*, will be a heavy brick in the construction of the House of Science. Please read it!

Dariusz Jacek Jakóbczak
Koszalin University of Technology, Poland
February 2017

Chapter 1
Introduction:
MHR Method

ABSTRACT

Computer vision needs suitable methods of shape representation and contour reconstruction. One of them, invented by the author and called method of Hurwitz-Radon Matrices (MHR), can be used in representation and reconstruction of shapes of the objects in the plane. Proposed method is based on a family of Hurwitz-Radon (HR) matrices. The matrices are skew-symmetric and possess columns composed of orthogonal vectors. 2D shape is represented by the set of successive nodes. It is shown how to create the orthogonal and discrete OHR operator and how to use it in a process of shape representation and reconstruction. Contour of the object, represented by successive contour points, consists of information which allows us to describe many important features of the object as shape coefficients. 2D curve modeling is a basic subject in many branches of industry and computer science.

INTRODUCTION

Method of Hurwitz-Radon Matrices (MHR), invented by the author, can be applied in reconstruction and interpolation of curves in the plane. The method is based on a family of Hurwitz-Radon (HR) matrices. The matrices are skew-symmetric and possess columns composed of orthogonal vectors. The operator of Hurwitz-Radon (OHR), built from these matrices, is described. Author explains how to create the orthogonal and discrete OHR

DOI: 10.4018/978-1-5225-2531-8.ch001

and how to use it in a process of curve interpolation and two-dimensional data modeling. Proposed method needs suitable choice of nodes, i.e. points of the 2D curve to be interpolated or extrapolated: nodes should be settled at each extremum (minimum or maximum) of one coordinate and at least one point between two successive local extrema, and nodes should be monotonic in one of coordinates (for example equidistance). Created from the family of N-1 HR matrices and completed with the identical matrix, system of matrices is orthogonal only for vector spaces of dimensions $N = 1, 2, 4$ or 8. Orthogonality of columns and rows is very important and significant for stability and high precision of calculations. MHR method is modeling the curve point by point without using any formula of function. Main features of MHR method are: accuracy of curve reconstruction depending on number of nodes and method of choosing nodes, interpolation of L points of the curve is connected with the computational cost of rank $O(L)$, MHR interpolation is not a linear interpolation (Ullman & Basri, 1991). The problem of curve length estimation is also considered. Algorithm of MHR method and the examples of data extrapolation are described. Value anticipation is the crucial feature in risk analyzing and decision making. Risk analysis needs suitable methods of data extrapolation and decision making. Proposed method of Hurwitz-Radon Matrices (MHR) can be used in extrapolation and interpolation of curves in the plane. For example quotations from the Stock Exchange, the market prices or rate of a currency form a curve. This chapter contains the way of data anticipation and extrapolation via MHR method and decision making: to buy or not, to sell or not. Proposed method is based on a family of Hurwitz-Radon (HR) matrices. The matrices are skew-symmetric and possess columns composed of orthogonal vectors. The operator of Hurwitz-Radon (OHR), built from these matrices, is described. Two-dimensional data are represented by the set of curve points. It is shown how to create the orthogonal and discrete OHR and how to use it in a process of data foreseeing and extrapolation. MHR method is interpolating and extrapolating the curve point by point without using any formula or function.

Computer vision needs suitable methods of shape representation and contour reconstruction. One of them, invented by the author and called method of Hurwitz-Radon Matrices (MHR), can be used in representation and reconstruction of shapes of the objects in the plane. Proposed method is based on a family of Hurwitz-Radon (HR) matrices. The matrices are skew-symmetric and possess columns composed of orthogonal vectors. 2D shape is represented by the set of successive nodes. It is shown how to create the orthogonal and discrete OHR operator and how to use it in a process of shape representation and reconstruction. Then MHR method is generalized to Probabilistic Nodes Combination (PNC) method.

This work clarifies the significance and novelty of the proposed method compared to existing methods (for example polynomial interpolations and Bézier curves). Previous published papers of the author were dealing with the method of Hurwitz-Radon Matrices (MHR method). Novelty of this monograph and proposed method consists in the fact that calculations are free from the family of Hurwitz-Radon Matrices. Problem statement of this monograph is: how to reconstruct (interpolate) missing points of 2D curve having the set of interpolation nodes (key points) and using the information about probabilistic distribution of unknown points. For example the simplest basic distribution leads to the easiest interpolation – linear interpolation. Apart from probability distribution, additionally there is the second factor of proposed interpolation method: nodes combination. The simplest nodes combination is zero. Thus proposed curve modeling is based on two agents: probability distribution and nodes combination. Significance of this book consists in generalization for MHR method: the computations are done without matrices in curve fitting and shape modeling, with clear point interpolation formula based on probability distribution function (continuous or discrete) and nodes combination. This book also consists of generalization for linear interpolation with different (no basic) probability distribution functions and nodes combinations. So this book answers the question: "Why and when should we use PNC method?". Curve interpolation represents one of the most important problems in mathematics and computer science: how to model the curve via discrete set of two-dimensional points? Also the matter of shape representation (as closed curve-contour) and curve parameterization is still opened. For example pattern recognition, signature verification or handwriting identification problems are based on curve modeling via the choice of key points. So interpolation is not only a pure mathematical problem but important task in computer vision and artificial intelligence. The monograph wants to approach a problem of curve modeling by characteristic points. Proposed method relies on nodes combination and functional modeling of curve points situated between the basic set of key points. The functions that are used in calculations represent whole family of elementary functions with inverse functions: polynomials, trigonometric, cyclometric, logarithmic, exponential and power function. These functions are treated as probability distribution functions in the range [0;1].

Significant problem in machine vision and computer vision is that of appropriate 2D shape representation and reconstruction. Classical discussion about shape representation is based on the problem: contour versus skeleton. This monograph is voting for contour which forms boundary of the object. Contour of the object, represented by successive contour points, consists of information which allows us to describe many important features of the object as shape coefficients. 2D curve modeling and generation is a basic subject in many branches of industry and computer science, for example in the cad/cam software. The representation of shape can have a great impact on the accuracy and effectiveness of object recognition. In the literature, shape has been represented by many options including curves, graph-based algorithms and medial axis to enable shape-based object recognition. Digital 2D curve (open or closed) can be represented by chain code (Freeman's code). Chain code depends on selection of the started point and transformations of the object. So Freeman's code is one of the method how to describe and to find contour of the object. Analog (continuous) version of Freeman's code is the curve α-s. Another contour representation and reconstruction is based on Fourier coefficients calculated in discrete Fourier transformation (DFT). These coefficients are used to fix similarity of the contours with different sizes or directions. If we assume that contour is built from segments of a line and fragments of circles or ellipses, hough transformation is applied to detect contour lines. Also geometrical moments of the object are used during the process of object shape representation. Contour is also applied in shape decomposition. Many branches of medicine, industry and manufacturing are looking for methods connected with geometry of the contour. Why and when should we use MHR and PNC methods? Interpolation methods and curve fitting represent so huge problem that each individual interpolation is exceptional and requires specific solutions. PNC method is such a novel tool with its all pros and cons. The user has to decide which interpolation method is the best in a single situation. The choice is yours if you have any choice. Presented method is such a new possibility for curve fitting and interpolation when specific data (for example handwritten symbol or character) starts up with no rules for polynomial interpolation. This book consists of two generalizations: generalization of previous MHR method with various nodes combinations and generalization of linear interpolation with different (no basic) probability distribution functions and nodes combinations.

BACKGROUND

The following question is important in mathematics and computer science: is it possible to find a method of curve interpolation and extrapolation in the plane without building the interpolation polynomials? This chapter aims at giving the positive answer to this question. Current methods of curve interpolation are based on classical polynomial interpolation: Newton, Lagrange or Hermite polynomials and spline curves which are piecewise polynomials (Dahlquist & Bjoerck, 1974). Classical methods are useless to interpolate the function that fails to be differentiable at one point, for example the absolute value function $f(x) = |x|$ at $x = 0$. If point $(0;0)$ is one of the interpolation nodes, then precise polynomial interpolation of the absolute value function is impossible. Also when the graph of interpolated function differs from the shape of polynomials considerably, for example $f(x) = 1/x$, interpolation is very hard because of existing local extrema of polynomial. We cannot forget about the Runge's phenomenon: when interpolation nodes are equidistance then high-order polynomial oscillates toward the end of the interval, for example close to -1 and 1 with function $f(x) = 1/(1+25x^2)$ (Ralston, 1965). MHR method is free of these bad feature. Computational algorithm is considered and then it is important to talk about time. Complexity of calculations for one unknown point in Lagrange or Newton interpolation based on n nodes is connected with the computational cost of rank $O(n^2)$. Proposed method has lower calculation complexity.

A significant problem in risk analysis and decision making is that of appropriate data representation and extrapolation (Brachman & Levesque, 2004). Two-dimensional data can be treated as points on the curve. Classical polynomial interpolations and extrapolations (Lagrange, Newton, Hermite) are useless for data anticipation, because the stock quotations or the market prices represent discrete data and they do not preserve a shape of the polynomial. Also Richardson extrapolation has some weak sides concerning discrete data. This chapter is dealing with the method of data foreseeing and value extrapolation by using a family of Hurwitz-Radon matrices. The quotations, prices or rate of a currency, represented by curve points, consist of information which allows us to extrapolate the next data and then to make a decision (Fagin et al, 1995).

If the probabilities of possible actions are known, then some criteria are ready to be applied in decision making and analyzing risk: for example criterion of Laplace, Bayes, Wald, Hurwicz, Savage, Hodge-Lehmann

(Straffin,1993) and others (Watson, 2002). But in this chapter author considers only two possibilities: to do something or not. For example to buy a share or not, to sell a currency or not. Proposed method of Hurwitz-Radon Matrices (MHR) is used in data extrapolation and then calculations for risk analyzing and decision making are described. MHR method presents new approach to extrapolation problem because it takes the interpolation nodes to create orthogonal basis as columns of matrix OHR operators. Then affine (convex) combination of such basis builds new orthogonal base for unknown coordinates of calculated points. MHR method uses two-dimensional data for knowledge representation (Markman, 1998) and for computational foundations (Sowa, 2000). Also medicine (Cierniak, 2005), industry (Jakóbczak & Kosiński, 2007) and manufacturing (Tang, 2005) are looking for the methods connected with geometry of the curves (Soussen & Mohammad-Djafari, 2004) . So suitable data representation and precise reconstruction (Latecki & Lakaemper, 1999) or extrapolation (Kozera, 2004) of the curve is a key factor in many applications of computational intelligence (Lowe, 1991 and 2001), knowledge representation and risk analysis. In comparison MHR method with Bézier curves, Hermite curves and B-curves (*B-splines*) or NURBS one unpleasant feature of these curves must be mentioned: small change of one characteristic point can make big change of whole reconstructed curve. Such an unwanted feature does not appear in MHR method. None of the methods, that are used nowadays, applies the orthogonal basis for unknown value extrapolation and foreseeing, but proposed MHR method does. Orthogonality means a very important feature for stability in calculations. Also point MHR interpolation and extrapolation via simple computations with matrices is something new in the problem of anticipation, risk analysis and decision making.

The considered problem statement looks as follow: let's assume there are given some 2D points of known data as the set of interpolation nodes. How the unknown value can be extrapolated and anticipated as the support in decision making and risk analysis, based on given characteristic (key) points?

THE METHOD OF HURWITZ-RADON MATRICES

Issues

This chapter deals with the problem of interpolation and extrapolation without computing the polynomial or any fixed function. The values of nodes are used to build the orthogonal matrix operators OHR and a linear (convex) combination of OHR operators leads to calculations of 2D curve points. Main idea of MHR method (Jakóbczak, 2006) is that the curve is interpolated or extrapolated point by point by computing the unknown coordinates of the points. The only significant factors in MHR method are: choosing the interpolation nodes and fixing the dimension of HR matrix ($N = 1, 2, 4$ or 8). Other characteristic features of function or curve, such as shape or similarity to polynomials, derivative or Runge's phenomenon, are not important in the process of MHR interpolation and extrapolation. The curve or function in MHR method is parameterized for value $\alpha \in [0;1]$ in each range of two successive interpolation nodes. Data extrapolation and foreseeing is calculated for $\alpha < 0$ or $\alpha > 1$. Estimation of the curve length with high precision is possible because of computing any number of curve points we want. Complexity of calculations for L unknown points in MHR interpolation and extrapolation, based on n nodes, is connected with the computational cost of rank $O(L)$. This is very important feature of MHR method.

The Origin of Hurwitz-Radon Matrices

Adolf Hurwitz (1859-1919) and Johann Radon (1887-1956) published separately the papers about specific class of matrices in 1923, working on the problem of quadratic forms. For example equation

$$(x_0^2 + x_1^2) \cdot (y_0^2 + y_1^2) = (z_0^2 + z_1^2)$$

is true when $z_0 = x_0 y_0 - x_1 y_1$, $z_1 = x_0 y_1 + x_1 y_0$. This result can be achieved from matrix equation:

$$\begin{bmatrix} x_0 & x_1 \\ -x_1 & x_0 \end{bmatrix} \cdot \begin{bmatrix} y_0 & y_1 \\ -y_1 & y_0 \end{bmatrix} = \begin{bmatrix} z_0 & z_1 \\ -z_1 & z_0 \end{bmatrix}.$$

Also equation

$$(x_0^2 + x_1^2 + x_2^2 + x_3^2) \cdot (y_0^2 + y_1^2 + y_2^2 + y_3^2) = z_0^2 + z_1^2 + z_2^2 + z_3^2$$

has solution:

$$z_0 = x_0 y_0 - x_1 y_1 - x_2 y_2 - x_3 y_3,$$

$$z_1 = x_0y_1 + x_1y_0 + x_2y_3\text{-}x_3y_2,$$

$$z_2 = x_0y_2\text{-}x_1y_3 + x_2y_0 + x_3y_1,$$

$$z_3 = x_0y_3 + x_1y_2\text{-}x_2y_1 + x_3y_0.$$

This result can be achieved from matrix equation of dimension $N = 4$:

$$\begin{bmatrix} x_0 & x_1 & x_2 & x_3 \\ -x_1 & x_0 & -x_3 & x_2 \\ -x_2 & x_3 & x_0 & -x_1 \\ -x_3 & -x_2 & x_1 & x_0 \end{bmatrix} \cdot \begin{bmatrix} y_0 & y_1 & y_2 & y_3 \\ -y_1 & y_0 & -y_3 & y_2 \\ -y_2 & y_3 & y_0 & -y_1 \\ -y_3 & -y_2 & y_1 & y_0 \end{bmatrix} = \begin{bmatrix} z_0 & z_1 & z_2 & z_3 \\ -z_1 & z_0 & -z_3 & z_2 \\ -z_2 & z_3 & z_0 & -z_1 \\ -z_3 & -z_2 & z_1 & z_0 \end{bmatrix} \cdot$$

Hurwitz and Radon proved that dimensions $N = 1, 2, 4$ and 8 are the only dimensions for these quadratic equations. When $N = 8$:

$$\left(\sum_{i=0}^{7} x_i^2\right) \cdot \left(\sum_{i=0}^{7} y_i^2\right) = \sum_{i=0}^{7} z_i^2$$

for

$$z_0 = x_0y_0\text{-}x_1y_1\text{-}x_2y_2\text{-}x_3y_3\text{-}x_4y_4\text{-}x_5y_5\text{-}x_6y_6\text{-}x_7y_7,$$

$$z_1 = x_0y_1 + x_1y_0\text{-}x_2y_3 + x_3y_2\text{-}x_4y_5 + x_5y_4 + x_6y_7\text{-}x_7y_6,$$

$$z_2 = x_0y_2 + x_1y_3 + x_2y_0\text{-}x_3y_1\text{-}x_4y_6\text{-}x_5y_7 + x_6y_4 + x_7y_5,$$

$$z_3 = x_0y_3\text{-}x_1y_2 + x_2y_1 + x_3y_0\text{-}x_4y_7 + x_5y_6\text{-}x_6y_5 + x_7y_4,$$

$$z_4 = x_0y_4 + x_1y_5 + x_2y_6 + x_3y_7 + x_4y_0\text{-}x_5y_1\text{-}x_6y_2\text{-}x_7y_3,$$

$$z_5 = x_0y_5\text{-}x_1y_4 + x_2y_7\text{-}x_3y_6 + x_4y_1 + x_5y_0 + x_6y_3\text{-}x_7y_2,$$

$$z_6 = x_0y_6\text{-}x_1y_7\text{-}x_2y_4 + x_3y_5 + x_4y_2\text{-}x_5y_3 + x_6y_0 + x_7y_1,$$

$$z_7 = x_0y_7 + x_1y_6\text{-}x_2y_5\text{-}x_3y_4 + x_4y_3 + x_5y_2\text{-}x_6y_1 + x_7y_0.$$

The matrices used to solve quadratic equations are defined: matrices A_i, $i = 1, 2, \ldots, m$ satisfying

$$A_j A_k + A_k A_j = 0, A_j^2 = -I, j \neq k, j, k = 1, 2, \ldots, m$$

are called a family of Hurwitz-Radon matrices.

A family of Hurwitz-Radon (HR) matrices has important features (Eckmann, 1999): HR matrices are skew-symmetric ($A_i^T = -A_i$) and reverse matrices are easy to find ($A_i^{-1} = -A_i$). Only for dimension $N = 1, 2, 4$ or 8 the family of HR matrices consists of N-1 matrices. When $N = 1$ there is no matrix, just calculations with real numbers. For $N = 2$ we have one matrix:

$$A_1 = \begin{bmatrix} 0 & 1 \\ -1 & 0 \end{bmatrix}.$$

For $N = 4$ there are three HR matrices with integer entries:

$$A_1 = \begin{bmatrix} 0 & 1 & 0 & 0 \\ -1 & 0 & 0 & 0 \\ 0 & 0 & 0 & -1 \\ 0 & 0 & 1 & 0 \end{bmatrix}, A_2 = \begin{bmatrix} 0 & 0 & 1 & 0 \\ 0 & 0 & 0 & 1 \\ -1 & 0 & 0 & 0 \\ 0 & -1 & 0 & 0 \end{bmatrix}, A_3 = \begin{bmatrix} 0 & 0 & 0 & 1 \\ 0 & 0 & -1 & 0 \\ 0 & 1 & 0 & 0 \\ -1 & 0 & 0 & 0 \end{bmatrix}.$$

For $N = 8$ we have seven HR matrices with elements $0, \pm 1$ (Jakóbczak, 2006).

So far HR matrices are applied in electronics (Citko, Jakóbczak & Sieńko, 2005): in Space-Time Block Coding (STBC) and orthogonal design (Tarokh, Jafarkhani & Calderbank, 1999), also in signal processing (Sieńko, Citko & Wilamowski, 2002) and Hamiltonian Neural Nets (Sieńko & Citko, 2002).

The Operator of Hurwitz-Radon

Here is the beginning of proposed MHR method. Let us consider a combination of identity matrix and HR matrix of dimension $N = 2$:

$$a \begin{bmatrix} 1 & 0 \\ 0 & 1 \end{bmatrix} + b \begin{bmatrix} 0 & 1 \\ -1 & 0 \end{bmatrix} = \begin{bmatrix} a & b \\ -b & a \end{bmatrix}.$$

For any points $(x_1, y_1) \in \mathbf{R}^2$, $(x_2, y_2) \in \mathbf{R}^2$ matrix equation

$$\begin{bmatrix} a & b \\ -b & a \end{bmatrix} \cdot \begin{bmatrix} x_1 \\ x_2 \end{bmatrix} = \begin{bmatrix} y_1 \\ y_2 \end{bmatrix}$$

is true with

$$a = \frac{x_1 y_1 + x_2 y_2}{x_1^2 + x_2^2}, \; b = \frac{x_2 y_1 - x_1 y_2}{x_1^2 + x_2^2} \text{ and } x_1^2 + x_2^2 > 0.$$

Reverse matrix equation

$$\begin{bmatrix} a & b \\ -b & a \end{bmatrix} \cdot \begin{bmatrix} y_1 \\ y_2 \end{bmatrix} = \begin{bmatrix} x_1 \\ x_2 \end{bmatrix}$$

is true with

$$a = \frac{x_1 y_1 + x_2 y_2}{y_1^2 + y_2^2}, \; b = \frac{-x_2 y_1 + x_1 y_2}{y_1^2 + y_2^2} \text{ and } y_1^2 + y_2^2 > 0.$$

Also we can consider a combination of identity matrix and three HR matrices of dimension $N = 4$:

$$a \begin{bmatrix} 1 & 0 & 0 & 0 \\ 0 & 1 & 0 & 0 \\ 0 & 0 & 1 & 0 \\ 0 & 0 & 0 & 1 \end{bmatrix} + b \begin{bmatrix} 0 & 1 & 0 & 0 \\ -1 & 0 & 0 & 0 \\ 0 & 0 & 0 & -1 \\ 0 & 0 & 1 & 0 \end{bmatrix} + c \begin{bmatrix} 0 & 0 & 1 & 0 \\ 0 & 0 & 0 & 1 \\ -1 & 0 & 0 & 0 \\ 0 & -1 & 0 & 0 \end{bmatrix}$$

$$+ d \begin{bmatrix} 0 & 0 & 0 & 1 \\ 0 & 0 & -1 & 0 \\ 0 & 1 & 0 & 0 \\ -1 & 0 & 0 & 0 \end{bmatrix} = \begin{bmatrix} a & b & c & d \\ -b & a & -d & c \\ -c & d & a & -b \\ -d & -c & b & a \end{bmatrix}.$$

For any points $(x_1, y_1) \in \mathbf{R}^2$, $(x_2, y_2) \in \mathbf{R}^2$, $(x_3, y_3) \in \mathbf{R}^2$, $(x_4, y_4) \in \mathbf{R}^2$ matrix equation

$$
\begin{bmatrix}
a & b & c & d \\
-b & a & -d & c \\
-c & d & a & -b \\
-d & -c & b & a
\end{bmatrix}
\cdot
\begin{bmatrix}
x_1 \\ x_2 \\ x_3 \\ x_4
\end{bmatrix}
=
\begin{bmatrix}
y_1 \\ y_2 \\ y_3 \\ y_4
\end{bmatrix}
$$

is satisfied with

$$
a = \frac{x_1 y_1 + x_2 y_2 + x_3 y_3 + x_4 y_4}{x_1^2 + x_2^2 + x_3^2 + x_4^2}, \quad
b = \frac{-x_1 y_2 + x_2 y_1 + x_3 y_4 - x_4 y_3}{x_1^2 + x_2^2 + x_3^2 + x_4^2},
$$

$$
c = \frac{-x_1 y_3 - x_2 y_4 + x_3 y_1 + x_4 y_2}{x_1^2 + x_2^2 + x_3^2 + x_4^2}, \quad
d = \frac{-x_1 y_4 + x_2 y_3 - x_3 y_2 + x_4 y_1}{x_1^2 + x_2^2 + x_3^2 + x_4^2}
$$

and $x_1^2 + x_2^2 + x_3^2 + x_4^2 > 0$.

Reverse matrix equation

$$
\begin{bmatrix}
a & b & c & d \\
-b & a & -d & c \\
-c & d & a & -b \\
-d & -c & b & a
\end{bmatrix}
\cdot
\begin{bmatrix}
y_1 \\ y_2 \\ y_3 \\ y_4
\end{bmatrix}
=
\begin{bmatrix}
x_1 \\ x_2 \\ x_3 \\ x_4
\end{bmatrix}
$$

is satisfied with

$$
a = \frac{x_1 y_1 + x_2 y_2 + x_3 y_3 + x_4 y_4}{y_1^2 + y_2^2 + y_3^2 + y_4^2}, \quad
b = \frac{x_1 y_2 - x_2 y_1 - x_3 y_4 + x_4 y_3}{y_1^2 + y_2^2 + y_3^2 + y_4^2},
$$

$$
c = \frac{x_1 y_3 + x_2 y_4 - x_3 y_1 - x_4 y_2}{y_1^2 + y_2^2 + y_3^2 + y_4^2}, \quad
d = \frac{x_1 y_4 - x_2 y_3 + x_3 y_2 - x_4 y_1}{y_1^2 + y_2^2 + y_3^2 + y_4^2}
$$

and $y_1^2 + y_2^2 + y_3^2 + y_4^2 > 0$.

A combination of identity matrix and seven HR matrices of dimension N = 8 looks as follows:

$$
\begin{bmatrix}
a_0 & a_1 & a_2 & a_3 & a_4 & a_5 & a_6 & a_7 \\
-a_1 & a_0 & a_3 & -a_2 & a_5 & -a_4 & -a_7 & a_6 \\
-a_2 & -a_3 & a_0 & a_1 & a_6 & a_7 & -a_4 & -a_5 \\
-a_3 & a_2 & -a_1 & a_0 & a_7 & -a_6 & a_5 & -a_4 \\
-a_4 & -a_5 & -a_6 & -a_7 & a_0 & a_1 & a_2 & a_3 \\
-a_5 & a_4 & -a_7 & a_6 & -a_1 & a_0 & -a_3 & a_2 \\
-a_6 & a_7 & a_4 & -a_5 & -a_2 & a_3 & a_0 & -a_1 \\
-a_7 & -a_6 & a_5 & a_4 & -a_3 & -a_2 & a_1 & a_0
\end{bmatrix}.
$$

Results for matrix equations with a combination of identity matrix and seven HR matrices of dimension

N = 8 are calculated in formulas (3), (4) and (8). Solutions of matrix equations (Sieńko, Citko & Jakóbczak, 2004) are used to build the matrix Operator of Hurwitz – Radon (OHR).

Let's assume there is given a finite set of points of the curve, called further nodes $(x_i, y_i) \in \boldsymbol{R}^2$ such as:

1. Nodes (interpolation points) are settled at local extrema (maximum or minimum) of one of coordinates and at least one point between two successive local extrema;
2. Each node (x_i, y_i) is monotonic in coordinates x_i or y_i (for example equidistance in one of coordinates).

Assume that the nodes belong to a curve in the plane. How the whole curve could be interpolated or extrapolated using this discrete set of nodes? Proposed method (Jakóbczak, 2007) is based on local, orthogonal matrix operators. The values of nodes' coordinates (x_i, y_i) are connected with HR matrices, built on N-dimensional vector space. It is important that HR matrices are skew-symmetric and only for dimensions N = 1, 2, 4 or 8 columns and rows of HR matrices are orthogonal (Eckmann, 1999).

If one curve is described by a set of nodes $\{(x_i, y_i), i = 1, 2, …, n\}$ monotonic (for example equidistance) in coordinates x_i, then HR matrices combined with identity matrix are used to build an orthogonal and discrete Hurwitz-Radon Operator (OHR). For nodes (x_1, y_1), (x_2, y_2) OHR of dimension

$N = 2$ is constructed:

$$M = \frac{1}{x_1^{\,2} + x_2^{\,2}} \begin{bmatrix} x_1 & x_2 \\ -x_2 & x_1 \end{bmatrix} \begin{bmatrix} y_1 & -y_2 \\ y_2 & y_1 \end{bmatrix},$$

$$M = \frac{1}{x_1^{\,2} + x_2^{\,2}} \begin{bmatrix} x_1 y_1 + x_2 y_2 & x_2 y_1 - x_1 y_2 \\ x_1 y_2 - x_2 y_1 & x_1 y_1 + x_2 y_2 \end{bmatrix}. \tag{1}$$

For nodes $(x_1, y_1), (x_2, y_2), (x_3, y_3), (x_4, y_4)$ monotonic (for example equidistance) in x_i OHR of dimension
$N = 4$ is constructed:

$$M = \frac{1}{x_1^{\,2} + x_2^{\,2} + x_3^{\,2} + x_4^{\,2}} \begin{bmatrix} u_0 & u_1 & u_2 & u_3 \\ -u_1 & u_0 & -u_3 & u_2 \\ -u_2 & u_3 & u_0 & -u_1 \\ -u_3 & -u_2 & u_1 & u_0 \end{bmatrix} \tag{2}$$

where

$$u_0 = x_1 y_1 + x_2 y_2 + x_3 y_3 + x_4 y_4,$$

$$u_1 = -x_1 y_2 + x_2 y_1 + x_3 y_4 - x_4 y_3,$$

$$u_2 = -x_1 y_3 - x_2 y_4 + x_3 y_1 + x_4 y_2,$$

$$u_3 = -x_1 y_4 + x_2 y_3 - x_3 y_2 + x_4 y_1.$$

For nodes $(x_1, y_1), (x_2, y_2), \ldots, (x_8, y_8)$ monotonic in x_i OHR of dimension $N = 8$ is equal with

$$M = \frac{1}{\sum\limits_{i=1}^{8} x_i^2} \begin{bmatrix} u_0 & u_1 & u_2 & u_3 & u_4 & u_5 & u_6 & u_7 \\ -u_1 & u_0 & u_3 & -u_2 & u_5 & -u_4 & -u_7 & u_6 \\ -u_2 & -u_3 & u_0 & u_1 & u_6 & u_7 & -u_4 & -u_5 \\ -u_3 & u_2 & -u_1 & u_0 & u_7 & -u_6 & u_5 & -u_4 \\ -u_4 & -u_5 & -u_6 & -u_7 & u_0 & u_1 & u_2 & u_3 \\ -u_5 & u_4 & -u_7 & u_6 & -u_1 & u_0 & -u_3 & u_2 \\ -u_6 & u_7 & u_4 & -u_5 & -u_2 & u_3 & u_0 & -u_1 \\ -u_7 & -u_6 & u_5 & u_4 & -u_3 & -u_2 & u_1 & u_0 \end{bmatrix} \tag{3}$$

where

$$u = \begin{bmatrix} y_1 & y_2 & y_3 & y_4 & y_5 & y_6 & y_7 & y_8 \\ -y_2 & y_1 & -y_4 & y_3 & -y_6 & y_6 & y_8 & -y_7 \\ -y_3 & y_4 & y_1 & -y_2 & -y_7 & -y_8 & y_5 & y_6 \\ -y_4 & -y_3 & y_2 & y_1 & -y_8 & y_7 & -y_6 & y_5 \\ -y_5 & y_6 & y_7 & y_8 & y_1 & -y_2 & -y_3 & -y_4 \\ -y_6 & -y_5 & y_8 & -y_7 & y_2 & y_1 & y_4 & -y_3 \\ -y_7 & -y_8 & -y_5 & y_6 & y_3 & -y_4 & y_1 & y_2 \\ -y_8 & y_7 & -y_6 & -y_5 & y_4 & y_3 & -y_2 & y_1 \end{bmatrix} \cdot \begin{bmatrix} x_1 \\ x_2 \\ x_3 \\ x_4 \\ x_5 \\ x_6 \\ x_7 \\ x_8 \end{bmatrix} \tag{4}$$

We can see here that the components of the vector $\mathbf{u} = (u_0, u_1, ..., u_7)^{\mathrm{T}}$, appearing in the matrix M in formula (3) are defined by (4) in the similar way to formula (2) but in terms of the coordinates of the above 8 nodes. Note that OHR operators (1)-(3) satisfy the condition of interpolation

$$M \cdot \mathbf{x} = \mathbf{y} \tag{5}$$

for $\mathbf{x} = (x_1, x_2...,x_N)^{\mathrm{T}} \in \mathbf{R}^N$, $\mathbf{x} \neq \mathbf{0}$, $\mathbf{y} = (y_1, y_2...,y_N)^{\mathrm{T}} \in \mathbf{R}^N$, $N = 1, 2, 4$ or 8.

If one curve is described by a set of nodes $\{(x_i, y_i), i = 1, 2, ..., n\}$ monotonic (for example equidistance) in coordinates y_i, then HR matrices combined with identity matrix are used to build an orthogonal and discrete reverse Hurwitz-Radon Operator (reverse OHR). For nodes (x_1, y_1), (x_2, y_2) reverse OHR of dimension $N = 2$ is constructed:

$$M^{-1} = \frac{1}{y_1{}^2 + y_2{}^2} \begin{bmatrix} x_1 & -x_2 \\ x_2 & x_1 \end{bmatrix} \begin{bmatrix} y_1 & y_2 \\ -y_2 & y_1 \end{bmatrix},$$

$$M^{-1} = \frac{1}{y_1{}^2 + y_2{}^2} \begin{bmatrix} x_1 y_1 + x_2 y_2 & -x_2 y_1 + x_1 y_2 \\ -x_1 y_2 + x_2 y_1 & x_1 y_1 + x_2 y_2 \end{bmatrix}. \tag{6}$$

For nodes (x_1,y_1), (x_2,y_2), (x_3,y_3), (x_4,y_4) monotonic in y_i the reverse OHR of dimension $N = 4$ is constructed with u_0, u_1, u_2 and u_3 from (2):

$$M^{-1} = \frac{1}{y_1{}^2 + y_2{}^2 + y_3{}^2 + y_4{}^2} \begin{bmatrix} u_0 & -u_1 & -u_2 & -u_3 \\ u_1 & u_0 & u_3 & -u_2 \\ u_2 & -u_3 & u_0 & u_1 \\ u_3 & u_2 & -u_1 & u_0 \end{bmatrix}. \tag{7}$$

For nodes (x_1,y_1), (x_2,y_2), ..., (x_8,y_8) monotonic in y_i the reverse OHR of dimension $N = 8$ is equal with

$$M^{-1} = \frac{1}{\sum\limits_{i=1}^{8} y_i{}^2} \begin{bmatrix} u_0 & -u_1 & -u_2 & -u_3 & -u_4 & -u_5 & -u_6 & -u_7 \\ u_1 & u_0 & -u_3 & u_2 & -u_5 & u_4 & u_7 & -u_6 \\ u_2 & u_3 & u_0 & -u_1 & -u_6 & -u_7 & u_4 & u_5 \\ u_3 & -u_2 & u_1 & u_0 & -u_7 & u_6 & -u_5 & u_4 \\ u_4 & u_5 & u_6 & u_7 & u_0 & -u_1 & -u_2 & -u_3 \\ u_5 & -u_4 & u_7 & -u_6 & u_1 & u_0 & u_3 & -u_2 \\ u_6 & -u_7 & -u_4 & u_5 & u_2 & -u_3 & u_0 & u_1 \\ u_7 & u_6 & -u_5 & -u_4 & u_3 & u_2 & -u_1 & u_0 \end{bmatrix}, \tag{8}$$

where the components of the vector $\mathbf{u} = (u_0, u_1,..., u_7)^{\mathrm{T}}$ are defined in terms of (4). Note that reverse OHR operators (6)-(8) satisfy the condition of interpolation

$$M^{-1} \cdot \mathbf{y} = \mathbf{x} \tag{9}$$

for $\mathbf{x} = (x_1, x_2..., x_N)^{\mathrm{T}} \in R^N$, $\mathbf{y} = (y_1, y_2..., y_N)^{\mathrm{T}} \in R^N$, $\mathbf{y} \neq \mathbf{0}$, $N = 1, 2, 4$ or 8.

Known values, for example currency rates or market prices, are represented on 2D curve by the set of nodes $(x_i, y_i) \in R^2$ (characteristic points) as follows in proposed MHR method:

1. Nodes (interpolation points) are settled at local extrema (maximum or minimum) of one of coordinates and at least one point between two successive local extrema;
2. Nodes (x_i, y_i) are monotonic in coordinates x_i ($x_i < x_{i+1}$ for all i) or y_i ($y_i < y_{i+1}$);
3. One curve is represented by at least four nodes.

Condition 1 is done for the most appropriate description of a curve. The quotations or prices are real data. Condition 2 according to a graph of function means that coordinates x_i represent for example the time. Condition 3 is adequate for extrapolation, but in the case of interpolation minimal number of nodes is five.

Data points are treated as interpolation nodes. How can we extrapolate continues values at time $x = 5.5$ for example or discrete data for next day $x = 6$ (Figure 1)? The anticipation of values is possible using proposed MHR method.

Figure 1. Five nodes of data and a curve
Source: author, 2016

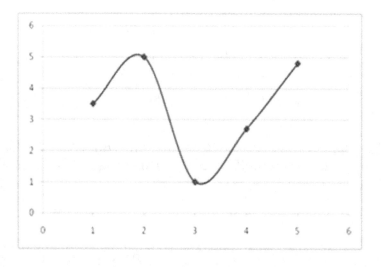

THE METHOD OF HURWITZ-RADON MATRICES

Key question looks as follows: how can we compute coordinates of points settled between interpolation nodes or beyond the nodes? The answer is connected with MHR method for interpolation and extrapolation. On a segment of a line every number "c" situated between "a" and "b" is described by a linear (convex) combination $c = \alpha \cdot a + (1-\alpha) \cdot b$ for

$$\alpha = \frac{b-c}{b-a} \in [0;1]. \tag{10}$$

If $c < a$ then $\alpha > 1$: there is extrapolation of points situated left of nodes. If $c > b$ then $\alpha < 0$: extrapolation of points situated right of nodes.

When the nodes are monotonic in coordinates x_i, average OHR operator M_2 of dimension $N = 1, 2, 4$ or 8 is constructed as follows:

$$M_2 = \alpha \cdot M_0 + (1 - \alpha) \cdot M_1 \tag{11}$$

with the operator M_0 built (1)-(3) by "odd" nodes $(x_1=a,y_1)$, (x_3,y_3), ..., (x_{2N-1},y_{2N-1}) and M_1 built (1)-(3) by "even" nodes $(x_2=b,y_2)$, (x_4,y_4), ..., (x_{2N},y_{2N}).

When the nodes are monotonic in coordinates y_i, average reverse OHR operator M_2^{-1} of dimension $N = 1, 2, 4$ or 8 is constructed as follows:

$$M_2^{-1} = \alpha \cdot M_0^{-1} + (1 - \alpha) \cdot M_1^{-1} \tag{12}$$

with the reverse operator M_0^{-1} built (6)-(8) by nodes $(x_1,y_1=a)$, (x_3,y_3), ..., (x_{2N-1},y_{2N-1}) and M_1^{-1} built (6)-(8) by nodes $(x_2,y_2=b)$, (x_4,y_4), ..., (x_{2N},y_{2N}).

Notice that having the operator M_2 for coordinates $x_i < x_{i+1}$ it is possible to reconstruct the second coordinates of points (x,y) in terms of the vector C defined with

$$c_i = \alpha \cdot x_{2i-1} + (1-\alpha) \cdot x_{2i}, \, i = 1, 2,..., N \tag{13}$$

as $C = [c_1, c_2,..., c_N]^{\mathrm{T}}$. The required formula is similar to (5):

$$Y(C) = M_2 \cdot C \tag{14}$$

in which components of vector $Y(C)$ give the second coordinate of the points (x,y) corresponding to the first coordinate, given in terms of components of the vector C.

On the other hand, having the operator M_2^{-1} for coordinates $y_i < y_{i+1}$ it is possible to reconstruct the first coordinates of points (x,y) in terms of the corresponding second coordinates given by components of the new vector C defined, as previously, with

$$c_i = \alpha \cdot y_{2i-1} + (1-\alpha) \cdot y_{2i} , \, i = 1, 2,..., N \tag{15}$$

and $C = [c_1, c_2,..., c_N]^T$. The final formula is similar to (9):

$$X(C) = M_2^{-1} \cdot C \tag{16}$$

in which components of the vector $X(C)$ give the first coordinate of the points (x,y) corresponding to the second coordinate, given in terms of components of the vector C.

After computing (14) or (16) for any $\alpha \in [0;1]$, we have a half of reconstructed points ($j = 1$ in algorithm 1). Now it is necessary to find second half of unknown coordinates ($j = 2$ in algorithm 1) for

$$c_i = \alpha \cdot x_{2i} + (1-\alpha) \cdot x_{2i+1}, \, i = 1, 2,..., N \tag{17}$$

or

$$c_i = \alpha \cdot y_{2i} + (1-\alpha) \cdot y_{2i+1}, \, i = 1, 2,..., N \tag{18}$$

depending on whether x_i (17) or y_i (18) is monotonic. There is no need to build the OHR for nodes $(x_2=a,y_2)$, (x_4,y_4), ..., (x_{2N},y_{2N}) or the reverse OHR for nodes $(x_2,y_2=a)$, (x_4,y_4), ..., (x_{2N},y_{2N}), because we have just found M_1 or M_1^{-1}. This operator will play the role as M_0 or M_0^{-1} in (11) or (12). New M_1 or M_1^{-1} must be computed for nodes $(x_3=b,y_3)$, ..., (x_{2N-1},y_{2N-1}), (x_{2N+1},y_{2N+1}) or $(x_3,y_3=b)$, ..., (x_{2N-1},y_{2N-1}), (x_{2N+1},y_{2N+1}).

As we see the minimum number of interpolation nodes $n = 2N+1 = 5, 9$ or 17 using OHR operators of dimension $N = 2, 4$ or 8 respectively. If there is more nodes than $2N+1$, the same calculations (10)-(18) have to be done for next range(s) or last range of $2N+1$ nodes. For example, if $n = 9$ then we

Figure 2. Twenty six interpolated points of function f(x) = 1/(1+25x²) using MHR method with 5 nodes
Source: Author, 2016.

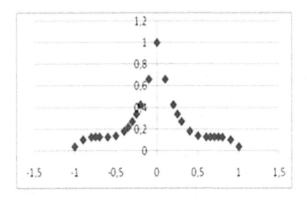

can use OHR operators of dimension $N = 4$ or OHR operators of dimension $N = 2$ for two subsets of nodes: $\{(x_1,y_1), \ldots, (x_5,y_5)\}$ and $\{(x_5,y_5), \ldots,(x_9,y_9)\}$.

Here is the application of MHR method for function $f(x)=1/(1+25x^2)$ with five nodes equidistance in first coordinate: $x_i = $ -1, -0.5, 0, 0.5, 1.

MHR interpolation of function $f(x) = 1/(1+25x^2)$ gives better result then polynomial interpolation: there is no Runge phenomenon. The same can be said for function $f(x) = 1/x$.

MHR extrapolation is valid for $\alpha < 0$ or $\alpha > 1$. In the case of continues data, parameter α is a real number. For example there are four nodes: (1;2), (1.3;5), (2;3), (2.5;6). MHR extrapolation with $\alpha = $ -0.01 gives the point (2.505;6.034) and with $\alpha = $ -0.1: (2.55;6.348). But the rate of a currency or the quotations are discrete data. If we assume that the rate of a currency is represented by equidistance nodes (day by day – fixed step of time $h = 1$ for coordinate x), next data or the rate on next day is extrapolated (anticipated) for $\alpha = $ -1. Calculation of unknown coordinates for data points using formulas (10)-(18) is called by author the method of Hurwitz-Radon Matrices (MHR).

ALGORITHM AND COMPLEXITY OF MHR CALCULATIONS

The algorithm of points reconstruction for $2N+1 = 5$, 9 or 17 successive nodes is presented.

Algorithm 1

Let $j = 1$. *Input: Set of interpolation nodes $\{(x_i, y_i),\ i = 1, 2, \ldots, n;\ n = 5, 9\ or\ 17\}$ such as:*

1. Nodes are settled at local extrema (maximum or minimum) of one of coordinates and at least one point between two successive local extrema;
2. Nodes (x_i, y_i) are monotonic in coordinates x_i or y_i.

   Step 1: *Determine the dimension N of OHR operators: $N = 2$ if $n = 5$, $N = 4$ if $n = 9$, $N = 8$ if $n = 17$.*

   Step 2: *If nodes are monotonic in x_i then build M_0 for nodes $(x_1 = a, y_1)$, $(x_3, y_3), \ldots, (x_{2N-1}, y_{2N-1})$ and M_1 for nodes $(x_2 = b, y_2), (x_4, y_4), \ldots, (x_{2N}, y_{2N})$ from (1)-(3). If nodes are monotonic in y_i then build M_0^{-1} for nodes $(x_1, y_1 = a), (x_3, y_3), \ldots, (x_{2N-1}, y_{2N-1})$ and M_1^{-1} for nodes $(x_2, y_2 = b), (x_4, y_4), \ldots, (x_{2N}, y_{2N})$ from (6)-(8).*

   Step 3: *Determine the number of points to be reconstructed $K_j > 0$ between two successive nodes, let $k = 1$.*

   Step 4: *Compute $\alpha \in [0;1]$ from (10) for $c_1 = c = \alpha \cdot a + (1-\alpha) \cdot b$.*

   Step 5: *Build M_2 from (11) or M_2^{-1} from (12).*

   Step 6: *Compute vector $C = [c_1, c_2, \ldots, c_N]^T$ from (13) or (15).*

   Step 7: *Compute unknown coordinates $Y(C)$ from (14) or $X(C)$ from (16).*

   Step 8: *If $k < K_j$, set $k = k + 1$ and go to Step 4. Otherwise if $j = 1$, set $M_0 = M_1$, $a = x_2$, $b = x_3$ (if nodes are monotonic in x_i) or $M_0^{-1} = M_1^{-1}$, $a = y_2$, $b = y_3$ (if nodes are monotonic in y_i), build new M_1 or M_1^{-1} for nodes $(x_3, y_3), (x_5, y_5), \ldots, (x_{2N+1}, y_{2N+1})$, let $j = 2$ and go to Step 3. Otherwise, stop.*

The number of reconstructed points in algorithm 1 is $K = N(K_1 + K_2)$. If there are more nodes than $2N+1 = 5$, 9 or 17, algorithm 1 has to be done for next range(s) or last range of $2N + 1$ nodes. Reconstruction of curve points using algorithm 1 is called by author the method of Hurwitz-Radon Matrices (MHR). If we have n interpolation nodes, then there is $K = L - n$ points to find using algorithm 1 and MHR method. The complexity of MHR calculations has to be considered.

Lemma 1: Let $n = 5$, 9 or 17 is the number of interpolation nodes, let MHR method (algorithm 1) is done for reconstruction of the curve consists of L points. Then MHR method is connected with the computational cost of rank $O(L)$.

Proof: Using algorithm 1 we have to reconstruct $K = L - n$ points of unknown curve. Counting the number of multiplications and divisions D in algorithm 1, for example in (20) in case $n = 5$ for each c_i at first and second half of reconstructed points, here are the results:

1. $D = 4L+7$ for $n = 5$ and $L = 2i + 5$;
2. $D = 6L+21$ for $n = 9$ and $L = 4i + 9$;
3. $D = 10L+73$ for $n = 17$ and $L = 8i + 17$; $i = 2,3,4...$

The lowest computational cost appears in MHR method with five nodes and OHR operators of dimension $N = 2$. Therefore whole set of n nodes can be divided into subsets of five nodes. Then whole curve is to be reconstructed by algorithm 1 with all subsets of five nodes: $\{(x_1,y_1), \ldots, (x_5,y_5)\}$, $\{(x_5,y_5), \ldots, (x_9,y_9)\}$,

$\{(x_9,y_9), \ldots, (x_{13},y_{13})\}\ldots$ If the last node (x_n,y_n) is indexed $n \neq 4i + 1$, then we have to use last five nodes $\{(x_{n-4},y_{n-4}), \ldots, (x_n,y_n)\}$ in algorithm 1.

The Formulas for a Single Point and Error Estimation

Now there are the formulas for computing one unknown coordinate of a single point. Assume there are given four nodes $(x_1,y_1), (x_2,y_2), (x_3,y_3), (x_4,y_4)$ monotonic in x_i. OHR operators of dimension $N = 2$ are built (1) as follows:

$$M_0 = \frac{1}{x_1^2 + x_3^2} \begin{bmatrix} x_1y_1 + x_3y_3 & x_3y_1 - x_1y_3 \\ x_1y_3 - x_3y_1 & x_1y_1 + x_3y_3 \end{bmatrix},$$

$$M_1 = \frac{1}{x_2^2 + x_4^2} \begin{bmatrix} x_2y_2 + x_4y_4 & x_4y_2 - x_2y_4 \\ x_2y_4 - x_4y_2 & x_2y_2 + x_4y_4 \end{bmatrix}.$$

Let first coordinate c_1 of reconstructed point is situated between x_1 and x_2:

$$c_1 = \alpha \cdot x_1 + \beta \cdot x_2 \text{ for } 0 \leq \beta = 1-\alpha \leq 1. \tag{19}$$

Compute second coordinate of reconstructed point $y(c_1)$ for $Y(C) = [y(c_1), y(c_2)]^T$ from (14):

$$\begin{bmatrix} y(c_1) \\ y(c_2) \end{bmatrix} = (\alpha \cdot M_0 + \beta \cdot M_1) \cdot \begin{bmatrix} \alpha \cdot x_1 + \beta \cdot x_2 \\ \alpha \cdot x_3 + \beta \cdot x_4 \end{bmatrix}. \tag{20}$$

After calculation (20):

$$y(c_1) = \alpha^2 \cdot y_1 + \beta^2 \cdot y_2 + \frac{\alpha \cdot \beta}{x_1^2 + x_3^2}(x_1 x_2 y_1 + x_2 x_3 y_3 + x_3 x_4 y_1 - x_1 x_4 y_3)$$
$$+ \frac{\alpha \cdot \beta}{x_2^2 + x_4^2}(x_1 x_2 y_2 + x_1 x_4 y_4 + x_3 x_4 y_2 - x_2 x_3 y_4)$$

(21)

So each point of the curve $P = (c_1, y(c_1))$ settled between nodes (x_1, y_1) and (x_2, y_2) is parameterized by $P(\alpha)$ for (19), (21) and $\alpha \in [0;1]$. Similar calculations are done for nodes (x_1, y_1), (x_2, y_2), (x_3, y_3), (x_4, y_4) monotonic in y_i to compute $x(c_1)$:

$$M_0^{-1} = \frac{1}{y_1^2 + y_3^2}\begin{bmatrix} x_1 y_1 + x_3 y_3 & -x_3 y_1 + x_1 y_3 \\ -x_1 y_3 + x_3 y_1 & x_1 y_1 + x_3 y_3 \end{bmatrix}$$

$$M_1^{-1} = \frac{1}{y_2^2 + y_4^2}\begin{bmatrix} x_2 y_2 + x_4 y_4 & -x_4 y_2 + x_2 y_4 \\ -x_2 y_4 + x_4 y_2 & x_2 y_2 + x_4 y_4 \end{bmatrix},$$

$$c_1 = \alpha \cdot y_1 + \beta \cdot y_2 \text{ for } 0 \le \beta = 1 - \alpha \le 1,$$

(22)

$$\begin{bmatrix} x(c_1) \\ x(c_2) \end{bmatrix} = (\alpha \cdot M_0^{-1} + \beta \cdot M_1^{-1}) \cdot \begin{bmatrix} \alpha \cdot y_1 + \beta \cdot y_2 \\ \alpha \cdot y_3 + \beta \cdot y_4 \end{bmatrix},$$

$$x(c_1) = \alpha^2 \cdot x_1 + \beta^2 \cdot x_2 + \frac{\alpha \cdot \beta}{y_1^2 + y_3^2} r_1 + \frac{\alpha \cdot \beta}{y_2^2 + y_4^2} r_2$$

(23)

for $r_1 = $ const., $r_2 = $ const. depending on nodes' coordinates: see formula (21). If nodes are monotonic in y_i, there is parameterization of curve points P settled between nodes (x_1, y_1) and (x_2, y_2): $P(\alpha) = (x(c_1), c_1)$ for (22), (23) and $\alpha \in [0;1]$.

If nodes (x_i, y_i) are equidistance in one coordinate, then calculation of one unknown coordinate is simpler. Let four successive nodes (x_1, y_1), (x_2, y_2), (x_3, y_3), (x_4, y_4) are equidistance in coordinate x_i and $a = x_1$, $h/2 = x_{i+1} - x_i = $ const. Calculations in formulas (20)-(21) are done for c_1 (19):

$$y(c_1) = \alpha y_1 + \beta y_2 + \alpha \beta s \tag{24}$$

and

$$s = h \left(\frac{2ay_1 + hy_1 + hy_3}{4a^2 + 4ah + 2h^2} - \frac{2ay_2 + 2hy_2 + hy_4}{4a^2 + 8ah + 5h^2} \right). \tag{25}$$

As we can see in formulas (21) and (23)-(25), MHR interpolation is not a linear interpolation. It is possible to estimate the interpolation error of MHR method (algorithm 1) for the class of linear function f:

$$\left| f(c_1) - y(c_1) \right| = \left| \alpha y_1 + \beta y_2 - y(c_1) \right| = \alpha \beta |s|. \tag{26}$$

Notice that estimation (26) has the biggest value $0.25|s|$ for $\beta = \alpha = 0.5$, when c_1 (19) is situated in the middle between x_1 and x_2.

Having four successive nodes (x_1,y_1), (x_2,y_2), (x_3,y_3), (x_4,y_4) equidistance in coordinate x_i ($a = x_1$, $h/2 = x_{i+1}-x_i$ = const.) we can compute polynomial $W_3(x) = m_3 x^3 + m_2 x^2 + m_1 x + t$ for these nodes and estimate the interpolation error of MHR method (algorithm 1) for the class of order three polynomials. After solving the system of equations:

$$y_1 = m_3 a^3 + m_2 a^2 + m_1 a + t,$$

$$y_2 = m_3 \left(a + \frac{h}{2} \right)^3 + m_2 \left(a + \frac{h}{2} \right)^2 + m_1 \left(a + \frac{h}{2} \right) + t,$$

$$y_3 = m_3 (a + h)^3 + m_2 (a + h)^2 + m_1 (a + h) + t,$$

$$y_4 = m_3 \left(a + \frac{3h}{2} \right)^3 + m_2 \left(a + \frac{3h}{2} \right)^2 + m_1 \left(a + \frac{3h}{2} \right) + t,$$

it is possible to compute m_3, m_2, m_1, t and the estimation for point c_1 (19):

$$\left| W_3(c_1) - y(c_1) \right| = \beta \left| \frac{1}{2} h(y_2 - y_1) \frac{12\alpha\beta a + 12a\beta^2 + 2h\beta^2 - \alpha\beta ah^2 - 12a - 2h}{6ha + 12a^2 + h^2} - \alpha \cdot s \right|. \tag{27}$$

Notice that estimations (26)-(27) are equal with zero for $\alpha = 0$ or $\beta = 0$ (in nodes). For eight successive nodes (x_i, y_i), $i = 1, 2, \ldots, 8$ equidistance in coordinate x_i, $a = x_1$, $h/2 = x_{i+1} - x_i = = \text{const.}$, using OHR of dimension $N = 4$ in formula (14) here is a formula of second coordinate reconstruction with first coordinate c_1 (19):

$$y(c_1) = \alpha y_1 + \beta y_2 - \frac{\beta h^2}{4a^2 + 16ah + 21h^2} \left[(\alpha y_3 + \beta y_4) + 2(\alpha y_7 + \beta y_8) \right]$$

$$+ \frac{\beta h}{(4a^2 + 16ah - 21h^2)(2a^2 + 6ah + 7h^2)} \begin{bmatrix} 2(\alpha y_1 + \beta y_2)(2a^3 + 10a^2h + 19ah^2 + 14h^3) \\ + \alpha h(ay_1 + hy_7)(2a + 7h) + 3.5\alpha h^3(y_1 + y_3) \\ + 2ah \begin{bmatrix} \alpha hy_3 + \alpha hy_7 + 17ay_2 - ay_4 \\ -2ay_8 - 3hy_4 - 6hy_8 \end{bmatrix} \\ + -7h^3(21y_2 + y_4 + 2y_8) \\ -2ay_2(2a^2 + 27ah + 19h^2) \end{bmatrix}$$

$$(28)$$

So we have another parameterization (28) of the point $P(\alpha) = (c_1, y(c_1))$ for $N = 4$ and $\beta = 1 - \alpha$. Formula (28) doesn't include values y_5 and y_6; algorithm 1 with nine successive nodes (x_i, y_i), $i = 1, 2, \ldots, 9$ equidistance in coordinate x_i is free of using y_5 and y_6 for computing second coordinate of the point settled between first and second node.

Algorithm 1 deals with average OHR operators (11)-(12) built with two OHR. This situation leads to parameterization of reconstructed point $P(\alpha) = (c_1, y(c_1))$ or $P(\alpha) = (x(c_1), c_1)$ settled between two successive nodes, where $\alpha \in [0;1]$ is order two in formulas (21), (23)-(25) and (28). The curve or data in MHR method are parameterized for value $\alpha \in [0;1]$ in the range of two successive interpolation nodes. MHR for data extrapolation is possible with $\alpha < 0$ or $\alpha > 1$.

Risk Analysis and Decision Making via Data Extrapolation

Example 1

MHR calculations are done for true rates of euro at National Bank of Poland (NBP) from January 24th to February 14th, 2011. If last four rates are considered: (1;3.8993), (2;3.9248), (3;3.9370) and (4;3.9337), MHR extrapolation with matrices of dimension $N = 2$ gives the result (5;3.9158). So anticipated rate of euro on the day February 15th is 3.9158 (Figure 3).

Figure 3. Extrapolated rate for day 5 (February 15th) using MHR method with 4 nodes
Source: Author, 2016.

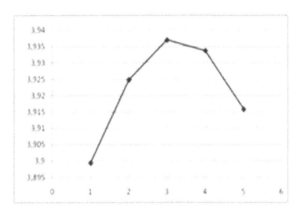

Figure 4. Extrapolated rate for day 9 (February 15th) using MHR method with 8 nodes
Source: Author, 2016.

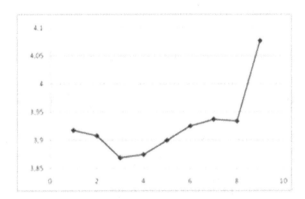

If last eight rates are considered: (1;3.9173), (2;3.9075), (3;3.8684), (4;3.8742), (5;3.8993), (6;3.9248), (7;3.9370) and (8;3.9337), MHR extrapolation with matrices of dimension $N = 4$ gives the result (9;4.0767). Anticipated rate of euro on the day February 15th is 4.0767 (Figure 4).

There are two extrapolated values for next day. This example gives us two anticipated rates for tomorrow: 3.9158 and 4.0767, which differs considerably. How these extrapolated values can be used in the process of decision making and analyzing risk: to buy euro or not, to sell euro or not? The proposal final anticipated rate of euro for the day February 15th (Figure 5) based on weighted mean value:

*Figure 5. Extrapolated rate for day 9 (February 15ᵗʰ) using MHR method with 8
nodes and weighted mean value (29)*
Source: Author, 2016.

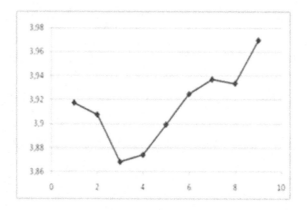

$$\frac{2 \cdot 3.9158 + 4.0767}{3} = 3.9694 \tag{29}$$

because the rate 3.9158 is calculated for $N = 2$, whereas 4.0767 is extrapolated
for $N = 4$. Formula (29) takes one fact into account: dimension $N = 4$ is two
times bigger than dimension $N = 2$ and the result 3.9158 has to be strengthen
multiplying by two.

If last sixteen rates are considered, MHR extrapolation with matrices of
dimension $N = 8$ has to be used. Here are the rates: (1;3.8765), (2;3.8777),
(3;3.8777), (4;3.9009), (5;3.9111), (6;3.9345), (7;3.9129), (8;3.9019),
(9;3.9173), (10;3.9075), (11;3.8684), (12;3.8742), (13;3.8993), (14;3.9248),
(15;3.9370) and (16;3.9337). Average OHR operator M_2 and MHR calculations
look as follows:

$$M_2 = \begin{bmatrix}
0.3226 & 0.0154 & 0.0286 & 0.0462 & -0.062 & 0.0444 & 0.0924 & 0.0461 \\
-0.0154 & 0.3226 & 0.0462 & -0.0286 & 0.0444 & 0.062 & -0.0461 & 0.0924 \\
-0.0286 & -0.0462 & 0.3226 & 0.0154 & 0.0924 & 0.0461 & 0.062 & -0.0444 \\
-0.0462 & 0.0286 & -0.0154 & 0.3226 & 0.0461 & -0.0924 & 0.0444 & 0.062 \\
0.062 & -0.0444 & -0.0924 & -0.0461 & 0.3226 & 0.0154 & 0.0286 & 0.0462 \\
-0.0444 & -0.062 & -0.0461 & 0.0924 & -0.0154 & 0.3226 & -0.0462 & 0.0286 \\
-0.0924 & 0.0461 & -0.062 & -0.0444 & -0.0286 & 0.0462 & 0.3226 & -0.0154 \\
-0.0461 & -0.0924 & 0.0444 & -0.062 & -0.0462 & -0.0286 & 0.0154 & 0.3226
\end{bmatrix},$$

Figure 6. Extrapolated rate for day 17 (February 15ᵗʰ) using MHR method with 16 nodes
Source: Author, 2016.

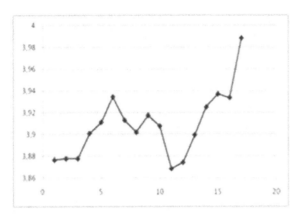

$$M_2 \cdot \begin{bmatrix} 3 \\ 5 \\ 7 \\ 9 \\ 11 \\ 13 \\ 15 \\ 17 \end{bmatrix} = \begin{bmatrix} 3.7252 \\ 3.8072 \\ 3.8704 \\ 3.8278 \\ 3.8653 \\ 3.8834 \\ 3.9825 \\ 3.9882 \end{bmatrix}$$

MHR extrapolation gives the result (17;3.9882). Anticipated rate of euro for the day February 15ᵗʰ is 3.9882 (Figure 6).

MHR extrapolation has been done for three times ($N = 2$, 4 or 8) and anticipated values are 3.9158, 4.0767 and 3.9882 respectively. The proposal final anticipated rate of euro for the day February 15ᵗʰ (Figure 7) based on weighted mean value:

$$\frac{4 \cdot 3.9158 + 2 \cdot 4.0767 + 3.9882}{7} = 3.9721 \tag{30}$$

because the rate 3.9158 is calculated with last four data points, 4.0767 is extrapolated for last eight data points and 3.9882 is computed for last sixteen

Figure 7. Extrapolated rate for day 17 (February 15th) using MHR method with 16 nodes and weighted mean value (30)
Source: Author, 2016.

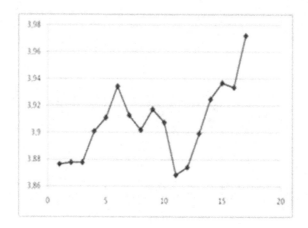

Figure 8. The true rate of euro for day 17 (February 15th)
Source: Author, 2016.

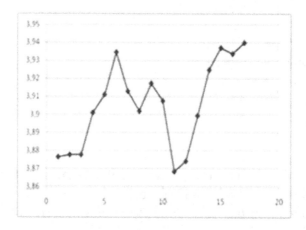

data points. Formula (30) takes one fact into account: number of sixteen points is four times bigger than four and two times bigger than eigth. The result 3.9158 has to be strengthen multiplying by four and the rate 4.0767 has to be strengthen multiplying by two.

The true rate of euro for the day February 15th is 3.9398 (Figure 8).

In author's opinion, values extrapolated for next day 3.9694 (13) and 3.9721 (14) are good enough to be one of the factors for making a decision of buying or selling the currency.

Example 2

MHR calculations are done for true rates of US dollar at National Bank of Poland (NBP) from June 16th to July 8th, 2011 (Friday). If last four rates are considered: (1;2.7266), (2;2.7531), (3;2.7597) and (4;2.7505), MHR extrapolation with matrices of dimension $N = 2$ gives the result (5;2.7239):

$$M_2 = \begin{bmatrix} 0.5503 & -9.13 \times 10^{-3} \\ -9.13 \times 10^{-3} & 0.5503 \end{bmatrix}, M_2 = \begin{bmatrix} 3 \\ 5 \end{bmatrix} = \begin{bmatrix} 1.6964 \\ 2.7239 \end{bmatrix}$$

So anticipated rate of US dollar on the day July 11th (Monday) is 2.7239.

If last eight rates are considered: (1;2.7877), (2;2.7517), (3;2.7273), (4;2.7156), (5;2.7266), (6; 2.7531), (7; 2.7597) and (8; 2.7505), MHR extrapolation with matrices of dimension $N = 4$ gives the result (9;2.8471):

$$M_2 = \begin{bmatrix} 0.3919 & -0.0032 & 0.0999 & 0.0527 \\ 0.0032 & 0.3919 & -0.0527 & 0.0999 \\ -0.0999 & 0.0527 & 0.3919 & 0.0032 \\ -0.0527 & -0.0999 & -0.0032 & 0.3919 \end{bmatrix}, M_2 \cdot \begin{bmatrix} 3 \\ 5 \\ 7 \\ 9 \end{bmatrix} = \begin{bmatrix} 2.3333 \\ 2.4999 \\ 2.7365 \\ 2.8471 \end{bmatrix}$$

Anticipated rate of US dollar on the day July 11th is 2.8471. There are two extrapolated values for next day. Example 2 gives us two anticipated rates for tomorrow: 2.7239 and 2.8471. How these extrapolated values can be used in the process of decision making: to buy dollar or not, to sell dollar or not? The proposal final anticipated rate of US dollar (Figure 9) on the day July 11th based on weighted mean value:

$$\frac{2 \cdot 2.7239 + 2.8471}{3} = 2.7650 \tag{31}$$

because the rate 2.7239 is calculated for $N = 2$, whereas 2.8471 is extrapolated for $N = 4$.

If last sixteen rates are considered, MHR extrapolation with matrices of dimension $N = 8$ has to be used. Here are the rates: (1;2.8069), (2;2.8077), (3;2.8058), (4;2.7776), (5;2.7661), (6;2.7914), (7;2.8201), (8;2.8055), (9;2.7877), (10;2.7517), (11;2.7273), (12;2.7156), (13;2.7266), (14;2.7531),

Figure 9. Extrapolated rate for day 9 (July 11ᵗʰ) using MHR method with 8 nodes and weighted mean value (31)
Source: Author, 2016.

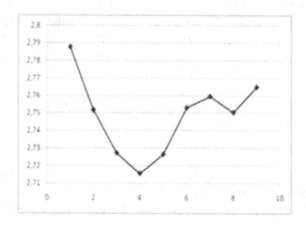

Figure 10. Extrapolated rate for day 17 (July 11ᵗʰ) using MHR method with 16 nodes and weighted mean value (32)
Source: Author, 2016.

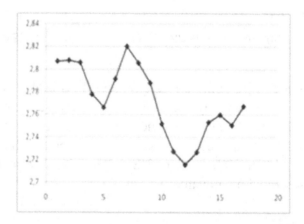

(15;2.7597) and (16;2.7505). MHR extrapolation gives the result (17;2.7808). Anticipated rate of US dollar on the day July 11ᵗʰ is 2.7808.

MHR extrapolation has been done for three times ($N = 2$, 4 or 8) and anticipated values are 2.7239, 2.8471 and 2.7808 respectively. The proposal final anticipated rate of US dollar (Figure 10) on the day July 11ᵗʰ based on weighted mean value:

Figure 11. The true rate of US dollar for day 17 (July 11th)
Source: Author, 2016.

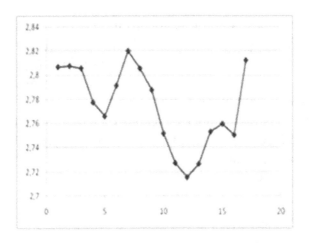

$$\frac{4 \cdot 2.7239 + 2 \cdot 2.8471 + 2.7808}{7} = 2.7672 \tag{32}$$

because the rate 2.7239 is calculated with last four data points, 2.8471 is extrapolated for last eight data points and 2.7808 is computed for last sixteen data points.

The true rate of US dollar on the day July 11th is 2.8123 (Figure 11).

In author's opinion, extrapolated values 2.7650 (15) and 2.7672 (16) and anticipated rates in example 1 preserve the increasing trend and they are good enough to be one of the factors for making a decision of buying or selling the currency. Anticipated values, calculated by MHR method, are applied in the process of risk analysis and decision making: to follow the action or not, to do one thing or another. Extrapolated values can be used to make a decision in many branches of science and economics.

Discussion of Examples

This chapter goes to first step of application for MHR method in point extrapolation and decision making. Figures and calculations show the trends of value: increasing or decreasing. This information could be used in analyzing risk and decision making, for example buying or selling when risk analysis is very difficult and very important.

THE LENGTH ESTIMATION

Selection of the nodes is a key factor in the process of interpolation and extrapolation. The length of a curve is significant feature. Also the length estimation depends on the nodes. Having nodes (x_1, y_1), (x_2, y_2),..., (x_n, y_n) in MHR method (algorithm 1), it is possible to compute as many curve points as we want for any parameter $\alpha \in [0;1]$.

Assume that L is the number of reconstructed points plus n nodes. So curve consists of L points that could be indexed (x_1', y_1'), (x_2', y_2'),..., (x_L', y_L'), where $(x_1', y_1') = (x_1, y_1)$ and $(x_L', y_L') = (x_n, y_n)$.

The length of curve, consists of L points, is estimated:

$$d(L) = \sum_{i=1}^{L-1} \sqrt{(x_{i+1}' - x_i')^2 + (y_{i+1}' - y_i')^2} \ . \tag{33}$$

For any accuracy of length estimation $\varepsilon > 0$, it is possible to use MHR method (algorithm 1) with suitable number and location of n nodes and reconstruct curve consists of L and L_1 points, where

$$\left| d(L) - d(L_1) \right| < \varepsilon \ .$$

So there is no need to compute

$$\int_{x_1}^{x_n} \sqrt{1 + [f'(x)]^2} \, dx \tag{34}$$

as the length of curve f. Formula (33) has lower computational cost then (34).

SOLUTIONS AND RECOMMENDATIONS

The chapter deals with the problem of data interpolation and anticipation. None of the methods, that are used nowadays, applies the orthogonal basis for unknown value extrapolation and foreseeing, but proposed MHR method does as the solution. Orthogonality means a very important feature for stability in calculations. Also MHR point interpolation and extrapolation via simple computations with matrices is something new in the problem of anticipation, risk analysis and decision making. Extrapolated values show increasing or decreasing trend during the process of analyzing risk and decision making. MHR method as the solution is recommended in artificial intelligence and operational research, for example in scheduling, time-tabling or planning.

FUTURE RESEARCH DIRECTIONS

Future works with MHR method are connected with the formula of extrapolated values. Also estimation of object area in the plane, using nodes of object contour, will be possible by MHR interpolation. Length of the curve and object area are significant features in many economic problems. Future works are dealing with smoothing the curve, parameterization of whole curve and possibility to apply MHR method to three-dimensional curves. Also case of equidistance nodes must be studied with all details. Another future research direction is to apply MHR method in artificial intelligence and operational research, for example scheduling, time-tabling, planning, identification of a specific person's face or fingerprint, character recognition (Lamdan, Schwartz & Wolfson, 1990) or image restoration (Pope & Lowe, 2004). There are several specialized tasks based on recognition to consider and it is important to use the shape of whole contour (Kriegman & Ponce, 1990) for identification and detection of persons, vehicles or other objects. Other applications of MHR method will be directed to computer graphics, modeling and image processing.

CONCLUSION

The method of Hurwitz-Radon Matrices leads to curve interpolation and value extrapolation depending on the number and location of data points. No characteristic features of curve are important in MHR method: failing to be differentiable at any point, the Runge's phenomenon or differences from the shape of polynomials. These features are very significant for classical polynomial interpolations and extrapolations. MHR method gives the possibility of reconstruction a curve and anticipation the data points. The only condition is to have a set of nodes according to assumptions in MHR method. Data representation and curve extrapolation by MHR method is connected with possibility of changing the nodes coordinates and reconstruction of new data or curve for new set of nodes. The same MHR interpolation and extrapolation is valid for discrete and continues data. Main features of MHR method are: accuracy of data reconstruction depending on number of nodes; interpolation or extrapolation of a curve consists of L points is connected with the computational cost of rank $O(L)$; MHR method is dealing with local operators: average OHR operators are built by successive 4, 8 or 16 data points, what is connected with smaller computational costs then using all nodes; MHR is not an affine interpolation.

Risk analysis needs suitable methods of data extrapolation and decision making. Proposed method of Hurwitz-Radon Matrices (MHR) can be used in extrapolation and interpolation of curves in the plane. For example quotations from the Stock Exchange, the market prices or rate of a currency form a curve. This chapter contains the way of data anticipation and extrapolation via MHR method and decision making: to buy or not, to sell or not. Proposed method is based on a family of Hurwitz-Radon (HR) matrices. The matrices are skew-symmetric and possess columns composed of orthogonal vectors. The operator of Hurwitz-Radon (OHR), built from these matrices, is described. Two-dimensional data are represented by the set of curve points. It is shown how to create the orthogonal and discrete OHR and how to use it in a process of data foreseeing and extrapolation. MHR method is interpolating and extrapolating the curve point by point without using any formula or function. Proposed method, called Probabilistic Nodes Combination (PNC), is the method of 2D curve interpolation and extrapolation using the set of key points (knots or nodes). Nodes can be treated as characteristic points of data for modeling and analyzing. The model of data can be built by choice of probability distribution function and nodes combination. PNC modeling via nodes combination and parameter γ as probability distribution function enables value anticipation in risk analysis and decision making. Two-dimensional curve is extrapolated and interpolated via nodes combination and different functions as discrete or continuous probability distribution functions: polynomial, sine, cosine, tangent, cotangent, logarithm, exponent, arc sin, arc cos, arc tan, arc cot or power function. Novelty of the paper consists of two generalizations: generalization of previous MHR method with various nodes combinations and generalization of linear interpolation with different (no basic) probability distribution functions and nodes combinations. Computer vision needs suitable methods of shape representation and contour reconstruction. One of them, invented by the author and called method of Hurwitz-Radon Matrices (MHR), can be used in representation and reconstruction of shapes of the objects in the plane. Proposed method is based on a family of Hurwitz-Radon (HR) matrices. The matrices are skew-symmetric and possess columns composed of orthogonal vectors. 2D shape is represented by the set of successive nodes. It is shown how to create the orthogonal and discrete OHR operator and how to use it in a process of shape representation and reconstruction. Then MHR method is generalized to Probabilistic Nodes Combination (PNC) method.

This work clarifies the significance and novelty of the proposed method compared to existing methods (for example polynomial interpolations and Bézier curves). Previous published papers of the author were dealing with the method of Hurwitz-Radon Matrices (MHR method). Novelty of this monograph and proposed method consists in the fact that calculations are free from the family of Hurwitz-Radon Matrices. Problem statement of this paper is: how to reconstruct (interpolate) missing points of 2D curve having the set of interpolation nodes (key points) and using the information about probabilistic distribution of unknown points. For example the simplest basic distribution leads to the easiest interpolation – linear interpolation. Apart from probability distribution, additionally there is the second factor of proposed interpolation method: nodes combination. The simplest nodes combination is zero. Thus proposed curve modeling is based on two agents: probability distribution and nodes combination. Significance of this paper consists in generalization for MHR method: the computations are done without matrices in curve fitting and shape modeling, with clear point interpolation formula based on probability distribution function (continuous or discrete) and nodes combination. This book also consists of generalization for linear interpolation with different (no basic) probability distribution functions and nodes combinations. So this chapter answers the question: "Why and when should we use PNC method?".

REFERENCES

Brachman, R. J., & Levesque, H. J. (2004). *Knowledge representation and reasoning*. San Francisco, CA: Morgan Kaufman.

Cierniak, R. (2005). *Computed tomography*. Warsaw, Poland: Exit.

Citko, W., Jakóbczak, D., & Sieńko, W. (2005, September). *On Hurwitz-Radon matrices based signal processing*. Paper presented at the workshop Signal Processing at Poznan University of Technology, Poznań, Poland.

Dahlquist, G., & Bjoerck, A. (1974). *Numerical methods*. Englewood Cliffs, NJ: Prentice Hall.

Eckmann, B. (1999). Topology, algebra, analysis- relations and missing links. *Notices of the American Mathematical Society, 5*(46), 520–527.

Fagin, R., Halpern, J. Y., Moses, Y., & Vardi, M. Y. (1995). *Reasoning about knowledge.* Cambridge, MA: MIT Press.

Jakóbczak, D. (2006). *Application of discrete, orthogonal operator of Hurwitz-Radon in compression and reconstruction of monochromatic images' contours* (Unpublished doctoral dissertation). Polish-Japanese Institute of Information Technology, Warsaw, Poland.

Jakóbczak, D. (2007). 2D and 3D image modeling using Hurwitz-Radon matrices. *Polish Journal of Environmental Studies, 4A*(16), 104–107.

Jakóbczak, D., & Kosiński, W. (2007a). Hurwitz-Radon operator in monochromatic medical image reconstruction. *Journal of Medical Informatics & Technologies, 11*, 69–78.

Jakóbczak, D., & Kosiński, W. (2007b). Application of Hurwitz-Radon matrices in monochromatic medical images decompression. In Z. Kowalczuk & B. Wiszniewski (Eds.), *Intelligent data mining in diagnostic purposes: Automatics and informatics* (pp. 389–398). Gdansk, Poland: PWNT.

Kozera, R. (2004). *Curve modeling via interpolation based on multidimensional reduced data.* Gliwice, Poland: Silesian University of Technology Press.

Kriegman, D. J., & Ponce, J. (1990). On recognizing and positioning curved 3-D objects from image contours. *IEEE Transactions on Pattern Analysis and Machine Intelligence, 12*(12), 1127–1137. doi:10.1109/34.62602

Lamdan, Y., Schwartz, J. T., & Wolfson, H. J. (1990). Affine invariant model-based object recognition. *IEEE Transactions on Robotics and Automation, 5*(6), 578–589. doi:10.1109/70.62047

Latecki, L. J., & Lakaemper, R. (1999). Convexity rule for shape decomposition based on Discrete Contour Evolution. *Computer Vision and Image Understanding, 3*(73), 441–454. doi:10.1006/cviu.1998.0738

Lowe, D. G. (1991). Fitting parameterized three-dimensional models to images. *IEEE Transactions on Pattern Analysis and Machine Intelligence, 5*(13), 441–450. doi:10.1109/34.134043

Lowe, D. G. (1999, September). *Object recognition from local scale-invariant features*. Paper presented at the International Conference on Computer Vision, Corfu, Greece.

Lowe, D. G. (2001). *Local feature view clustering for 3D object recognition*. Paper presented at the IEEE Conference on Computer Vision and Pattern Recognition, Kauai, HI. doi:10.1109/CVPR.2001.990541

Markman, A. B. (1998). *Knowledge representation*. Mahwah, NJ: Lawrence Erlbaum Associates.

Pope, A. R., & Lowe, D. G. (2004). Probabilistic models of appearance for 3-D object recognition. *International Journal of Computer Vision*, 2(40), 149–167.

Ralston, A. (1965). *A first course in numerical analysis*. New York: McGraw-Hill Book Company.

Sieńko, W., & Citko, W. (2002). *Hamiltonian Neural Net based signal processing*. Paper presented at the International Conference on Signal and Electronic System ICSES, Wrocław – Świeradów Zdrój, Poland.

Sieńko, W., Citko, W., & Jakóbczak, D. (2004). Learning and system modeling via Hamiltonian Neural Networks. In L. Rutkowski, J. Siekmann, R. Tadeusiewicz, & A. Zadeh (Eds.), *Lecture notes on artificial intelligence: Artificial intelligence and soft computing-ICAISC 2004* (pp. 266–271). Berlin: Springer-Verlag. doi:10.1007/978-3-540-24844-6_36

Sieńko, W., Citko, W., & Wilamowski, B. (2002). *Hamiltonian Neural Nets as a universal signal processor*. Paper presented at the 28th Annual Conference of the IEEE Industrial Electronics Society IECON, Sevilla, Spain. doi:10.1109/IECON.2002.1182910

Soussen, C., & Mohammad-Djafari, A. (2004). Polygonal and polyhedral contour reconstruction in computed tomography. *IEEE Transactions on Image Processing*, *11*(13), 1507–1523. doi:10.1109/TIP.2004.836159 PMID:15540458

Sowa, J. F. (2000). *Knowledge representation: logical, philosophical and computational foundations*. New York: Brooks/Cole.

Straffin, P. D. (1993). *Game theory and strategy*. Washington, DC: Mathematical Association of America.

Tang, K. (2005). Geometric optimization algorithms in manufacturing. *Computer-Aided Design and Applications*, 2(6), 747–757. doi:10.1080/168 64360.2005.10738338

Tarokh, V., Jafarkhani, H., & Calderbank, R. (1999). Space-Time Block Codes from orthogonal designs. *IEEE Transactions on Information Theory*, 5(45), 1456–1467. doi:10.1109/18.771146

Ullman, S., & Basri, R. (1991). Recognition by linear combinations of models. *IEEE Transactions on Pattern Analysis and Machine Intelligence*, 10(13), 992–1006. doi:10.1109/34.99234

Watson, J. (2002). *Strategy – an introduction to game theory*. San Diego, CA: University of California Press.

ADDITIONAL READING

Ballard, D. H. (1982). *Computer Vision*. New York: Prentice Hall.

Basu, S., & Bresler, Y. (2000). $O(N^2\log_2 N)$ filtered backprojection reconstruction algorithm for tomography. *IEEE Transactions on Image Processing*, 9(10), 1760–1773. doi:10.1109/83.869187 PMID:18262914

Brankov, J. G., Yang, Y., & Wernick, M. N. (2004). Tomographic image reconstruction based on a Content – Adaptive Mesh Model. *IEEE Transactions on Medical Imaging*, 2(23), 202–212. doi:10.1109/TMI.2003.822822 PMID:14964565

Brasse, D., & Defrise, M. (2004). Fast fully 3-D image reconstruction in PET using planograms. *IEEE Transactions on Medical Imaging*, 4(23), 413–425. doi:10.1109/TMI.2004.824231 PMID:15084067

Cetin, M., Karl, W. C., & Willsky, A. S. (2002, September). *Edge – preserving image reconstruction for coherent imaging application*. Paper presented at the IEEE International Conference on Image Processsing, Rochester, NY. doi:10.1109/ICIP.2002.1039992

Chapra, S. C. (2012). *Applied Numerical Methods*. McGraw-Hill.

Chlebus, E., & Cholewa, M. (1999). Rapid prototyping – rapid tooling. *CADCAM Forum, 11*, 23-28.

Choraś, R. S. (2005). *Computer Vision*. Warsaw, Poland: Exit.

Cocozza-Thivent, C., Eymard, R., Mercier, S., & Roussignol, M. (2006). Characterization of the Marginal Distributions of Markov Processes Used in Dynamic Reliability. *Journal of Applied Mathematics and Stochastic Analysis. Article ID*, *92156*, 1–18.

Collins, G. W. II. (2003). *Fundamental Numerical Methods and Data Analysis*. Case Western Reserve University.

Cormen, T. H., Leiserson, C. E., & Rivest, R. L. (1996). *Introduction to algorithms*. Massachusetts, USA: the Massachusetts Institute of Technology Press and McGraw-Hill.

Defrise, M. (2001). A short readers guide to 3D tomographic reconstruction. *Computerized Medical Imaging and Graphics*, *25*(2), 113–116. doi:10.1016/S0895-6111(00)00061-6 PMID:11137787

Dejdumrong, N. (2007). A Shape Preserving Verification Techniques for Parametric Curves. *Computer Graphics, Imaging and Visualization. CGIV*, *2007*, 163–168.

Dryja, M., Jankowska, J., & Jankowski, M. (1982). *Survey of numerical methods and algorithms. Part II*. Warsaw, Poland: WNT.

Dyn, N., Levin, D., & Gregory, J. A. (1987). A 4-Point Interpolatory Subdivision Scheme for Curve Design. *Computer Aided Geometric Design*, *4*(4), 257–268. doi:10.1016/0167-8396(87)90001-X

Eldar, Y. C. (2001). *Quantum Signal Processing*. (Unpublished doctoral dissertation). Massachusetts Institute of Technology, USA.

Eldar, Y. C., & Oppenheim, A. V. (2002). Quantum Signal Processing. *IEEE Signal Processing Magazine*, *6*(19), 12–32. doi:10.1109/MSP.2002.1043298

Fortuna, Z., Macukow, B., & Wąsowski, J. (1982). *Numerical methods*. Warsaw, Poland: WNT.

Jakóbczak, D. (2005). Hurwitz-Radon matrices and their children. *Computer Science*, *5*(8), 29–38.

Jakóbczak, D. (2009). Curve Interpolation Using Hurwitz-Radon Matrices. *Polish Journal of Environmental Studies*, *3B*(18), 126–130.

Jakóbczak, D. (2010). Shape Representation and Shape Coefficients via Method of Hurwitz-Radon Matrices. *Lecture Notes in Computer Science, 6374*, 411–419. doi:10.1007/978-3-642-15910-7_47

Jakóbczak, D. (2010). Object Modeling Using Method of Hurwitz-Radon Matrices of Rank k. In W. Wolski & M. Borawski (Eds.), *Computer Graphics: Selected Issues* (pp. 79–90). Szczecin, Poland: University of Szczecin Press.

Jakóbczak, D. (2011). Curve Parameterization and Curvature via Method of Hurwitz-Radon Matrices. *Image Processing & Communications-. International Journal (Toronto, Ont.), 1-2*(16), 49–56.

Jakóbczak, D. (2011). Data Extrapolation and Decision Making via Method of Hurwitz-Radon Matrices. *Lecture Notes in Computer Science, 6922*, 173–182. doi:10.1007/978-3-642-23935-9_17

Jakóbczak, D. (2011). Curve Extrapolation and Data Analysis using the Method of Hurwitz-Radon Matrices. *Folia Oeconomica Stetinensia.* 9(17)/2010, 121-138.

Jakóbczak, D. (2013). Probabilistic Modeling of Signature using the Method of Hurwitz-Radon Matrices. *Global Perspectives on Artificial Intelligence, 1*(1), 1–7.

Jankowska, J., & Jankowski, M. (1981). *Survey of numerical methods and algorithms. Part I.* Warsaw, Poland: WNT.

Kontaxakis, G., & Strauss, L. G. (1998). Maximum likelihood algorithms for image reconstruction in Positron Emission Tomography. *Radionuclides for Oncology – Current Status and Future Aspects, 1998*, 73-106.

Kowalczuk, Z., & Wiszniewski, B. (Eds.). (2007). *Intelligent data mining in diagnostic purposes: Automatics and informatics.* Gdansk, Poland: PWNT.

Kundur, D., & Hatzinakos, D. (1998). A novel blind deconvolution scheme for image restoration using recursive filtering. *IEEE Transactions on Signal Processing, 2*(46), 375–390. doi:10.1109/78.655423

Laine, A., & Zong, X. (1996). *Border identification of echocardiograms via multiscale edge detection and shape modeling.* Paper presented at the IEEE International Conference on Image Processsing, Lausanne, Switzerland. doi:10.1109/ICIP.1996.560486

Lang, S. (1970). *Algebra.* Reading, MA: Addison-Wesley Publishing Company.

Le Buhan Jordan, C., Bossen, F., & Ebrahimi, T. (1997). *Scalable shape representation for content based visual data compression*. Paper presented at the International Conference on Image Processing, Santa Barbara, CA. doi:10.1109/ICIP.1997.647962

Liu, T., & Geiger, D. (1999). Approximate tree matching and shape similarity. *Int. Conf. Computer Vision*. Corfu, Greece.

Lorton, A., Fouladirad, M., & Grall, A. (2013). A Methodology for Probabilistic Model-based Prognosis. *European Journal of Operational Research, 225*(3), 443–454. doi:10.1016/j.ejor.2012.10.025

Marker, J., Braude, I., Museth, K., & Breen, D. (2006). Contour-based surface reconstruction using implicit curve fitting, and distance field filtering and interpolation. *Volume Graphics, 2006*, 1–9.

Meyer, Y. (1993). *Wavelets: algorithms & applications*. Philadelphia: Society for Industrial and Applied Mathematics.

Pergler, M., & Freeman, A. (2008). Probabilistic Modeling as an Exploratory Decision-Making Tool. *McKinsey Working Papers on Risk*. 6, 1-18.

Poggio, T., & Smale, S. (2003). The mathematics of learning: Dealing with data. *Notices of the American Mathematical Society, 5*(50), 537–544.

Przelaskowski, A. (2005). *Data compression*. Warsaw, Poland: BTC.

Ralston, A., & Rabinowitz, P. (2001). *A First Course in Numerical Analysis* (2nd ed.). New York: Dover Publications.

Rogers, D. F. (2001). *An Introduction to NURBS with Historical Perspective*. Morgan Kaufmann Publishers.

Rutkowski, L., Siekmann, J., Tadeusiewicz, R., & Zadeh, A. (Eds.). (2004). *Lecture notes on artificial intelligence: Artificial intelligence and soft computing*. Berlin: Springer-Verlag.

Saber, E., Xu, Y., & Murat Tekalp, A. (2005). Partial shape recognition by sub-matrix matching for partial matching guided image labeling. *Pattern Recognition, 38*(10), 1560–1573. doi:10.1016/j.patcog.2005.03.027

Schumaker, L. L. (2007). *Spline Functions: Basic Theory*. Cambridge Mathematical Library. doi:10.1017/CBO9780511618994

Sebastian, T. B., Klein, P. N., & Kimia, B. B. (2003). On aligning curves. *IEEE Transactions on Pattern Analysis and Machine Intelligence*, 25(1), 116–124. doi:10.1109/TPAMI.2003.1159951

Tadeusiewicz, R., & Flasiński, M. (1991). *Image Recognition*. Warsaw, Poland: PWN.

Vakhania, N. (1993). Orthogonal random vectors and the Hurwitz – Radon-Eckmann theorem. *Proc. of the Georgian Academy of Sciences-Mathematics, 1(1)*, 109-125.

Willis, M. (2000). *Algebraic reconstruction algorithms for remote sensing image enhancement*. Unpublished doctoral dissertation, Department of Electrical and Computer Engineering, Brigham Young University.

Xu, Fang, & Mueller, K. (2005). Accelerating popular tomographic reconstruction algorithms on commodity PC graphics hardware. *IEEE Transactions on Nuclear Science*, 3(52), 654–661.

Zaletelj, J., & Tasic, J. F. (2003). *Optimization and tracking of polygon vertices for shape coding*. Berlin: Springer-Verlag. doi:10.1007/978-3-540-45179-2_52

Zhang, D., & Lu, G. (2004). Review of Shape Representation and Description Techniques. *Pattern Recognition*, 1(37), 1–19. doi:10.1016/j. patcog.2003.07.008

Zhang, J. K., Davidson, T., & Wong, K. M. (2004). Efficient design of orthonormal wavelet bases for signal representation. *IEEE Transactions on Signal Processing*, 7(52), 1983–1996. doi:10.1109/TSP.2004.828923

KEY TERMS AND DEFINITIONS

Artificial Intelligence: Intelligence of machines and computers, as a connection of algorithms and hardware, which makes that a man – human being can be simulated by the machines in analyzing risk, decision making, reasoning, knowledge, planning, learning, communication, perception and the ability to move and manipulate objects.

Contour Modeling: Calculation of unknown points of the object contour having information about some points of the object contour.

Curve Interpolation: Computing new and unknown points of a curve and creating a graph of a curve using existing data points – interpolation nodes.

Data Extrapolation: Calculation of unknown values for the points situated outside the ranges of nodes.

Hurwitz – Radon Matrices: A family of skew – symmetric and orthogonal matrices with columns and rows that create, together with identical matrix, the base in vector spaces of dimensions $N = 2, 4$ or 8.

OHR Operator: Matrix operator of Hurwitz – Radon built from coordinates of interpolation nodes.

MHR Method: The method of curve interpolation and extrapolation using linear (convex) combinations of OHR operators.

Value Anticipation: Foreseeing next value when last value is known.

Chapter 2
Probabilistic Nodes Combination (PNC):
Formulas and Examples

ABSTRACT

The method of Probabilistic Nodes Combination (PNC) enables interpolation and modeling of two-dimensional curves using nodes combinations and different coefficients γ: polynomial, sinusoidal, cosinusoidal, tangent, cotangent, logarithmic, exponential, arc sin, arc cos, arc tan, arc cot or power function, also inverse functions. This probabilistic view is novel approach a problem of modeling and interpolation. Computer vision and pattern recognition are interested in appropriate methods of shape representation and curve modeling. PNC method represents the possibilities of shape reconstruction and curve interpolation via the choice of nodes combination and probability distribution function for interpolated points. It seems to be quite new look at the problem of contour representation and curve modeling in artificial intelligence and computer vision. Function for γ calculations is chosen individually at each curve modeling and it is treated as probability distribution function: γ depends on initial requirements and curve specifications.

DOI: 10.4018/978-1-5225-2531-8.ch002

INTRODUCTION

Probabilistic modeling is still a developing branch of economic and computer sciences: operational research (for example probabilistic model-based prognosis) (Lorton, Fouladirad & Grall, 2013), decision making techniques and probabilistic modeling (Pergler & Freeman, 2008), artificial intelligence and machine learning. Different aspects of probabilistic methods are used: stochastic processes and stochastic model-based techniques, Markov processes (Cocozza-Thivent, Eymard, Mercier & Roussignol, 2006), Poisson processes, Gamma processes, Monte Carlo methods, Bayes rule, conditional probability and many probability distributions. In this chapter the goal of a probability distribution function is to describe the position of unknown points between given interpolation nodes. Two-dimensional curve is used to represent the data points and extrapolation of the unknown values enables analyzing risk and then decision making.

The chapter clarifies the significance and novelty of the proposed method compared to existing methods (for example polynomial interpolations and Bézier curves). Previous published papers of the author were dealing with the method of Hurwitz-Radon Matrices (MHR method). Novelty of this chapter and proposed method consists in the fact that calculations are free from the family of Hurwitz-Radon Matrices. Problem statement of this chapter is: how to reconstruct (interpolate) missing points of 2D curve and how to anticipate (extrapolate) unknown values or data having the set of interpolation nodes (key points) and using the information about probabilistic distribution of unknown points. For example the simplest basic (uniform) distribution leads to the easiest interpolation – linear interpolation. Apart from probability distribution, additionally there is the second factor of proposed interpolation method: nodes combination. The simplest nodes combination is zero. Thus proposed curve modeling and extrapolation is based on two agents: probability distribution and nodes combination. First trial of probabilistic modeling in MHR version was described in (Jakóbczak, 2013). Significance of this chapter consists in generalization for MHR method: the computations are done without matrices in curve fitting and data anticipation, with clear point interpolation formula based on probability distribution function (continuous or discrete) and nodes combination. The chapter also consists of generalization for linear interpolation with different (non-uniform) probability distribution functions and nodes combinations. So this chapter answers the question: "Why and when should we use Probabilistic Nodes Combination (PNC) method in extrapolation and interpolation?".

Curve interpolation (Collins, 2003) represents one of the most important problems in mathematics and computer science: how to model the curve (Chapra, 2012) via discrete set of two-dimensional points (Ralston & Rabinowitz, 2001)? Also the matter of shape representation (as closed curve-contour) and curve parameterization is still opened (Zhang & Lu, 2004). Operational research in planning and scheduling, also decision making systems in risk analysis, solve the problems which are based on data modeling and extrapolation via the choice of key points. So interpolation and extrapolation is not only a pure mathematical problem but important task in economic and artificial intelligence. The chapter wants to approach a problem of curve modeling by characteristic points. Proposed method relies on nodes combination and functional modeling of curve points situated between the basic set of key points and outside of this set. The functions that are used in calculations represent whole family of elementary functions with inverse functions: polynomials, trigonometric, cyclometric, logarithmic, exponential and power function. These functions are treated as probability distribution functions in the range [0;1].

An important problem in operational research and computer sciences (Ballard, 1982) is that of appropriate shape representation and reconstruction. Classical discussion about shape representation is based on the problem: contour versus skeleton. This chapter is voting for contour which forms boundary of the object. Contour of the object, represented by contour points, consists of information which allows us to describe many important features of the object as shape coefficients (Tadeusiewicz & Flasiński, 1991). In the chapter contour is dealing with a set of curves. Curve modeling and generation is a basic subject in many branches of industry and computer science, for example in the CAD/CAM software.

The representation of shape has a great impact on the accuracy and effectiveness of object recognition (Saber, Yaowu & Murat, 2005). In the literature, shape has been represented by many options including curves (Sebastian & Klein, 2003), graph-based algorithms and medial axis (Liu & Geiger, 1999) to enable shape-based object recognition. Digital curve (open or closed) can be represented by chain code (Freeman's code). Chain code depends on selection of the started point and transformations of the object. So Freeman's code is one of the methods how to describe and to find contour of the object. An analog (continuous) version of Freeman's code is the curve α-s. Another contour representation and reconstruction is based on Fourier coefficients calculated in Discrete Fourier Transformation (DFT). These coefficients are used to fix similarity of the contours with different sizes or directions. If we assume that contour is built from segments of a line and fragments of circles or ellipses, Hough transformation is applied to detect contour lines. Also geometrical moments of the object are used during the process of object shape representation (Choraś, 2005). Proposed method, called Probabilistic Nodes Combination (PNC), is the method of 2D curve interpolation and extrapolation using the set of key points (knots or nodes). Nodes can be treated as characteristic points of data for modeling and analyzing. The model of data can be built by choice of probability distribution function and nodes combination. PNC modeling via nodes combination and parameter γ as probability distribution function enables value anticipation in risk analysis and decision making. Two-dimensional curve is extrapolated and interpolated via nodes combination and different functions as discrete or continuous probability distribution functions: polynomial, sine, cosine, tangent, cotangent, logarithm, exponent, arc sin, arc cos, arc tan, arc cot or power function. Novelty of this book consists of two generalizations: generalization of previous MHR method with various nodes combinations and generalization of linear interpolation with different (no basic) probability distribution functions and nodes combinations.

Curve interpolation represents one of the most important problems in mathematics and computer science: how to model the curve via discrete set of two-dimensional points? Also the matter of shape representation (as closed curve-contour) and curve parameterization is still opened. For example pattern recognition, signature verification or handwriting identification problems are based on curve modeling via the choice of key points. So interpolation is not only a pure mathematical problem but important task in computer vision and artificial intelligence. The monograph wants to approach a problem of curve modeling by characteristic points. Proposed method relies on nodes combination and functional modeling of curve points situated between the basic set of key points. The functions that are used in calculations represent whole family of elementary functions with inverse functions: polynomials, trigonometric, cyclometric, logarithmic, exponential and power function. These functions are treated as probability distribution functions in the range [0;1]. The method of Probabilistic Nodes Combination (PNC) enables interpolation and modeling of two-dimensional curves using nodes combinations and different coefficients γ: polynomial, sinusoidal, cosinusoidal, tangent, cotangent, logarithmic, exponential, arc sin, arc cos, arc tan, arc cot or power function, also inverse functions. This probabilistic view is novel approach a problem of modeling and interpolation. Computer vision and pattern recognition are interested in appropriate methods of shape representation and curve modeling. PNC method represents the possibilities of shape reconstruction and curve interpolation via the choice of nodes combination and probability distribution function for interpolated points. It seems to be quite new look at the problem of contour representation and curve modeling in artificial intelligence and computer vision.

BACKGROUND

All interpolation theory is based on polynomials. But why? Many kinds of polynomials are used for interpolation: classical polynomials, trigonometric polynomials, orthogonal polynomials (Tschebyscheff, Legendre, Laguerre), rational polynomials. But what about the exceptional situations with unexpected features of curve, data or nodes. Then polynomials are not the solution, for example when:

1. The curve is not a graph of function (no matter – opened or closed curve);
2. The curve does not have to be smooth at interpolation nodes: for example curve representing symbols, signature, handwriting or other specific data;
3. Nodes are fixed and there is no possibility to choose "better" nodes as for orthogonal polynomials;
4. The curve differs considerably from any interpolation polynomial;
5. The curve fails to be differentiable at some points;
6. Between each pair of nodes we are not interested in linear interpolation (uniform probability distribution and zero nodes combination) but there ought to be some generalization (even for two nodes only) with other probability distributions and nodes combinations;
7. Interpolated points depend on some chosen nodes (two nearest nodes or more) via nodes combination $h(p_1, p_2, ..., p_m)$ in (1);
8. We are not interested in the formula of interpolation function (for lower computational costs) but only calculated points of modeled curve are ready to be used in numerical computations;
9. The formula of curve or function is known but from some reason (for example high computational costs or hard polynomial interpolation) the curve has to be modeled or fitted in some way for numerical calculations

– the examples for PNC interpolation (in MHR version) of functions $f(x)$ = $2/x$ and $f(x) = 1/(1+5x^2)$ with quantified measures and experimental comparison with classical polynomial interpolation in (Jakóbczak, 2010);

10. Extrapolation problem is also a big numerical challenge and PNC interpolation enables the extension into extrapolation (Jakóbczak, 2011) with α outside of [0;1] and $\gamma = F(\alpha)$ still strictly monotonic, $F(0) = 0$, $F(1) = 1$. So for example $\gamma = \alpha^2$ is impossible for extrapolation if $\alpha <$ 0 (Jakóbczak, 2011). Polynomial or other interpolations are sometimes useless for extrapolation;

11. Having only nodes the user may have "negative" information (from specific character of data): no polynomial interpolation;

12. All calculations are numerical (discrete) – even $\gamma = F(\alpha)$ is to be given in tabular (discrete) form. There is no need to build continuous function: polynomial or others;

13. Parametric version of modeled curve is to be found.

Above thirteen important and heavy individual and characteristic features of some curves and their interpolations show that there may exist the situations with unexpected assumptions for interpolation.

Why not classical interpolation? Classical methods are useless to interpolate the function that fails to be differentiable at one point, for example the absolute value function $f(x) = |x|$ at $x = 0$. If point (0;0) is one of the interpolation nodes, then precise polynomial interpolation of the absolute value function is impossible. Also when the graph of interpolated function differs from the shape of polynomial considerably, for example $f(x) = 1/x$, interpolation is very hard because of existing local extrema and the roots of polynomial. We cannot forget about the Runge's phenomenon: when nodes are equidistance then high-order polynomial oscillates toward the end of the interval, for example close to -1 and 1 with function $f(x) = 1/(1+25x^2)$ (Ralston & Rabinowitz, 2001). These classical negative cases do not appear in proposed PNC method. Experimental comparison for PNC with polynomial interpolation is to be found in (Jakóbczak, 2009).

Nowadays methods apply mainly polynomial functions in different versions (trigonometric, orthogonal, rational) and for example Bernstein polynomials in Bezier curves, splines (Schumaker, 2007) and NURBS (Rogers, 2001). But Bezier curves don't represent the interpolation method (rather interpolation-approximation method) and cannot be used for example in handwriting modeling with key points (interpolation nodes). In comparison PNC method with Bézier curves, Hermite curves and B-curves (*B-splines*) or NURBS one unpleasant feature of these curves has to be mentioned: small change of one characteristic point can result in unwanted change of whole reconstructed curve. Such a feature does not appear in proposed PNC method which is more stable than Bézier curves. Only first and last characteristic point is situated on the Bézier curve (interpolation), the rest characteristic points lay outside the Bézier curve (approximation). Numerical methods for data interpolation are based on polynomial or trigonometric functions, for example Lagrange, Newton, Aitken and Hermite methods. These methods have many weak sides (Dahlquist & Bjoerck, 1974) and are not sufficient for curve interpolation in the situations when the curve cannot be build by polynomials or trigonometric functions. Also there exists several well established methods of curve modeling, for example shape-preserving techniques (Dejdumrong, 2007), subdivision algorithms (Dyn, Levin & Gregory, 1987) and others (Kozera, 2004) to overcome difficulties of polynomial interpolation, but probabilistic interpolation with nodes combination seems to be quite novel in the area of shape modeling. Proposed 2D curve interpolation is the functional modeling via any elementary functions and it helps us to fit the curve during the computations.

This chapter presents novel Probabilistic Nodes Combination (PNC) method of curve interpolation. This chapter takes up new PNC method of two-dimensional curve modeling via the examples using the family of Hurwitz-Radon matrices (MHR method) (Jakóbczak, 2007), but not only this method (other nodes combinations). The method of PNC requires minimal assumptions: the only information about a curve is the set of at least two nodes. Proposed PNC method is applied in curve modeling via different coefficients: polynomial, sinusoidal, cosinusoidal, tangent, cotangent, logarithmic, exponential, arc sin, arc cos, arc tan, arc cot or power. Function for PNC calculations is chosen individually at each interpolation and it represents probability distribution function of parameter $\alpha \in [0;1]$ for every point situated between two interpolation knots. PNC method uses two-dimensional vectors (x,y) for curve modeling-knots $p_i = (x_i,y_i) \in R^2$ in PNC method, $i = 1,2,...n$:

1. PNC needs 2 knots or more ($n \geq 2$);
2. If first node and last node are the same ($p_1 = p_n$), then curve is closed (contour);
3. For more precise modeling knots ought to be settled at key points of the curve, for example local minimum or maximum and at least one node between two successive local extrema.

Figure 1. Five knots of the curve before modeling
Source: Author, 2016.

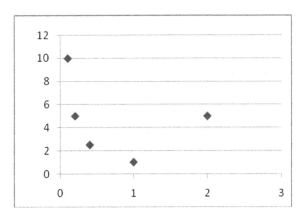

Condition 3 means for example the highest point of the curve in a particular orientation, convexity changing or curvature extrema. So this chapter wants to answer the question: how to interpolate the curve by a set of knots (Jakóbczak, 2010)?

Nodes on Figure 1 represent characteristic points of the handwritten letter or symbol: if $n = 5$ then curve is opened and if $n = 6$ then curve is closed (contour). The examples of PNC curve modeling for these nodes are described later in this chapter. Coefficients for PNC curve modeling are computed using nodes combinations and probability distribution functions: polynomials, power functions, sine, cosine, tangent, cotangent, logarithm, exponent or arc sin, arc cos, arc tan or arc cot.

NOVELTY OF PROBABILISTIC INTERPOLATION AND EXTRAPOLATION

Issues

The method of PNC enables to compute points between two successive nodes of the curve: calculated points are interpolated and parameterized for real number $\alpha \in [0;1]$ in the range of two successive nodes. PNC method uses the combinations of nodes $p_1=(x_1,y_1)$, $p_2=(x_2,y_2),\ldots, p_n=(x_n,y_n)$ as $h(p_1,p_2,\ldots,p_m)$ and $m = 1,2,\ldots n$. Nodes combination h is defined individually for each curve to interpolate points (x,y) with second coordinate $y = y(c)$ for any first coordinate $x = c$ situated between nodes (x_i,y_i) and (x_{i+1},y_{i+1}):

$$c = \alpha \cdot x_i + (1-\alpha) \cdot x_{i+1}, \; i = 1,2,...n-1,$$

$$y(c) = \gamma \cdot y_i + (1 - \gamma)y_{i+1} + \gamma(1 - \gamma) \cdot h(p_1, p_2, ..., p_m), \tag{1}$$

$\alpha \in [0;1], \gamma = F(\alpha) \in [0;1], F:[0;1] \to [0;1], F(0)=0, F(1)=1$ and F is strictly monotonic.

PNC extrapolation requires α outside of $[0;1]$: $\alpha < 0$ (anticipating points right of last node for $c > x_n$) or $\alpha > 1$ (extrapolating values left of first node for $c < x_1$), $\gamma = F(\alpha), F:P \to \mathbf{R}, \; P \supset [0;1], F(0)=0, F(1)=1$ and F is still strictly monotonic for the arguments from P. So c and α represent the same – coordinate x of any point (x,y) between two successive nodes (x_i,y_i) and (x_{i+1},y_{i+1}): having c we can calculate α and vice versa. PNC curve modeling relies on two factors: function $\gamma = F(\alpha)$ and nodes combination $h(p_1,p_2,...,p_m)$. Function F is a probabilistic distribution function for random variable $\alpha \in [0;1]$ and parameter γ leads PNC interpolation into probabilistic modeling. Second factor, the combination of nodes h, is responsible for making dependent a reconstructed point on the coordinates of several nodes. The simplest case is for $h = 0$. Here are the examples of h computed for MHR method (Jakóbczak, 2009):

$$h(p_1, p_2) = \frac{y_1}{x_1} x_2 + \frac{y_2}{x_2} x_1$$

(only two neighboring nodes are taken for PNC calculations) or

$$h(p_1, p_2, p_3, p_4) = \frac{1}{x_1^2 + x_3^2}(x_1 x_2 y_1 + x_2 x_3 y_3 + x_3 x_4 y_1 - x_1 x_4 y_3)$$
$$+ \frac{1}{x_2^2 + x_4^2}(x_1 x_2 y_2 + x_1 x_4 y_4 + x_3 x_4 y_2 - x_2 x_3 y_4)$$

(more than two neighboring nodes are used in PNC interpolation).

The examples of other nodes combinations are presented below. Formula (1) represents curve parameterization $(x(\alpha),y(\alpha))$ between two successive nodes (x_i,y_i) and (x_{i+1},y_{i+1}) as $\alpha \in [0;1]$:

$$x(\alpha) = \alpha \cdot x_i + (1-\alpha) \cdot x_{i+1}$$

and

$$y(\alpha) = F(\alpha) \cdot y_i + (1 - F(\alpha))y_{i+1} + F(\alpha)(1 - F(\alpha)) \cdot h(p_1, p_2, ..., p_m),$$

$$y(\alpha) = F(\alpha) \cdot (y_i - y_{i+1} + (1 - F(\alpha)) \cdot h(p_1, p_2, ..., p_m)) + y_{i+1}.$$

Proposed parameterization gives us the infinite number of possibilities for curve calculations (determined by choice of F and h) as there is the infinite number of human handwritten letters and symbols. Nodes combination is the individual feature of each modeled curve (for example a handwritten character). Coefficient $\gamma = F(\alpha)$ and nodes combination h are key factors in PNC curve interpolation and data extrapolation.

Distribution Functions in PNC Interpolation and Extrapolation

Points settled between the nodes are computed using PNC method. Each real number $c \in [a;b]$ is calculated by a convex combination $c = \alpha \cdot a + (1 - \alpha) \cdot b$ for

$$\alpha = \frac{b - c}{b - a} \in [0;1].$$

Key question is dealing with coefficient γ in (1). The simplest way of PNC calculation means $h = 0$ and $\gamma = \alpha$ (basic probability distribution – uniform distribution). Then PNC represents a linear interpolation. MHR method (Jakóbczak, 2010) is not a linear interpolation. MHR is the example of PNC modeling.

Each interpolation requires specific distribution of parameter α and γ (1) depends on parameter $\alpha \in [0;1]$:

$$\gamma = F(\alpha), F:[0;1] \rightarrow [0;1], F(0) = 0, F(1) = 1 \text{ and F is strictly monotonic.}$$

Coefficient γ is calculated using different functions (polynomials, power functions, sine, cosine, tangent, cotangent, logarithm, exponent, arc sin, arc cos, arc tan or arc cot, also inverse functions) and choice of function is connected with initial requirements and curve specifications. Different values of coefficient γ are connected with applied functions $F(\alpha)$. The functions (2)-(34) represent the examples of probability distribution functions for random variable $\alpha \in [0;1]$ and real number $s > 0$:

1. **Power Function:**

$$\gamma = \alpha^s \text{ with } s > 0. \tag{2}$$

For $s = 1$: basic version of PNC and MHR (Jakóbczak, 2010) methods when $\gamma = \alpha$.

2. **Sine:**

$$\gamma = sin(\alpha^s \cdot \pi/2), s > 0 \tag{3}$$

or

$$\gamma = sin^s(\alpha \cdot \pi/2), s > 0. \tag{4}$$

For $s = 1$:

$$\gamma = sin(\alpha \cdot \pi/2). \tag{5}$$

3. **Cosine:**

$$\gamma = 1\text{-}cos(\alpha^s \cdot \pi/2), s > 0 \tag{6}$$

or

$$\gamma = 1\text{-}cos^s(\alpha \cdot \pi/2), s > 0. \tag{7}$$

For $s = 1$:

$$\gamma = 1\text{-}cos(\alpha \cdot \pi/2). \tag{8}$$

4. **Tangent:**

$$\gamma = tan(\alpha^s \cdot \pi/4), s > 0 \tag{9}$$

or

$$\gamma = tan^s(\alpha \cdot \pi/4), s > 0. \tag{10}$$

For $s = 1$:

$$\gamma = tan(\alpha \cdot \pi/4). \tag{11}$$

5. **Logarithm:**

$$\gamma = log_2(\alpha^s + 1),\ s > 0 \tag{12}$$

or

$$\gamma = log_2{}^s(\alpha + 1),\ s > 0. \tag{13}$$

For $s = 1$:

$$\gamma = log_2(\alpha + 1). \tag{14}$$

6. **Exponent:**

$$\gamma = \left(\frac{a^\alpha - 1}{a - 1}\right)^s,\ s > 0 \text{ and } a > 0 \text{ and } a \neq 1. \tag{15}$$

For $s = 1$ and $a = 2$:

$$\gamma = 2^\alpha - 1. \tag{16}$$

7. **Arc Sine:**

$$\gamma = (2/\pi) \cdot arcsin(\alpha^s),\ s > 0 \tag{17}$$

or

$$\gamma = (2/\pi \cdot arcsin\ \alpha)^s,\ s > 0. \tag{18}$$

For $s = 1$:

$$\gamma = (2/\pi) \cdot arcsin(\alpha). \tag{19}$$

8. **Arc Cosine:**

$$\gamma = 1\text{-}(2/\pi)\cdot arccos(\alpha^s), s > 0 \tag{20}$$

   or

$$\gamma = 1\text{-}(2/\pi\cdot arccos\ \alpha)^s, s > 0. \tag{21}$$

   For $s = 1$:

$$\gamma = 1\text{-}(2/\pi)\cdot arccos(\alpha). \tag{22}$$

9. **Arc Tangent:**

$$\gamma = (4/\pi)\cdot arctan(\alpha^s), s > 0 \tag{23}$$

   or

$$\gamma = (4/\pi\cdot arctan\ \alpha)^s, s > 0. \tag{24}$$

   For $s = 1$:

$$\gamma = (4/\pi)\cdot arctan(\alpha). \tag{25}$$

10. **Cotangent:**

$$\gamma = ctg(\pi/2 - \alpha^s \cdot \pi/4), s > 0 \tag{26}$$

   or

$$\gamma = ctg^s\ (\pi/2\text{-}\alpha \cdot \pi/4), s > 0. \tag{27}$$

   For $s = 1$:

$$\gamma = ctg(\pi/2\text{-}\alpha \cdot \pi/4). \tag{28}$$

11. **Arc Cotangent:**

$$\gamma = 2 - (4/\pi)\cdot arcctg(\alpha^s), s > 0 \tag{29}$$

or

$$\gamma = (2 - 4/\pi \cdot arcctg\ \alpha)^s,\ s > 0. \tag{30}$$

For $s = 1$:

$$\gamma = 2 - (4/\pi) \cdot arcctg(\alpha). \tag{31}$$

Functions used in γ calculations (2)-(31) are strictly monotonic for random variable $\alpha \in [0;1]$ as $\gamma = F(\alpha)$ is probability distribution function. Of course any monotonic combination of functions (2)-(31) between points (0;0) and (1;1) is also good, for example

$$\gamma = \alpha^5 \cdot (4/\pi) \cdot arctan(\alpha)$$

or

$$\gamma = \tfrac{1}{2}(\alpha^{7.6} + sin^3(\alpha \cdot \pi/2))$$

or

$$\gamma = \tfrac{1}{4}(\alpha^{1.6} + \alpha^{0.6} + \alpha^6 + sin^{3.9}(\alpha \cdot \pi/2))$$

or

$$\gamma = \tfrac{1}{2}(\alpha^{7.98} + \alpha^3 \cdot (4/\pi) \cdot arctan(\alpha))$$

or other modeling functions.

Also inverse function $F^{-1}(\alpha)$ is appropriate for γ calculations. Choice of function and value s depends on curve specifications and individual requirements. Proposed (2)-(31) probability distributions are continuous, but of course parameter γ can represent discrete probability distributions, for example: $F(0.1)=0.23$, $F(0.2)=0.3$, $F(0.3)=0.42$, $F(0.4)=0.52$, $F(0.5)=0.63$, $F(0.6)=0.69$, $F(0.7)=0.83$, $F(0.8)=0.942$, $F(0.9)=0.991$. What is very important in PNC method: two curves (for example a handwritten letter) may have the same set of nodes but different h or γ results in different interpolations (Figure 2-10).

Algorithm of PNC interpolation and modeling (1) looks as follows:

Step 1: Choice of knots p_i at key points.

Step 2: Choice of nodes combination $h(p_1, p_2, \ldots, p_m)$.

Step 3: Choice of distribution $\gamma = F(\alpha)$: (2)-(31) or others (continuous or discrete).

Step 4: Determining values of α: $\alpha = 0.1, 0.2\ldots0.9$ (nine points) or 0.01, 0.02\ldots0.99 (99 points) or others.

Step 5: The computations (1).

These five steps can be treated as the algorithm of PNC method of curve modeling and interpolation (1). Without knowledge about the formula of curve or function, PNC interpolation has to implement the coefficients γ (2)-(31), but PNC is not limited only to these coefficients. Each strictly monotonic function F between points (0;0) and (1;1) can be used in PNC modeling.

Data Modeling and Curve Fitting

Curve knots $p_1 = (0.1;10)$, $p_2 = (0.2;5)$, $p_3 = (0.4;2.5)$, $p_4 = (1;1)$ and $p_5 = (2;5)$ from Figure 1 are used in some examples of PNC method in handwritten character modeling. Figures 2-9 represent PNC as MHR interpolation (Jakóbczak, 2011) with different γ. Points of the curve are calculated with no matrices ($N = 1$) and $\gamma = \alpha$ in example 1 and with matrices of dimension $N = 2$ in examples 2-8 for $\alpha = 0.1, 0.2, \ldots, 0.9$.

Example 1

PNC curve interpolation (1) for $\gamma = \alpha$ and

$$h(p_1, p_2) = \frac{y_1}{x_1} x_2 + \frac{y_2}{x_2} x_1 :$$

For $N = 2$ (examples 2 – 8) MHR version (Jakóbczak, 2011) as PNC method gives us

$$h(p_1, p_2, p_3, p_4) = \frac{1}{x_1^2 + x_3^2} (x_1 x_2 y_1 + x_2 x_3 y_3 + x_3 x_4 y_1 - x_1 x_4 y_3)$$
$$+ \frac{1}{x_2^2 + x_4^2} (x_1 x_2 y_2 + x_1 x_4 y_4 + x_3 x_4 y_2 - x_2 x_3 y_4)$$

Figure 2. PNC character modeling for nine reconstructed points between nodes
Source: Author, 2016.

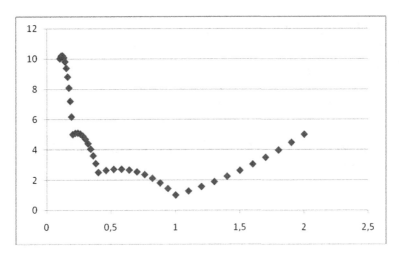

Example 2

PNC sinusoidal interpolation with $\gamma = sin(\alpha \cdot \pi/2)$.

Example 3

PNC tangent interpolation for $\gamma = tan(\alpha \cdot \pi/4)$.

Figure 3. Sinusoidal modeling with nine reconstructed curve points between nodes
Source: Author, 2016.

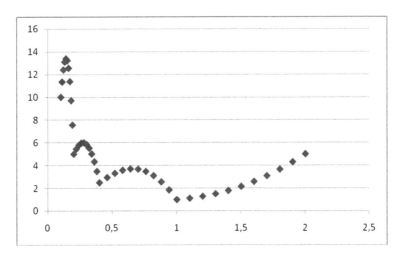

Example 4

PNC tangent interpolation with $\gamma = tan(\alpha^s \cdot \pi/4)$ and $s = 1.5$.

Example 5

PNC tangent curve interpolation for $\gamma = tan(\alpha^s \cdot \pi/4)$ and $s = 1.797$.

Figure 4. Tangent character modeling with nine interpolated points between nodes
Source: Author, 2016

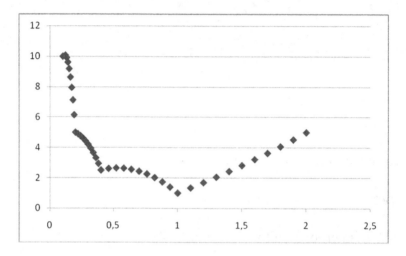

Figure 5. Tangent curve modeling with nine recovered points between nodes
Source: Author, 2016.

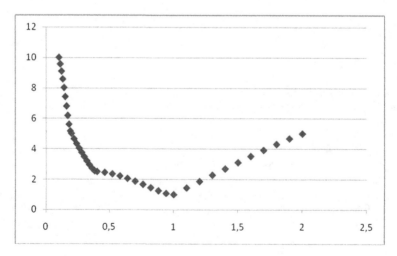

Example 6

PNC sinusoidal interpolation with $\gamma = sin(\alpha^s \cdot \pi/2)$ and $s = 2.759$.

Example 7

PNC power function modeling for $\gamma = \alpha^s$ and $s = 2.1205$.

Figure 6. Tangent symbol modeling with nine reconstructed points between nodes
Source: Author, 2016.

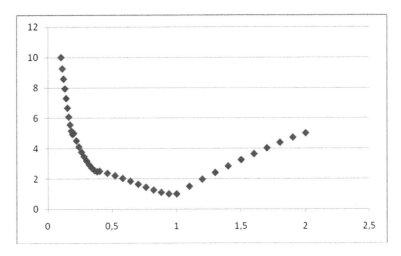

Figure 7. Sinusoidal modeling with nine interpolated curve points between nodes
Source: Author, 2016.

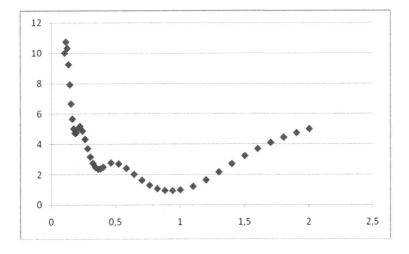

Example 8

PNC logarithmic curve modeling with $\gamma = log_2(\alpha^s + 1)$ and $s = 2.533$.

These eight examples demonstrate possibilities of PNC curve interpolation and handwritten character modeling for key nodes in MHR version. And here are other examples of PNC modeling (but not MHR):

Figure 8. Power function curve modeling with nine recovered points between nodes
Source: Author, 2016.

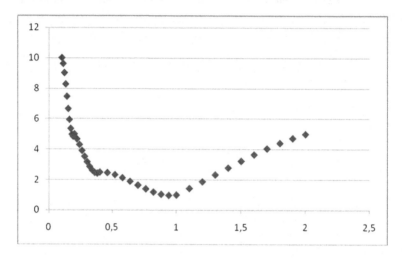

Figure 9. Logarithmic character modeling with nine reconstructed points between nodes
Source: Author, 2016.

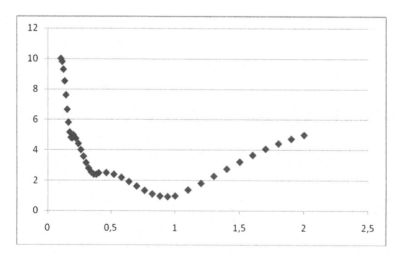

Example 9

PNC for $\gamma = \alpha^2$ and $h(p_1, p_2) = x_1 y_1 + x_2 y_2$:

Example 10

PNC for $\gamma = \alpha^3$ and $h(p_1, p_2) = x_1 y_1 + x_2 y_2$:

Figure 10. Quadratic symbol modeling with nine reconstructed points between nodes
Source: Author, 2016.

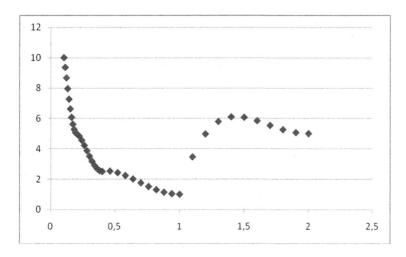

Figure 11. Cubic character modeling with nine reconstructed points between nodes
Source: Author, 2016.

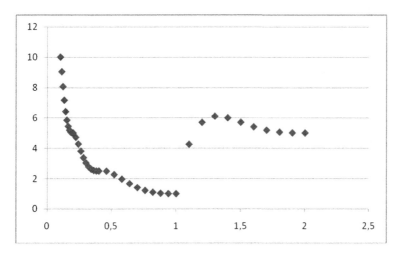

If there is considered Figure 1 as closed curve (contour) with the node p_6 = p_1 = (0.1;10) then examples 9 and 10 give the shapes:

Example 11

PNC for $\gamma = \alpha^2$ and $h(p_1, p_2) = x_1 y_1 + x_2 y_2$:

Example 12

PNC for $\gamma = \alpha^3$ and $h(p_1, p_2) = x_1 y_1 + x_2 y_2$:

Every man has individual style of handwriting. Recognition of handwritten letter or symbol need modeling and the model of each individual symbol or character can be built by choice of γ and h in (1). PNC modeling via nodes combinations h and parameter γ as probability distribution function enables curve interpolation for each specific letter or symbol.

Number of reconstructed points depends on a user by value α. If for example $\alpha = 0.01, 0.02,...,0.99$ then 99 points are interpolated for each pair of nodes. Reconstructed values and interpolated points, calculated by PNC method, are applied in the process of curve modeling. Every curve can be interpolated by some distribution function as parameter γ and nodes combination h. Parameter γ is treated as probability distribution function for each curve.

Figure 12. Quadratic contour modeling with nine reconstructed points between nodes
Source: Author, 2016.

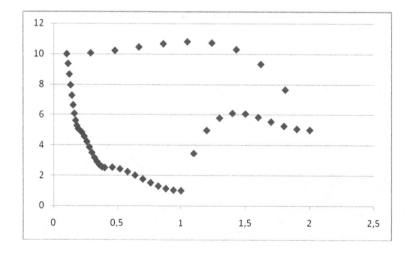

Figure 13. Cubic shape modeling with nine reconstructed points between nodes
Source: Author, 2016.

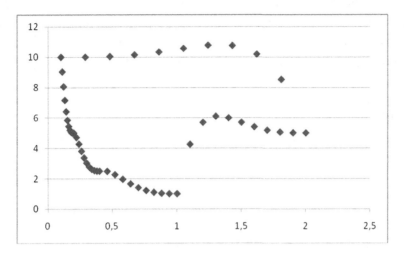

Beta Distribution

Considering nowadays used probability distribution functions for random variable $\alpha \in [0;1]$-one distribution is dealing with the range $[0;1]$: beta distribution. Probability density function f for random variable $\alpha \in [0;1]$ is:

$$f(\alpha) = c \cdot \alpha^s \cdot (1-\alpha)^r, s \geq 0, r \geq 0. \tag{32}$$

When $r = 0$ probability density function (32) represents $f(\alpha) = c \cdot \alpha^s$ and then probability distribution function F is like (2), for example $f(\alpha) = 3\alpha^2$ and $\gamma = \alpha^3$. If s and r are positive integer numbers then γ is the polynomial, for example $f(\alpha) = 6\alpha(1-\alpha)$ and $\gamma = 3\alpha^2 - 2\alpha^3$. So beta distribution gives us coefficient γ in (1) as polynomial because of interdependence between probability density f and distribution F functions:

$$f(\alpha) = F'(\alpha), \ F(\alpha) = \int_0^\alpha f(t)dt. \tag{33}$$

For example (33):

$$f(\alpha) = \alpha \cdot e^\alpha \text{ and } \gamma = F(\alpha) = 1 - (1-\alpha)e^\alpha. \tag{34}$$

Basic (uniform) distribution ($\gamma = \alpha$) with nodes combination $h = 0$ turns PNC interpolation (1) to linear interpolation. What about PNC in the case of yet another distribution on the range [0;1]: beta distribution (32)? Power functions as γ used in examples 1, 7 and 9-12 are also connected with beta distribution. Here are the examples of PNC modeling for beta distribution with nodes combination $h = 0$.

Example 13

PNC for $\gamma = 3\alpha^2$-$2\alpha^3$ and $h(p_1, p_2) = 0$:

Example 14

PNC for $\gamma = 4\alpha^3$-$3\alpha^4$ and $h(p_1, p_2) = 0$:

Example 15

PNC for $\gamma = 2\alpha$-α^2 and $h(p_1, p_2) = 0$:

Examples 9-12 represent beta distribution with $h(p_1, p_2) = x_1 y_1 + x_2 y_2$.

Figure 14. Beta distribution in handwritten character modeling
Source: Author, 2016.

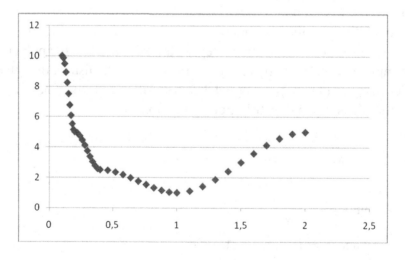

Figure 15. Beta distribution in handwritten symbol modeling
Source: Author, 2016.

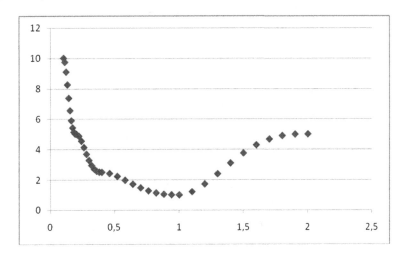

Figure 16. Beta distribution in handwritten letter modeling
Source: Author, 2016.

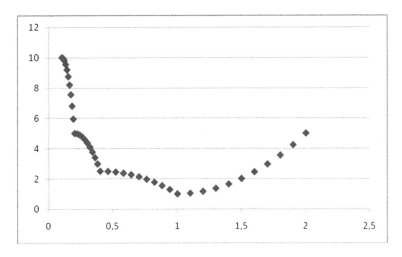

Exponential Distribution

Exponential distribution is dealing with random variable ≥ 0, but in PNC interpolation random variable $\alpha \in [0;1]$. Then exponential distribution is represented by distribution function (34):

$$\gamma = F(\alpha) = 1 - (1 - \alpha)e^{\alpha}.$$

Example 16

PNC for $\gamma = 1-(1-\alpha)e^{\alpha}$ and $h(p_1, p_2) = 0$:

Example 17

PNC for $\gamma = 1-(1-\alpha)e^{\alpha}$ and $h(p_1, p_2) = \dfrac{y_2}{y_1} + \dfrac{x_2}{x_1}$:

These examples show the variety of possibilities in curve modeling via the choice of nodes combination and probability distribution function for interpolated points.

PNC Extrapolation as the Support in Planning

Unknown data, important for planning or decision making, are modeled (interpolated or extrapolated) by the choice of nodes, determining specific nodes combination and characteristic probabilistic distribution function. Less complicated models take $h(p_1, p_2, \ldots, p_m) = 0$ and then the formula of interpolation (2) looks as follows:

$$y(c) = \gamma \cdot y_i + (1 - \gamma)y_{i+1} .$$

Figure 17. Exponential distribution in handwritten character modeling
Source: Author, 2016

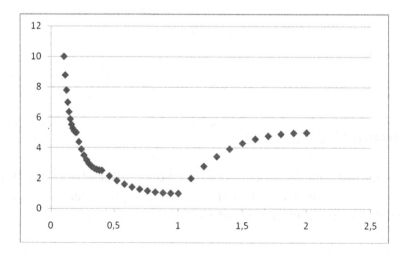

Figure 18. Exponential distribution in handwritten symbol modeling
Source: Author, 2016.

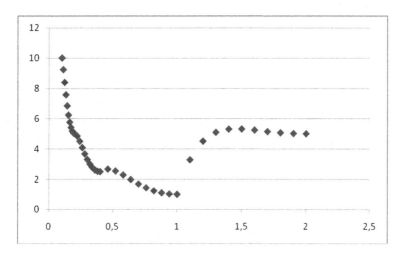

It is linear interpolation for basic (uniform) probability distribution ($\gamma = \alpha$).

Example 1

Nodes (1;3), (3;1), (5;3), (7;3) and $h = 0$, $\gamma = F(\alpha) = \alpha^2$. This function F requires $\alpha > 1$ and extrapolation is computed with (4)-(5):

Figure 19. PNC modeling for nine interpolated points between successive nodes and nine extrapolated points right of the last node
Source: Author, 2016.

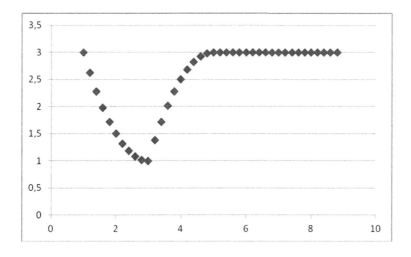

Extrapolated points: (7.2;3), (7.4;3), (7.6;3), (7.8;3), (8;3), (8.2;3), (8.4;3), (8.6;3), (8.8;3).

Example 2

Nodes (1;3), (3;1), (5;3), (7;2) and $h = 0$, $\gamma = F(\alpha) = \alpha^2$. This function F requires $\alpha > 1$ and extrapolation is computed with (4)-(5) too:

Extrapolated points: (7.2;1.79), (7.4;1.56), (7.6;1.31), (7.8;1.04), (8;0.75), (8.2;0.44), (8.4;0.11), (8.6;-0.24), (8.8;-0.61).

Example 3

Nodes (1;3), (3;1), (5;3), (7;4) and $h = 0$, $\gamma = F(\alpha) = \alpha^3$:

Extrapolated points: (7.2;4.331), (7.4;4.728), (7.6;5.197), (7.8;5.744), (8;6.375), (8.2;7.096), (8.4;7.913), (8.6;8.832), (8.8;9.859).

These three examples 1-3 (Figures 1-3) with nodes combination $h = 0$ differ at fourth node and probability distribution functions $\gamma = F(\alpha)$. Much more possibilities of modeling are connected with a choice of nodes combination $h(p_1, p_2, \ldots, p_m)$. MHR method uses the combination (3) with good features because of orthogonal rows and columns at Hurwitz-Radon family of matrices:

Figure 20. PNC modeling with nine interpolated points between successive nodes and nine extrapolated points right of the last node
Source: Author, 2016.

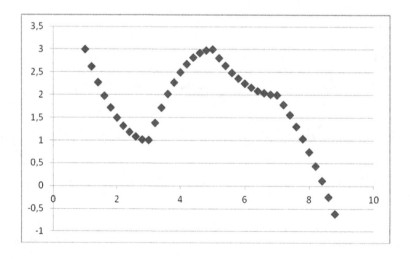

Figure 21. PNC modeling for nine interpolated points between successive nodes and nine extrapolated points right of the last node
Source: Author, 2016.

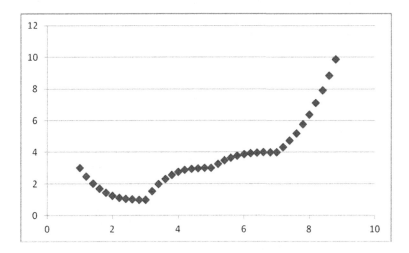

$$h(p_i, p_{i+1}) = \frac{y_i}{x_i} x_{i+1} + \frac{y_{i+1}}{x_{i+1}} x_i$$

and then (2):

$$y(c) = \gamma \cdot y_i + (1 - \gamma) y_{i+1} + \gamma(1 - \gamma) \cdot h(p_i, p_{i+1}).$$

Here are two examples 4 and 5 of PNC method with MHR combination (3).

Example 4

Nodes (1;3), (3;1), (5;3) and $\gamma = F(\alpha) = \alpha^2$. This function F requires $\alpha > 1$ and extrapolation is computed with (4)-(5):
Extrapolated points: (5.2;2.539), (5.4;1.684), (5.6;0.338), (5.8;-1.603), (6;-4.25), (6.2;-7.724), (6.4;-12.155), (6.6;-17.68), (6.8;-24.443).

Example 5

Nodes (1;3), (3;1), (5;3) and $\gamma = F(\alpha) = \alpha^{1.5}$. This function F requires $\alpha > 1$ and extrapolation is computed with (4)-(5):

Figure 22. PNC modeling with nine interpolated points between successive nodes and nine extrapolated points right of the last node
Source: Author, 2016.

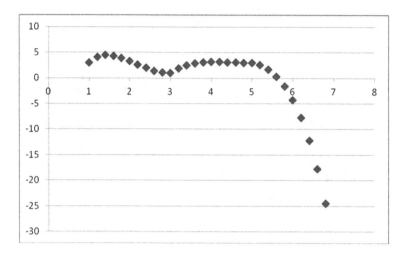

Figure 23. PNC modeling with nine interpolated points between successive nodes and nine extrapolated points right of the last node
Source: Author, 2016.

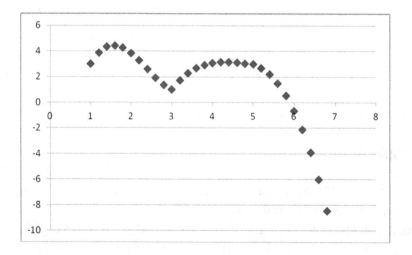

Extrapolated points: (5.2;2.693), (5.4;2.196), (5.6;1.487), (5.8;0.543), (6;-0.657), (6.2;-2.136), (6.4;-3.915), (6.6;-6.016), (6.8;-8.461).

Now let us consider PNC method with other functions F than power functions, $\alpha < 0$ for extrapolation (1)-(2) and nodes combination $h = 0$.

Example 6

Nodes (2;2), (3;1), (4;2), (5;1), (6;2) and $\gamma = F(\alpha) = sin(\alpha \cdot \pi/2)$, $h = 0$:
   Extrapolated points: (6.1;2.156), (6.2;2.309), (6.3;2.454), (6.4;2.588), (6.5;2.707), (6.6;2.809), (6.7;2.891), (6.8;2.951), (6.9;2.988).

Example 7

Nodes (2;2), (3;1), (4;2), (5;1), (6;2) and $\gamma = F(\alpha) = sin^3(\alpha \cdot \pi/2)$, $h = 0$:
   Extrapolated points: (6.1;2.004), (6.2;2.03), (6.3;2.094), (6.4;2.203), (6.5;2.354), (6.6;2.53), (6.7;2.707), (6.8;2.86), (6.9;2.964).
   These two examples 6 and 7 (Figures 6-7) with nodes combination $h = 0$ and the same set of nodes differ only at probability distribution functions $\gamma = F(\alpha)$. Figure 8 is the example of nodes combination h as (3) in MHR method.

Example 8

Nodes (2;2), (3;1), (4;1), (5;1), (6;2) and $\gamma = F(\alpha) = 2^{\alpha}-1$:
   Extrapolated points: (6.1;2.067), (6.2;2.129), (6.3;2.188), (6.4;2.242), (6.5;2.293), (6.6;2.34), (6.7;2.384), (6.8;2.426), (6.9;2.464).

Figure 24. PNC modeling with nine interpolated points between successive nodes and nine extrapolated points right of the last node
Source: Author, 2016.

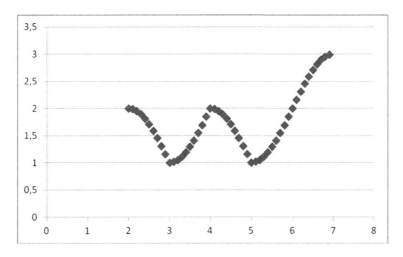

Figure 25. PNC modeling with nine interpolated points between successive nodes and nine extrapolated points right of the last node
Source: Author, 2016.

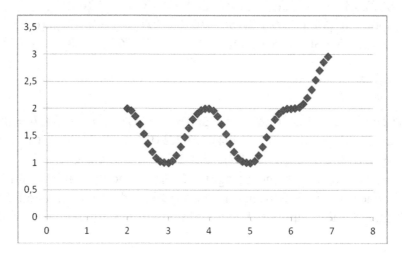

Figure 26. PNC modeling with nine interpolated points between successive nodes and nine extrapolated points right of the last node
Source: Author, 2016.

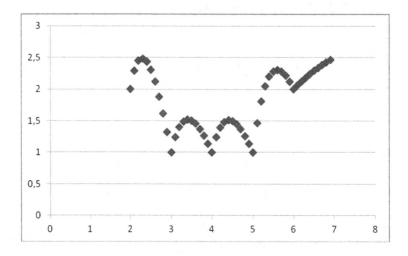

Examples that are calculated above have one function $\gamma = F(\alpha)$ and one combination h for all ranges between nodes. But it is possible to create a model with functions $\gamma_i = F_i(\alpha)$ and combinations h_i individually for a range of nodes $(p_i; p_{i+1})$. Then it enables very precise modeling of data between each successive pair of nodes. Each data point is interpolated or extrapolated by PNC via three factors: the set of nodes, probability distribution function $\gamma = F(\alpha)$ and nodes combination h. These three factors are chosen individually for each data, therefore this information about modeled points seems to be enough for specific PNC curve interpolation and extrapolation. Function γ is selected via the analysis of known points before extrapolation, we may assume $h = 0$ at the beginning and after some time exchange h by more adequate.

These eight examples illustrate the extrapolation of some important values in planning process, for example anticipation of some costs or expenses and foreseeing the prices or other significant data in the process of planning.

SOLUTIONS AND RECOMMENDATIONS

Proposed method, called Probabilistic Nodes Combination (PNC), is the method of 2D curve interpolation and extrapolation using the set of key points (knots or nodes). Nodes can be treated as characteristic points of data for modeling and analyzing. The model of data can be built by choice of probability distribution function and nodes combination. PNC modeling via nodes combination and parameter γ as probability distribution function enables value anticipation in risk analysis and decision making. Two-dimensional curve is extrapolated and interpolated via nodes combination and different functions as discrete or continuous probability distribution functions: polynomial, sine, cosine, tangent, cotangent, logarithm, exponent, arc sin, arc cos, arc tan, arc cot or power function. Novelty of the chapter consists of two generalizations: generalization of previous MHR method with various nodes combinations and generalization of linear interpolation with different (no uniform) probability distribution functions and nodes combinations.

FUTURE RESEARCH DIRECTIONS

Future trends will go to various directions: how to fix the best probability distribution function for the nodes, how to calculate the most appropriate nodes combination and what extrapolation is the most valuable in decision making and risk analysis.

CONCLUSION

Planning process requires the anticipation of unknown values or data and foreseeing some important factors. The method of Probabilistic Nodes Combination (PNC) enables interpolation and extrapolation of two-dimensional curves using nodes combinations and different coefficients γ: polynomial, sinusoidal, cosinusoidal, tangent, cotangent, logarithmic, exponential, arc sin, arc cos, arc tan, arc cot or power function, also inverse functions. Function for γ calculations is chosen individually at each planning and it is treated as probability distribution function: γ depends on initial requirements and data specifications. PNC method leads to point extrapolation and interpolation via discrete set of fixed knots. Main features of PNC method are:

1. The smaller distance between knots the better;
2. PNC method develops a linear interpolation and extrapolation into other functions as probability distribution functions;
3. PNC is a generalization of MHR method via different nodes combinations;
4. Interpolation and extrapolation of L points is connected with the computational cost of rank $O(L)$ as in MHR method;
5. Nodes combination and coefficient γ are crucial in the process of data probabilistic anticipation and foreseeing.

Proposed method, called Probabilistic Nodes Combination (PNC), is the method of 2D curve interpolation and extrapolation using the set of key points (knots or nodes). Nodes can be treated as characteristic points of data for modeling and analyzing. The model of data can be built by choice of probability distribution function and nodes combination. PNC modeling via nodes combination and parameter γ as probability distribution function enables value anticipation in risk analysis and decision making. Two-dimensional curve is extrapolated and interpolated via nodes combination and different functions as discrete or continuous probability distribution functions: polynomial, sine, cosine, tangent, cotangent, logarithm, exponent, arc sin, arc cos, arc tan, arc cot or power function. Novelty of the chapter consists of two generalizations: generalization of previous MHR method with various nodes combinations and generalization of linear interpolation with different (no basic) probability distribution functions and nodes combinations. Computer vision needs suitable methods of shape representation and contour reconstruction. One of them, invented by the author and called method of Hurwitz-Radon Matrices (MHR), can be used in representation and reconstruction of shapes of the objects in the plane. Proposed method is based on a family of Hurwitz-Radon (HR) matrices. The matrices are skew-symmetric and possess columns composed of orthogonal vectors. 2D shape is represented by the set of successive nodes. It is shown how to create the orthogonal and discrete OHR operator and how to use it in a process of shape representation and reconstruction. Then MHR method is generalized to Probabilistic Nodes Combination (PNC) method. This work clarifies the significance and novelty of the proposed method compared to existing methods (for example polynomial interpolations and Bézier curves). Previous published papers of the author were dealing with the method of Hurwitz-Radon Matrices (MHR method). Novelty of this monograph and proposed method consists in the fact that calculations are free from the family of Hurwitz-Radon Matrices. Problem statement of this chapter is: how to reconstruct (interpolate) missing points of 2D curve having the set of interpolation nodes (key points) and using the information about probabilistic distribution of unknown points. For example the simplest basic distribution leads to the easiest interpolation – linear interpolation. Apart from probability distribution, additionally there is the second factor of proposed interpolation method: nodes combination. The simplest nodes combination is zero. Thus proposed curve modeling is based on two agents: probability distribution and nodes combination. Significance of this book consists in generalization for MHR method: the computations are done without matrices in curve fitting and shape modeling, with clear point interpolation formula based on probability distribution function (continuous or discrete) and nodes combination. This book also consists of generalization for linear interpolation with different (no basic) probability distribution functions and nodes combinations. So this chapter answers the question: "Why and when should we use PNC method?".

Curve interpolation represents one of the most important problems in mathematics and computer science: how to model the curve via discrete set of two-dimensional points? Also the matter of shape representation (as closed curve-contour) and curve parameterization is still opened. For example pattern recognition, signature verification or handwriting identification problems are based on curve modeling via the choice of key points. So interpolation is not only a pure mathematical problem but important task in computer vision and artificial intelligence. The book wants to approach a problem of curve modeling by characteristic points. Proposed method relies on nodes combination and functional modeling of curve points situated between the basic set of key points. The functions that are used in calculations represent whole family of elementary functions with inverse functions: polynomials, trigonometric, cyclometric, logarithmic, exponential and power function. These functions are treated as probability distribution functions in the range [0;1]. Significant problem in machine vision and computer vision is that of appropriate 2D shape representation and reconstruction. Classical discussion about shape representation is based on the problem: contour versus skeleton. This monograph is voting for contour which forms boundary of the object. Contour of the object, represented by successive contour points, consists of information which allows us to describe many important features of the object as shape coefficients. 2D curve modeling and generation is a basic subject in many branches of industry and computer science, for example in the cad/cam software. The representation of shape can have a great impact on the accuracy and effectiveness of object recognition. In the literature, shape has been represented by many options including curves, graph-based algorithms and medial axis to enable shape-based object recognition. Digital 2D curve (open or closed) can be represented by chain code (Freeman's code). Chain code depends on selection of the started point and transformations of the object. So Freeman's code is one of the method how to describe and to find contour of the object. Analog (continuous) version of Freeman's code is the curve $\alpha\text{-}s$. Another contour representation and reconstruction is based on Fourier coefficients calculated in discrete Fourier transformation (DFT). These coefficients are used to fix similarity of the contours with different sizes or directions. If we assume that contour is built from segments of a line and fragments of circles or ellipses, hough transformation is applied to detect contour lines. Also geometrical moments of the object are used during the process of object shape representation. Contour is also applied in shape decomposition. Many branches of medicine, industry and manufacturing are looking for methods connected with geometry of the contour.

Future works are going to: application of PNC method in decision making, choice and features of nodes combinations and coefficient γ, implementation of PNC in computer vision and artificial intelligence: shape geometry, contour modelling, object recognition and curve parameterization.

REFERENCES

Ballard, D. H. (1982). *Computer Vision*. New York: Prentice Hall.

Chapra, S. C. (2012). *Applied Numerical Methods*. McGraw-Hill.

Choraś, R. S. (2005). *Computer Vision*. Warsaw, Poland: Exit.

Cocozza-Thivent, C., Eymard, R., Mercier, S., & Roussignol, M. (2006). Characterization of the Marginal Distributions of Markov Processes Used in Dynamic Reliability. *Journal of Applied Mathematics and Stochastic Analysis*, 1–18.

Collins, G. W. II. (2003). *Fundamental Numerical Methods and Data Analysis*. Case Western Reserve University.

Dahlquist, G., & Bjoerck, A. (1974). *Numerical Methods*. New York: Prentice Hall.

Dejdumrong, N. (2007). A Shape Preserving Verification Techniques for Parametric Curves. *Computer Graphics, Imaging and Visualization, 2007*, 163–168.

Dyn, N., Levin, D., & Gregory, J. A. (1987). A 4-Point Interpolatory Subdivision Scheme for Curve Design. *Computer Aided Geometric Design, 4*(4), 257–268. doi:10.1016/0167-8396(87)90001-X

Jakóbczak, D. (2007). 2D and 3D Image Modeling Using Hurwitz-Radon Matrices. *Polish Journal of Environmental Studies, 4A*(16), 104–107.

Jakóbczak, D. (2009). Curve Interpolation Using Hurwitz-Radon Matrices. *Polish Journal of Environmental Studies, 3B*(18), 126–130.

Jakóbczak, D. (2010a). Shape Representation and Shape Coefficients via Method of Hurwitz-Radon Matrices. *Lecture Notes in Computer Science, 6374*, 411–419. doi:10.1007/978-3-642-15910-7_47

Jakóbczak, D. (2010b). Object Modeling Using Method of Hurwitz-Radon Matrices of Rank k. In W. Wolski & M. Borawski (Eds.), *Computer Graphics: Selected Issues* (pp. 79–90). Szczecin, Poland: University of Szczecin Press.

Jakóbczak, D. (2011a). Curve Parameterization and Curvature via Method of Hurwitz-Radon Matrices. *Image Processing & Communications- International Journal (Toronto, Ont.), 1-2*(16), 49–56.

Jakóbczak, D. (2011b). Data Extrapolation and Decision Making via Method of Hurwitz-Radon Matrices. *Lecture Notes in Computer Science, 6922*, 173–182. doi:10.1007/978-3-642-23935-9_17

Jakóbczak, D. (2011c). Curve Extrapolation and Data Analysis using the Method of Hurwitz-Radon Matrices. *Folia Oeconomica Stetinensia, 9*(17), 121-138.

Jakóbczak, D. (2013). Probabilistic Modeling of Signature using the Method of Hurwitz-Radon Matrices. *Global Perspectives on Artificial Intelligence*, *1*(1), 1–7.

Kozera, R. (2004). *Curve Modeling via Interpolation Based on Multidimensional Reduced Data*. Gliwice, Poland: Silesian University of Technology Press.

Liu, T., & Geiger, D. (1999). Approximate tree matching and shape similarity. *Int. Conf. Computer Vision,* Corfu, Greece.

Lorton, A., Fouladirad, M., & Grall, A. (2013). A Methodology for Probabilistic Model-based Prognosis. *European Journal of Operational Research*, *225*(3), 443–454. doi:10.1016/j.ejor.2012.10.025

Pergler, M., & Freeman, A. (2008). Probabilistic Modeling as an Exploratory Decision-Making Tool. *McKinsey Working Papers on Risk*, *6*, 1-18.

Ralston, A., & Rabinowitz, P. (2001). *A First Course in Numerical Analysis* (2nd ed.). New York: Dover Publications.

Rogers, D. F. (2001). *An Introduction to NURBS with Historical Perspective*. Morgan Kaufmann Publishers.

Saber, E., Xu, Y., & Murat Tekalp, A. (2005). Partial shape recognition by sub-matrix matching for partial matching guided image labeling. *Pattern Recognition*, *38*(10), 1560–1573. doi:10.1016/j.patcog.2005.03.027

Schumaker, L. L. (2007). *Spline Functions: Basic Theory*. Cambridge Mathematical Library. doi:10.1017/CBO9780511618994

Sebastian, T. B., Klein, P. N., & Kimia, B. B. (2003). On aligning curves. *IEEE Transactions on Pattern Analysis and Machine Intelligence*, *25*(1), 116–124. doi:10.1109/TPAMI.2003.1159951

Tadeusiewicz, R., & Flasiński, M. (1991). *Image Recognition*. Warsaw, Poland: PWN.

Zhang, D., & Lu, G. (2004). Review of Shape Representation and Description Techniques. *Pattern Recognition*, *1*(37), 1–19. doi:10.1016/j. patcog.2003.07.008

ADDITIONAL READING

Basu, S., & Bresler, Y. (2000). O($N^2\log_2 N$) filtered backprojection reconstruction algorithm for tomography. *IEEE Transactions on Image Processing*, 9(10), 1760–1773. doi:10.1109/83.869187 PMID:18262914

Brankov, J. G., Yang, Y., & Wernick, M. N. (2004). Tomographic image reconstruction based on a Content–Adaptive Mesh Model. *IEEE Transactions on Medical Imaging*, 2(23), 202–212. doi:10.1109/TMI.2003.822822 PMID:14964565

Brasse, D., & Defrise, M. (2004). Fast fully 3-D image reconstruction in PET using planograms. *IEEE Transactions on Medical Imaging*, 4(23), 413–425. doi:10.1109/TMI.2004.824231 PMID:15084067

Bulacu, M., & Schomaker, L. (2007). Text-independent writer identification and verification using textural and allographic features. *IEEE Transactions on Pattern Analysis and Machine Intelligence*, 29(4), 701–717. doi:10.1109/TPAMI.2007.1009 PMID:17299226

Bulacu, M., Schomaker, L., & Brink, A. (2007). *Text-independent writer identification and verification on off-line Arabic handwriting*. In: *International Conference on Document Analysis and Recognition*. 769–773.

Cetin, M., Karl, W. C., & Willsky, A. S. (2002, September). *Edge–preserving image reconstruction for coherent imaging application*. Paper presented at the IEEE International Conference on Image Processsing, Rochester, NY, USA. doi:10.1109/ICIP.2002.1039992

Chen, J., Cheng, W., & Lopresti, D. (2011). Using perturbed handwriting to support writer identification in the presence of severe data constraints. In: Document Recognition and Retrieval. 1–10. doi:10.1117/12.876497

Chen, J., Lopresti, D., & Kavallieratou, E. (2010). *The impact of ruling lines on writer identification*. In: *International Conference on Frontiers in Handwriting Recognition*. 439–444. doi:10.1109/ICFHR.2010.75

Chlebus, E., & Cholewa, M. (1999). Rapid prototyping – rapid tooling. *CADCAM Forum, 11*, 23-28.

Cormen, T. H., Leiserson, C. E., & Rivest, R. L. (1996). *Introduction to algorithms*. Massachusetts, USA: the Massachusetts Institute of Technology Press and McGraw-Hill.

Defrise, M. (2001). A short readers guide to 3D tomographic reconstruction. *Computerized Medical Imaging and Graphics, 25*(2), 113–116. doi:10.1016/S0895-6111(00)00061-6 PMID:11137787

Djeddi, C., & Souici-Meslati, L. (2010). *A texture based approach for Arabic writer identification and verification*. In: *International Conference on Machine and Web Intelligence*. 115–120.

Djeddi, C., & Souici-Meslati, L. (2011). *Artificial immune recognition system for Arabic writer identification*. In: *International Symposium on Innovation in Information and Communication Technology*. 159–165. doi:10.1109/ISIICT.2011.6149612

Dryja, M., Jankowska, J., & Jankowski, M. (1982). *Survey of numerical methods and algorithms. Part II*. Warsaw, Poland: WNT.

Eldar, Y. C. (2001). *Quantum Signal Processing*. (Unpublished doctoral dissertation). Massachusetts Institute of Technology, USA.

Eldar, Y. C., & Oppenheim, A. V. (2002). Quantum Signal Processing. *IEEE Signal Processing Magazine, 6*(19), 12–32. doi:10.1109/MSP.2002.1043298

Fortuna, Z., Macukow, B., & Wąsowski, J. (1982). *Numerical methods*. Warsaw, Poland: WNT.

Galloway, M. M. (1975). Texture analysis using gray level run lengths. *Computer Graphics and Image Processing, 4*(2), 172–179. doi:10.1016/S0146-664X(75)80008-6

Garain, U., & Paquet, T. (2009). *Off-line multi-script writer identification using AR coefficients*. In: *International Conference on Document Analysis and Recognition*. 991–995. doi:10.1109/ICDAR.2009.222

Ghiasi, G., & Safabakhsh, R. (2013). Offline text-independent writer identification using codebook and efficient code extraction methods. *Image and Vision Computing, 31*(5), 379–391. doi:10.1016/j.imavis.2013.03.002

Jakóbczak, D. (2005). Hurwitz-Radon matrices and their children. *Computer Science, 5*(8), 29–38.

Jakóbczak, D. J. (2014). *2D Curve Modeling via the Method of Probabilistic Nodes Combination-Shape Representation, Object Modeling and Curve Interpolation-Extrapolation with the Applications.* Saarbrucken: LAP Lambert Academic Publishing.

Jankowska, J., & Jankowski, M. (1981). *Survey of numerical methods and algorithms. Part I.* Warsaw, Poland: WNT.

Kontaxakis, G., & Strauss, L. G. (1998). Maximum likelihood algorithms for image reconstruction in Positron Emission Tomography. *Radionuclides for Oncology – Current Status and Future Aspects, 1998,* 73-106.

Kowalczuk, Z., & Wiszniewski, B. (Eds.). (2007). *Intelligent data mining in diagnostic purposes: Automatics and informatics.* Gdansk, Poland: PWNT.

Kundur, D., & Hatzinakos, D. (1998). A novel blind deconvolution scheme for image restoration using recursive filtering. *IEEE Transactions on Signal Processing, 2*(46), 375–390. doi:10.1109/78.655423

Laine, A., & Zong, X. (1996). *Border identification of echocardiograms via multiscale edge detection and shape modeling.* Paper presented at the IEEE International Conference on Image Processsing, Lausanne, Switzerland. doi:10.1109/ICIP.1996.560486

Lang, S. (1970). *Algebra.* Reading, Massachusetts, USA: Addison-Wesley Publishing Company.

Le Buhan Jordan, C., Bossen, F., & Ebrahimi, T. (1997). *Scalable shape representation for content based visual data compression.* Paper presented at the International Conference on Image Processing, Santa Barbara, CA, USA. doi:10.1109/ICIP.1997.647962

Marker, J., Braude, I., Museth, K., & Breen, D. (2006). Contour-based surface reconstruction using implicit curve fitting, and distance field filtering and interpolation. *Volume Graphics, 2006,* 1–9.

Marti, U.-V., & Bunke, H. (2002). The IAM-database: An English sentence database for offline handwriting recognition. *Int. J. Doc. Anal. Recognit., 5*(1), 39–46. doi:10.1007/s100320200071

Meyer, Y. (1993). *Wavelets: algorithms & applications.* Philadelphia, USA: Society for Industrial and Applied Mathematics.

Nosary, A., Heutte, L., & Paquet, T. (2004). Unsupervised writer adaption applied to handwritten text recognition. *Pattern Recognition Letters, 37*(2), 385–388. doi:10.1016/S0031-3203(03)00185-7

Ozaki, M., Adachi, Y., & Ishii, N. (2006). *Examination of effects of character size on accuracy of writer recognition by new local arc method.* In: *International Conference on Knowledge-Based Intelligent Information and Engineering Systems.* 1170–1175. doi:10.1007/11893004_148

Poggio, T., & Smale, S. (2003). The mathematics of learning: Dealing with data. *Notices of the American Mathematical Society, 5*(50), 537–544.

Przelaskowski, A. (2005). *Data compression.* Warsaw, Poland: BTC.

Rutkowski, L., Siekmann, J., Tadeusiewicz, R., & Zadeh, A. (Eds.). (2004). *Lecture notes on artificial intelligence: Artificial intelligence and soft computing.* Berlin-Heidelberg, Germany: Springer-Verlag.

Schlapbach, A., & Bunke, H. (2004). *Using HMM based recognizers for writer identification and verification. 9th Int. Workshop on Frontiers in Handwriting Recognition.* 167–172. doi:10.1109/IWFHR.2004.107

Schlapbach, A., & Bunke, H. (2006). *Off-line writer identification using Gaussian mixture models.* In: *International Conference on Pattern Recognition.* 992–995.

Schlapbach, A., & Bunke, H. (2007). A writer identification and verification system using HMM based recognizers. *Pattern Analysis & Applications, 10*(1), 33–43. doi:10.1007/s10044-006-0047-5

Schomaker, L., Franke, K., & Bulacu, M. (2007). Using codebooks of fragmented connected-component contours in forensic and historic writer identification. *Pattern Recognition Letters, 28*(6), 719–727. doi:10.1016/j.patrec.2006.08.005

Shahabinejad, F., & Rahmati, M. (2007). A new method for writer identification and verification based on Farsi/Arabic handwritten texts, *Ninth International Conference on Document Analysis and Recognition (ICDAR 2007).* 829–833.

Siddiqi, I., Cloppet, F., & Vincent, N. (2009). Contour based features for the classification of ancient manuscripts. In: Conference of the International Graphonomics Society. 226–229.

Siddiqi, I., & Vincent, N. (2010). Text independent writer recognition using redundant writing patterns with contour-based orientation and curvature features. *Pattern Recognition Letters*, *43*(11), 3853–3865. doi:10.1016/j.patcog.2010.05.019

Vakhania, N. (1993). Orthogonal random vectors and the Hurwitz – Radon-Eckmann theorem. *Proc. of the Georgian Academy of Sciences-Mathematics, 1(1)*, 109-125.

Van, E. M., Vuurpijl, L., Franke, K., & Schomaker, L. (2005). The WANDA measurement tool for forensic document examination. *J. Forensic Doc. Exam.*, *16*, 103–118.

Willis, M. (2000). *Algebraic reconstruction algorithms for remote sensing image enhancement*. Unpublished doctoral dissertation, Department of Electrical and Computer Engineering, Brigham Young University.

Xu, Fang, & Mueller, K. (2005). Accelerating popular tomographic reconstruction algorithms on commodity PC graphics hardware. *IEEE Transactions on Nuclear Science*, *3*(52), 654–661.

Zaletelj, J., & Tasic, J. F. (2003). *Optimization and tracking of polygon vertices for shape coding*. Berlin-Heidelberg, Germany: Springer-Verlag. doi:10.1007/978-3-540-45179-2_52

Zhang, J. K., Davidson, T., & Wong, K. M. (2004). Efficient design of orthonormal wavelet bases for signal representation. *IEEE Transactions on Signal Processing*, *7*(52), 1983–1996. doi:10.1109/TSP.2004.828923

KEY TERMS AND DEFINITIONS

Artificial Intelligence: Intelligence of machines and computers, as a connection of algorithms and hardware, which makes that a man – human being can be simulated by the machines in analyzing risk, decision making, reasoning, knowledge, planning, learning, communication, perception and the ability to move and manipulate objects.

Curve Interpolation: Computing new and unknown points of a curve and creating a graph of a curve using existing data points – interpolation nodes.

Data Extrapolation: Calculation of unknown values for the points situated outside the ranges of nodes.

Hurwitz – Radon Matrices: A family of skew – symmetric and orthogonal matrices with columns and rows that create, together with identical matrix, the base in vector spaces of dimensions $N = 2$, 4 or 8.

MHR Method: The method of curve interpolation and extrapolation using linear (convex) combinations of OHR operators.

OHR Operator: Matrix operator of Hurwitz – Radon built from coordinates of interpolation nodes.

Value Anticipation: Foreseeing next value when last value is known.

Chapter 3

PNC in 2D Curve Modeling:
Interpolation and Extrapolation

ABSTRACT

Interpolation methods and curve fitting represent so huge problem that each individual interpolation is exceptional and requires specific solutions. PNC method is such a novel tool with its all pros and cons. The user has to decide which interpolation method is the best in a single situation. The choice is yours if you have any choice. Presented method is such a new possibility for curve fitting and interpolation when specific data (for example handwritten symbol or character) starts up with no rules for polynomial interpolation. This chapter consists of two generalizations: generalization of previous MHR method with various nodes combinations and generalization of linear interpolation with different (no basic) probability distribution functions and nodes combinations. This probabilistic view is novel approach a problem of modeling and interpolation. Computer vision and pattern recognition are interested in appropriate methods of shape representation and curve modeling.

INTRODUCTION

The problem of multidimensional data modeling appears in many branches of science and industry. Image retrieval, data reconstruction, object identification or pattern recognition are still the open problems in artificial intelligence and computer vision. The chapter is dealing with these questions via modeling of high-dimensional data for applications of image segmentation in image

DOI: 10.4018/978-1-5225-2531-8.ch003

retrieval and recognition tasks. Handwriting based author recognition offers a huge number of significant implementations which make it an important research area in pattern recognition. There are so many possibilities and applications of the recognition algorithms that implemented methods have to be concerned on a single problem: retrieval, identification, verification or recognition. This chapter is concerned with two parts: image retrieval and recognition tasks. Image retrieval is based on probabilistic modeling of unknown features via combination of N-dimensional probability distribution function for each feature treated as random variable. Handwriting and signature recognition and identification represents a significant problem. In the case of biometric writer recognition, each person is represented by the set of modeled letters or symbols. The sketch of proposed Probabilistic Features Combination (PFC) method consists of three steps: first handwritten letter or symbol must be modeled by a vector of features (N-dimensional data), then compared with unknown letter and finally there is a decision of identification. Author recognition of handwriting and signature is based on the choice of feature vectors and modeling functions. So high-dimensional data interpolation in handwriting identification (Marti & Bunke, 2002) is not only a pure mathematical problem but important task in pattern recognition and artificial intelligence such as: biometric recognition (Nosary, Heutte & Paquet, 2004), personalized handwriting recognition (Djeddi & Souici-Meslati, 2010 & 2011), automatic forensic document examination (Van, Vuurpijl, Franke & Schomaker, 2005; Schomaker, Franke & Bulacu, 2007), classification of ancient manuscripts (Siddiqi, Cloppet & Vincent, 2009). Also writer recognition (Garain & Paquet, 2009) in monolingual handwritten texts (Ozaki, Adachi & Ishii, 2006) is an extensive area of study (Chen, Lopresti & Kavallieratou, 2010) and the methods independent from the language (Chen, Cheng & Lopresti, 2011) are well-seen (Bulacu, Schomaker & Brink, 2007). Proposed method represents language-independent and text-independent approach because it identifies the author via a single letter or symbol from the sample. The method of Probabilistic Nodes Combination (PNC) enables interpolation and modeling of two-dimensional curves using nodes combinations and different coefficients γ: polynomial, sinusoidal, cosinusoidal, tangent, cotangent, logarithmic, exponential, arc sin, arc cos, arc tan, arc cot or power function, also inverse functions. This probabilistic view is novel approach a problem of modeling and interpolation. Computer vision and pattern recognition are interested in appropriate methods of shape representation and curve modeling. PNC method represents the possibilities of shape reconstruction and curve interpolation via the choice of nodes combination and probability distribution function for interpolated points. It seems to be quite new look at the problem of contour representation and curve modeling in artificial intelligence and computer vision. Proposed method, called Probabilistic Nodes Combination (PNC), is the method of 2D curve interpolation and extrapolation using the set of key points (knots or nodes). Nodes can be treated as characteristic points of data for modeling and analyzing. The model of data can be built by choice of probability distribution function and nodes combination. PNC modeling via nodes combination and parameter γ as probability distribution function enables value anticipation in risk analysis and decision making. Two-dimensional curve is extrapolated and interpolated via nodes combination and different functions as discrete or continuous probability distribution functions: polynomial, sine, cosine, tangent, cotangent, logarithm, exponent, arc sin, arc cos, arc tan, arc cot or power function. Novelty of this book consists of two generalizations: generalization of previous MHR method with various nodes combinations and generalization of linear interpolation with different (no basic) probability distribution functions and nodes combinations.

BACKGROUND

Writer recognition methods in the recent years are going to various directions (Galloway, 1975): writer recognition using multi-script handwritten texts, introduction of new features (Ghiasi & Safabakhsh, 2013), combining different types of features (Siddiqi & Vincent, 2010), studying the sensitivity of character size on writer identification, investigating writer identification in multi-script environments (Shahabinejad & Rahmati, 2007), impact of ruling lines on writer identification, model perturbed handwriting, methods based on run-length features, the edge-direction and edge-hinge features, a combination of codebook and visual features extracted from chain code and polygonized representation of contours, the autoregressive coefficients, codebook and efficient code extraction methods, texture analysis with Gabor filters and extracting features (Schlapbach & Bunke, 2007), using Hidden Markov Model (Schlapbach & Bunke, 2004) or Gaussian Mixture Model (Schlapbach & Bunke, 2006). So hybrid soft computing is essential: no method is dealing with writer identification via N-dimensional data modeling or interpolation and multidimensional points comparing as it is presented in this chapter. The chapter wants to approach a problem of curve interpolation and shape modeling by characteristic points in handwriting identification (Bulacu & Schomaker, 2007). Proposed method relies on nodes combination and functional modeling of curve points situated between the basic set of key points. The functions that are used in calculations represent whole family of elementary functions with inverse functions: polynomials, trigonometric, cyclometric, logarithmic, exponential and power function. These functions are treated as probability distribution functions in the range [0;1]. Nowadays methods apply mainly polynomial functions, for example Bernstein polynomials in Bezier curves, splines (Schumaker, 2007) and NURBS. But Bezier curves don't represent the interpolation method and cannot be used for example in signature and handwriting modeling with characteristic points (nodes). Numerical methods (Collins, 2003) for data interpolation are based on polynomial or trigonometric functions (Chapra, 2012), for example Lagrange, Newton, Aitken and Hermite methods (Ralston & Rabinowitz, 2001). These methods have some weak sides and are not sufficient for curve interpolation in the situations when the curve cannot be build by polynomials or trigonometric functions (Zhang & Lu, 2004).

This chapter presents novel Probabilistic Features Combination (PFC) method of high-dimensional interpolation in hybrid soft computing and takes up PFC method of multidimensional data modeling. The method of PFC requires information about data (image, object, curve) as the set of N-dimensional feature vectors. Proposed PFC method is applied in image retrieval and recognition tasks via different coefficients for each feature as random variable: polynomial, sinusoidal, cosinusoidal, tangent, cotangent, logarithmic, exponential, arc sin, arc cos, arc tan, arc cot or power. Modeling functions for PFC calculations are chosen individually for every task and they represent probability distribution functions of random variable $\alpha_i \in [0;1]$ for every feature $i=1,2,\ldots N$-1. So this chapter wants to answer the question: how to retrieve the image using N-dimensional feature vectors and to recognize a handwritten letter or symbol by a set of high-dimensional nodes via hybrid soft computing?

POINT RETRIEVAL

Issues

The method of PFC is computing (interpolating) unknown (unclear, noised or destroyed) values of features between two successive nodes (N-dimensional vectors of features) using hybridization of probabilistic methods and numerical methods. Calculated values (unknown or noised features such as coordinates, colors, textures or any coefficients of pixels, voxels and doxels or image parameters) are interpolated and parameterized for real number $\alpha_i \in [0;1]$ ($i = 1,2,...N\text{-}1$) between two successive values of feature. PFC method uses the combinations of nodes (N-dimensional feature vectors) $p_1=(x_1,y_1,...,z_1)$, $p_2=(x_2,y_2,...,z_2)$,..., $p_n=(x_n,y_n,...z_n)$ as $h(p_1,p_2,...,p_m)$ and $m=1,2,...n$ to interpolate unknown value of feature (for example y) for the rest of coordinates:

$$c_1 = \alpha_1 \cdot x_k + (1-\alpha_1) \cdot x_{k+1},\ ......\ c_{N-1} = \alpha_{N-1} \cdot z_k + (1-\alpha_{N-1}) \cdot z_{k+1},\ k = 1,2,...n\text{-}1,$$

$$c = (c_1,..., c_{N-1}),\ \alpha = (\alpha_1,..., \alpha_{N-1}),\ \gamma_i = F_i(\alpha_i) \in [0;1],\ i = 1,2,...N\text{-}1$$

$$y(c) = \gamma \cdot y_k + (1 - \gamma)y_{k+1} + \gamma(1 - \gamma) \cdot h(p_1, p_2, ..., p_m) \qquad (1)$$

$$\alpha_i \in [0;1],\ \gamma = F(\alpha) = F(\alpha_1,..., \alpha_{N-1}) \in [0;1].$$

Then N-1 features $c_1,..., c_{N-1}$ are parameterized by $\alpha_1,..., \alpha_{N-1}$ between two nodes and the last feature (for example y) is interpolated via formula (1). Of course there can be calculated $x(c)$ or $z(c)$ using (1). Two examples of h (when $N = 2$) computed for MHR method (Jakóbczak, 2014) with good features because of orthogonal rows and columns at Hurwitz-Radon family of matrices:

$$y(c) = \gamma \cdot y_k + (1 - \gamma)y_{k+1} + \gamma(1 - \gamma) \cdot h(p_1, p_2, ..., p_m)\ h(p_1, p_2) = \frac{y_1}{x_1} x_2 \qquad (2)$$

or

$$+ \frac{y_2}{x_2} x_1.$$

The simplest nodes combination is

$$h(p_1, p_2, p_3, p_4) = \frac{1}{x_1^2 + x_3^2}(x_1 x_2 y_1 + x_2 x_3 y_3 + x_3 x_4 y_1 - x_1 x_4 y_3)$$
$$+ \frac{1}{x_2^2 + x_4^2}(x_1 x_2 y_2 + x_1 x_4 y_4 + x_3 x_4 y_2 - x_2 x_3 y_4)$$

(3)

and then there is a formula of interpolation:

$$h(p_1, p_2, ..., p_m) = 0 .$$

Formula (1) gives the infinite number of calculations for unknown feature (determined by choice of *F* and *h*) as there is the infinite number of objects to recognize or the infinite number of images to rerieve. Nodes combination is the individual feature of each modeled data. Coefficient $\gamma = F(\alpha)$ and nodes combination *h* are key factors in PFC data interpolation and object modeling.

N-Dimensional Probability Distribution Functions in PFC Modeling

Unknown values of features, settled between the nodes, are computed using PFC method as in (1). Key question is dealing with coefficient γ. The simplest way of PFC calculation means $h = 0$ and $\gamma_i = \alpha_i$ (basic probability distribution for each random variable α_i). Then PFC represents a linear interpolation. Figure 1 is the example of curve (data) modeling when the formula is known: $y = 2^x$.

Figure 1. PFC linear 2D modeling of function $y=2^x$ with seven nodes (in left window) and options in right window (modeling functions γ and nodes combination h)

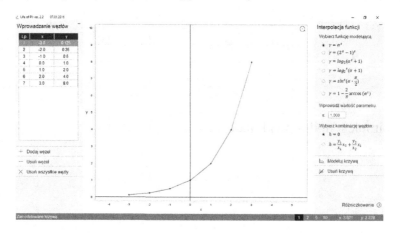

MHR method (Jakóbczak, 2014) is the example of PFC modeling for feature vector of dimension $N = 2$. Each interpolation requires specific distributions of random variables α_i and γ in (1) depends on parameters $\alpha_i \in [0;1]$:

$$\gamma = F(\alpha),\ F:[0;1]^{N-1} \to [0;1],\ F(0,\dots,0) = 0,\ F(1,\dots,1) = 1$$

and F is strictly monotonic for each random variable α_i separately. Coefficient γ_i are calculated using appropriate function and choice of function is connected with initial requirements and data specifications. Different values of coefficients γ_i are connected with applied functions $F_i(\alpha_i)$. These functions $\gamma_i = F_i(\alpha_i)$ represent the examples of probability distribution functions for random variable $\alpha_i \in [0;1]$ and real number $s>0$, $i = 1,2,\dots N-1$:

$$\gamma_i = \alpha_i^s,$$

$$\gamma_i = \sin(\alpha_i^s \cdot \pi/2),$$

$$\gamma_i = \sin^s(\alpha_i \cdot \pi/2),$$

$$\gamma_i = 1 - \cos(\alpha_i^s \cdot \pi/2),$$

$$\gamma_i = 1 - \cos^s(\alpha_i \cdot \pi/2),$$

$$\gamma_i = \tan(\alpha_i^s \cdot \pi/4),$$

$$\gamma_i = \tan^s(\alpha_i \cdot \pi/4),$$

$$\gamma_i = \log_2(\alpha_i^s + 1),$$

$$\gamma_i = \log_2^s(\alpha_i + 1),$$

$$\gamma_i = (2^\alpha - 1)^s,$$

$$\gamma_i = 2/\pi \cdot \arcsin(\alpha_i^s),$$

$$\gamma_i = (2/\pi \cdot \arcsin\alpha_i)^s,$$

$$\gamma_i = 1 - 2/\pi \cdot \arccos(\alpha_i^s),$$

$\gamma_i = 1-(2/\pi \cdot arccos\alpha_i)^s,$

$\gamma_i = 4/\pi \cdot arctan(\alpha_i^s),$

$\gamma_i = (4/\pi \cdot arctan\alpha_i)^s,$

$\gamma_i = ctg(\pi/2-\alpha_i^s \cdot \pi/4),$

$\gamma_i = ctg^s(\pi/2-\alpha_i \cdot \pi/4),$

$\gamma_i = 2-4/\pi \cdot arcctg(\alpha_i^s),$

$\gamma_i = (2-4/\pi \cdot arcctg\alpha_i)^s$

or any strictly monotonic function between points $(0;0)$ and $(1;1)$ – for example combinations of these functions (see Chapter 2). In some cases it is possible to take modeling function $G(\alpha)$ as opposite to F:

$$G(\alpha) = \gamma = 1-F(\alpha),\ G{:}[0;1]^{N-1} \to [0;1],\ G(0,\ldots,0) = 1,\ G(1,\ldots,1) = 0.$$

Then G is also strictly monotonic function between points $(0;1)$ and $(1;0)$. So formula of PNC interpolation-extrapolation is given in the alternative version:

$$y(c) = \gamma \cdot y_i + (1 - \gamma)y_{i+1}.$$

Interpolations of function $y=2^x$ for $N = 2$, $h = 0$ and $\gamma = \alpha^s$ with $s = 0.8$ (Figure 2) or $\gamma=log_2(\alpha+1)$ (Figure 3) are quite better then linear interpolation (Figure 1).

Functions γ_i are strictly monotonic for each random variable $\alpha_i \in [0;1]$ as $\gamma=F(\alpha)$ is N-dimensional probability distribution function, for example:

$$y(c) = (1 - \gamma) \cdot y_k + \gamma \cdot y_{k+1} + \gamma(1 - \gamma) \cdot h(p_1, p_2, \ldots, p_m),\ \gamma = \frac{1}{N-1}\sum_{i-1}^{N-1}\gamma_i$$

and every monotonic combination of γ_i such as

$$\gamma = F(\alpha),\ F{:}[0;1]^{N-1} \to [0;1],\ F(0,\ldots,0) = 0,\ F(1,\ldots,1) = 1.$$

Figure 2. PFC two-dimensional modeling of function $y=2^x$ with seven nodes as Figure 1 and h=0, $\gamma=\alpha^{0.8}$

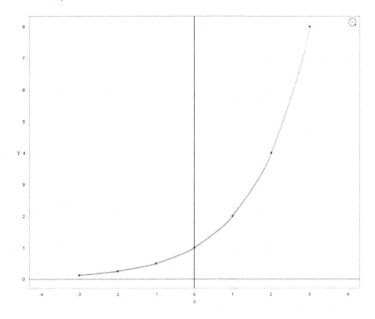

Figure 3. PFC two-dimensional reconstruction of function $y=2^x$ with seven nodes as Figure 1 and h=0, $\gamma = log_2(\alpha+1)$

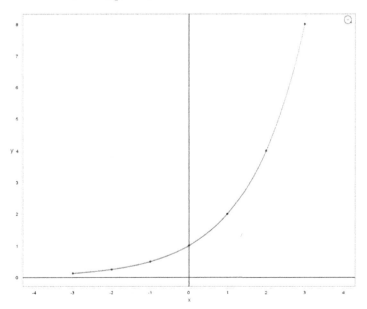

For example when $N = 3$ there is a bilinear interpolation:

$$\gamma_1 = \alpha_1, \gamma_2 = \alpha_2, \gamma = \tfrac{1}{2}(\alpha_1 + \alpha_2) \tag{4}$$

or a bi-quadratic interpolation:

$$\gamma_1 = \alpha_1^2, \gamma_2 = \alpha_2^2, \gamma = \tfrac{1}{2}(\alpha_1^2 + \alpha_2^2) \tag{5}$$

or a bi-cubic interpolation:

$$\gamma_1 = \alpha_1^3, \gamma_2 = \alpha_2^3, \gamma = \tfrac{1}{2}(\alpha_1^3 + \alpha_2^3) \tag{6}$$

or others modeling functions γ. Choice of functions γ_i and value s depends on the specifications of feature vectors and individual requirements. What is very important in PFC method: two data sets (for example a handwritten letter or signature) may have the same set of nodes (feature vectors: pixel coordinates, pressure, speed, angles) but different h or γ results in different interpolations (Figures 4-6). Here are three examples of PFC reconstruction (Figures 4-6) for $N = 2$ and four nodes: (-1.5;-1), (1.25;3.15), (4.4;6.8) and (8;7). Formula of the curve is not given.

Figure 4. PFC 2D modeling for $\gamma = \alpha^2$ and $h = 0$

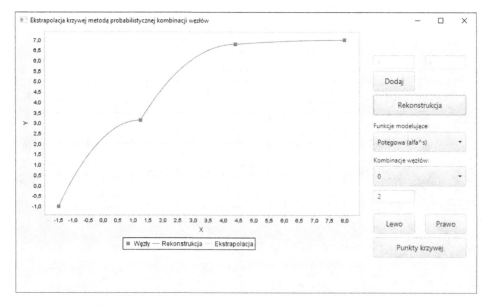

Figure 5. PFC 2D reconstruction for $\gamma = sin(\alpha^2 \cdot \pi/2)$ and h in (2)

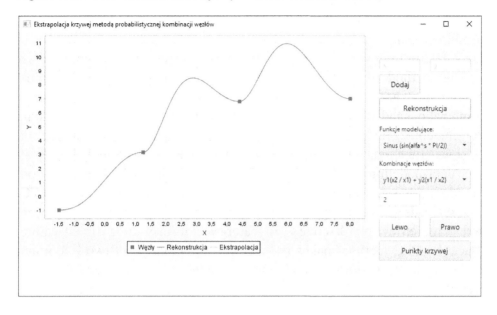

Figure 6. PFC 2D interpolation for $\gamma = tan(\alpha^2 \cdot \pi/4)$ and $h = (x_2/x_1) + (y_2/y_1)$

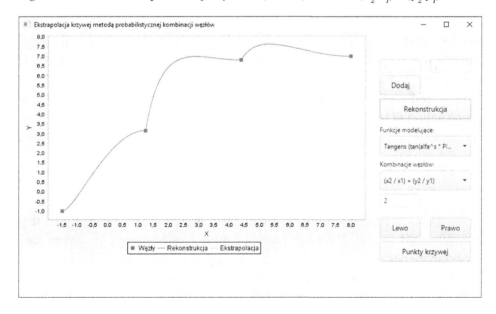

Algorithm of PFC retrieval, interpolation and modeling consists of five steps: first choice of nodes p_i (feature vectors), then choice of nodes combination $h(p_1,p_2,...,p_m)$, choice of distribution (modeling function) $\gamma = F(\alpha)$, determining values of $\alpha_i \in [0;1]$ and finally the computations (1).

The method of Probabilistic Features Combination (PFC) enables interpolation and modeling of high-dimensional N data using features' combinations and different coefficients γ: polynomial, sinusoidal, cosinusoidal, tangent, cotangent, logarithmic, exponential, arc sin, arc cos, arc tan, arc cot or power function. Functions for γ calculations are chosen individually at each data modeling and it is treated as N-dimensional probability distribution function: γ depends on initial requirements and features' specifications. PFC method leads to data interpolation as handwriting or signature identification and image retrieval via discrete set of feature vectors in N-dimensional feature space. So PFC method makes possible the combination of two important problems: interpolation and modeling in a matter of image retrieval or writer identification.

Signature Modeling

Human signature or handwriting consists mainly of non-typical curves and irregular shapes. So how to model two-dimensional handwritten characters via PFC method? Each model has to be described (1) by the set of nodes, nodes combination h and a function $\gamma = F(\alpha)$ for each letter. Other features in multi-dimensional feature space are not visible but used in recognition process (for example p-pen pressure, s-speed of writing, a- pen angle). Less complicated models can take $h(p_1,p_2,...,p_m) = 0$ and then the formula of interpolation (1) looks as follows:

$$\gamma = \prod_{i=1}^{N-1} \gamma_i \qquad (7)$$

Formula (7) represents the simplest linear interpolation for basic probability distribution if $\gamma = \alpha$. Here are some examples of non-typical curves and irregular shapes as the whole signature or a part of signature, reconstructed via PFC method for seven nodes (x,y) – see Figures 1-3:

Proposed method, called Probabilistic Features Combination (PFC), is the method of N-dimensional data interpolation and extrapolation using the set of key points (knots or nodes). Nodes can be treated as characteristic

Figure 7.

Lp.	x	y
1	-3.0	0.125
2	-2.0	0.25
3	-1.0	0.5
4	0.0	1.0
5	1.0	2.0
6	2.0	4.0
7	3.0	8.0

points of data for modeling and analyzing. The model of data can be built by choice of probability distribution function and nodes combination. PFC modeling via nodes combination and parameter γ as probability distribution function enables value anticipation in risk analysis and decision making. *N*-dimensional object is extrapolated and interpolated via nodes combination and different functions as discrete or continuous probability distribution functions: polynomial, sine, cosine, tangent, cotangent, logarithm, exponent, arc sin, arc cos, arc tan, arc cot or power function.

Nodes are treated as characteristic points of data for modeling and analyzing. The model of data can be built by choice of probability distribution function and nodes combination. PFC modeling via nodes combination and parameter γ as probability distribution function enables value anticipation in risk analysis and decision making. Two-dimensional object is extrapolated and interpolated via nodes combination and different functions as discrete or continuous probability distribution functions: polynomial, sine, cosine, tangent, cotangent, logarithm, exponent, arc sin, arc cos, arc tan, arc cot or power function.

Functions for γ calculations are chosen individually at each data modeling and it is treated as 2-dimensional probability distribution function: γ depends on initial requirements and features' specifications. PFC method leads to data interpolation as handwriting or signature identification and image retrieval via discrete set of feature vectors in 2-dimensional feature space. So PFC method makes possible the combination of two important problems: interpolation and modeling in a matter of image retrieval or writer identification. PFC interpolation develops a linear interpolation in multidimensional feature spaces into other functions as two-dimensional probability distribution functions. Future works are going to applications of PFC method in biometric recognition, computer vision and artificial intelligence.

Figure 8. PFC 2D interpolation for $y(c) = \gamma \cdot y_i + (1 - \gamma)y_{i+1}$

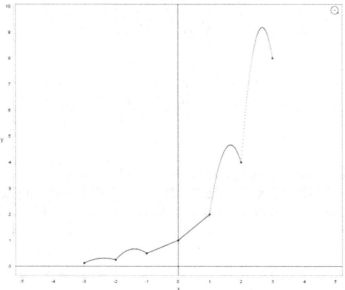

Figure 9. PFC 2D modeling for $\gamma = \alpha^s, s = 1, h = \dfrac{y_1}{x_1}x_2 + \dfrac{y_2}{x_2}x_1$

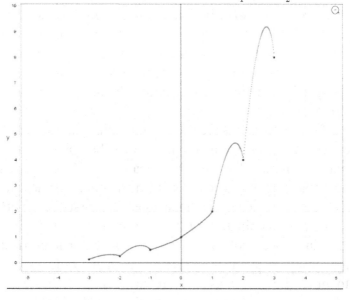

Figure 10. PFC 2D reconstruction for $\gamma = \alpha^s, s = 0,8, h = \dfrac{y_1}{x_1}x_2 + \dfrac{y_2}{x_2}x_1$

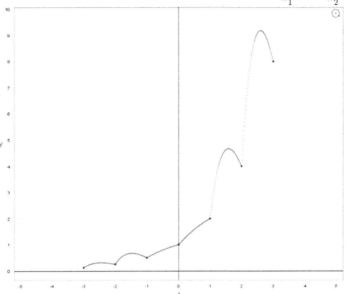

Figure 11. PFC 2D reconstruction for $\gamma = \left(2^\alpha - 1\right)^s, s = 1, h = \dfrac{y_1}{x_1}x_2 + \dfrac{y_2}{x_2}x_1$

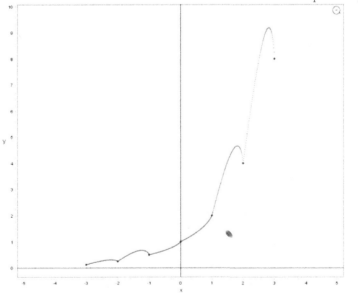

Figure 12. PFC 2D interpolation for $\gamma = \log_2\left(\alpha^s + 1\right), s = 0,8, h = \dfrac{y_1}{x_1}x_2 + \dfrac{y_2}{x_2}x_1$

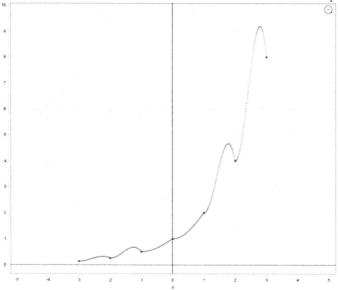

Figure 13. PFC 2D modeling for $\gamma = \sin^s\left(\alpha \cdot \dfrac{\pi}{2}\right), s = 1, h = \dfrac{y_1}{x_1}x_2 + \dfrac{y_2}{x_2}x_1$

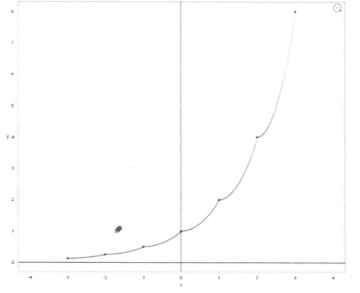

Figure 14. PFC 2D modeling for $\gamma = \sin^s\left(\alpha \cdot \dfrac{\pi}{2}\right), s = 0, 8, h = 0$

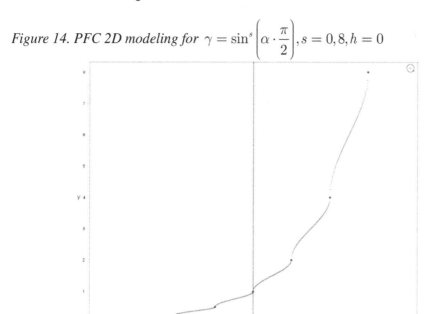

Modeling and Interpolation of Non-Typical Curves and Irregular Shapes

PFC two dimensional interpolation and modeling enables to solve classic problem in numerical methods: how to parameterize and to model any given function. But having the set of nodes there is another problem connected with handwriting and human signing: how to model or to reconstruct the curve which is the part of signature or handwriting but which is non-typical or irregular. Human signature and handwriting consists of non-typical curves and irregular shapes. PFC method (1) is the way of modeling and interpolation for non-typical curves and irregular shapes – contours as closed curves (if first node and last node is the same). Here are some examples of modeled non-typical or irregular curves as a part of signature or handwriting for five nodes:

$$\gamma = 1 - \frac{2}{\pi}\arccos\left(\alpha^s\right), s = 0, 5, h = 0.$$

Figure 14-16 are the examples of very specific modeling for non-typical and irregular curves as a signature. PFC interpolation is used for parameterization and reconstruction of curves in the plane.

Figure 15. PFC 2D interpolation for
$$\left(-0.9; 4.736\right), \left(-0.5; 0.666\right), \left(0; 0\right), \left(0.5; -0.666\right), \left(0.9; -4.736\right),$$
$$\gamma = \log_2^{s}\left(\alpha + 1\right), \ s = 0.8$$

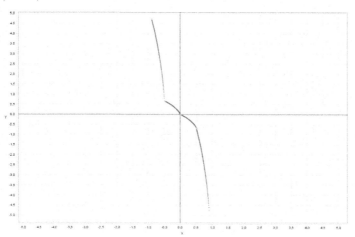

Figure 16. PFC 2D interpolation for $h = 0, \ \gamma = \sin\left(\alpha^{s} * \dfrac{\pi}{2}\right), \ s = 1.8$

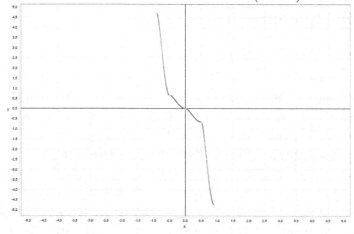

DATA EXTRAPOLATION

Extrapolation of values is valid with the same formulas and algorithms as methods of MHR, PNC and PFC, but for $\alpha \notin [0;1]$. It is possible to extrapolate not only coordinates of points in the function, but also any other curves with

Figure 17. PFC 2D interpolation for $h = 0$, $\gamma = \left(2^{\alpha} - 1\right)^{s}$, $s = 1.2$

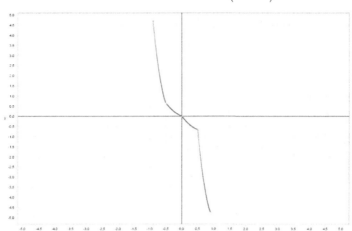

nodes in the range $[a;b]$ of one coordinate. When extrapolated point $(c;y_c)$ is situated before the first node ($c < a$ if there is a graph of function – left extrapolation) then parameter $\alpha > 1$: for example $\alpha = 1.01$; 1.02; …; 1.99; 2.00 and so on. When extrapolated point is situated behind the last node ($c > b$ if there is a graph of function – right extrapolation) then parameter $\alpha < 0$: for example $\alpha = -0.01$; -0.02;…; -0.99; -1.00 and so on. If for any modeling function $\alpha < 0$ is beyond the domain, for example $h = 0$ with $s=0.5$, then in the case of extrapolation it is possible to take alternative version of PNC:

$$\gamma = F\left(\alpha\right) = \alpha^{s}.$$

Then right extrapolation is done for $\alpha > 1$, but left extrapolation is done for $\alpha < 0$.

Some Examples of PNC Extrapolation and Interpolation

Curve extrapolation via PNC method for nodes (1;1), (2;3), (3;4), (6;6) and modelingfunction $y(c) = (1 - \gamma) \cdot y_k + \gamma \cdot y_{k+1} + \gamma(1 - \gamma) \cdot h(p_1, p_2,..., p_m)$,nodes combination $h = (\gamma = F\left(\alpha\right) = \alpha^s) + (\dfrac{x_2}{x_1})$, $s = 1$:

1. Left of first node: See Figure 18.

2.   Right of last node: See Figure 19.

And now there are PNC examples for nodes:

$x = -1.5; y = -1;$

$x = 1.25; y = 3.15;$

$x = 4.4 ; y = 6.8;$

$x = 8; y = 7$

and parameter $s = 2$ (for exponential modeling function $a = 3$).
Modeling functions:

$F(\alpha) = \alpha^s;$

$F(\alpha) = \sin(\alpha^s \cdot \dfrac{y_2}{y_1});$

$F(\alpha) = 1-\cos(\alpha^s \cdot \dfrac{\text{À}}{2});$

$F(\alpha) = \tan(\alpha^s \cdot \dfrac{\text{À}}{2});$

$F(\alpha) = ctg(\dfrac{\pi}{4} -\alpha^s \cdot \dfrac{\pi}{2});$

$F(\alpha) = \log_2(\alpha^s + 1);$

$F(\alpha) = (\dfrac{\pi}{4})^s;$

$F(\alpha) = \dfrac{a^\alpha -1}{a - 1} \cdot \arcsin(\alpha^s);$

Figure 18. Data extrapolation before the first node

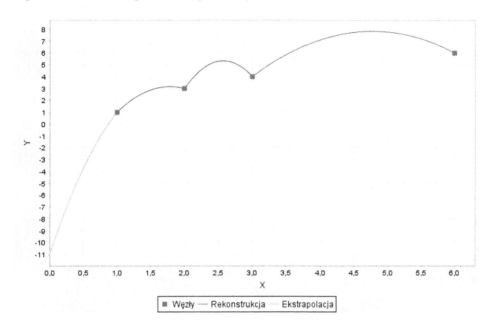

Figure 19. Data extrapolation behind the last node

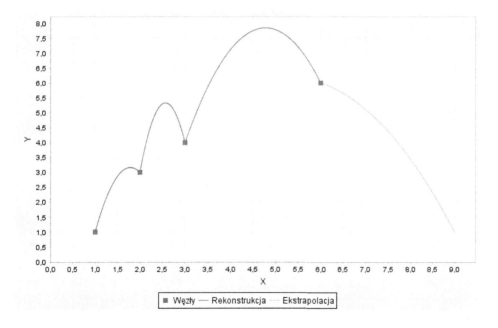

$$F(\alpha) = 1 - \frac{2}{\pi} \cdot \arccos(\alpha^s);$$

$$F(\alpha) = \frac{2}{\pi} \cdot \arctan(\alpha^s);$$

$$F(\alpha) = 2 - \frac{4}{\pi} \cdot \text{arcctg}(\alpha^s).$$

Nodes combination:

$h = 0,$

$$\frac{4}{\pi}$$

$h = x_1 x_2 + y_1 y_2,$

Figure 20. Interpolation with $F(\alpha) = \alpha^2$ and $h = 0$

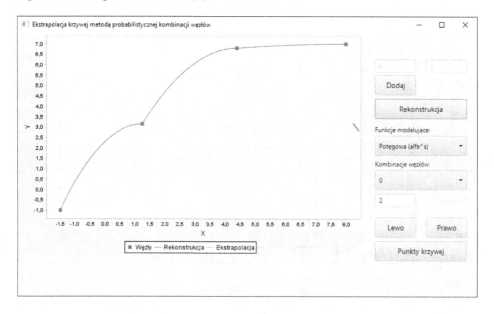

$$h = (h = y_1(\frac{x_2}{x_1}) + y_2(\frac{x_1}{x_2})) + (\frac{x_2}{x_1}).$$

Figures 20-22:

$F(\alpha) = \alpha^2 \; ; h = 0$

Figures 23-25:

$$F(\alpha) = \sin(\alpha^2 \cdot \frac{y_2}{y_1}) \text{ and } h = y_1(\frac{\pi}{2}) + y_2(\frac{x_2}{x_1})$$

Figures 26-28:

$$F(\alpha) = 1\text{-}\cos(\alpha^2 \cdot \frac{x_1}{x_2}) \text{ and } h = x_1 x_2 + y_1 y_2$$

Figures 29-31:

Figure 21. Left extrapolation with $F(\alpha) = \alpha^2$ and $h = 0$

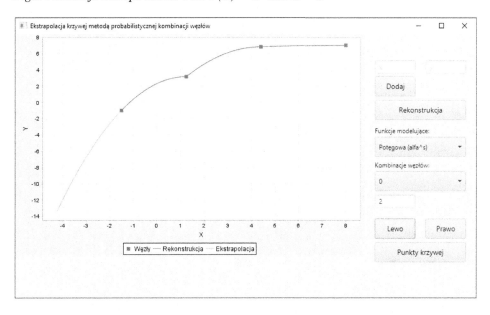

Figure 22. Right extrapolation for $F(\alpha) = \alpha^2$ and $h = 0$

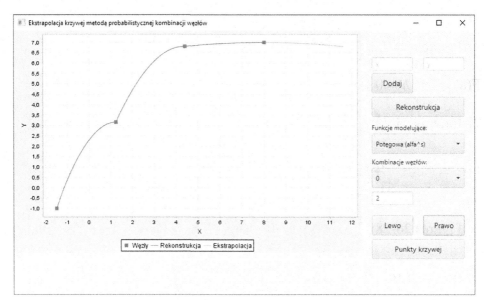

Figure 23. Interpolation with $F(\alpha) = sin(\alpha^2 \cdot \pi/2)$ and $h = y_1(\dfrac{x_1}{x_2}) + y_2(\dfrac{x_2}{x_1})$

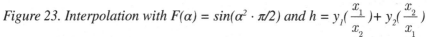

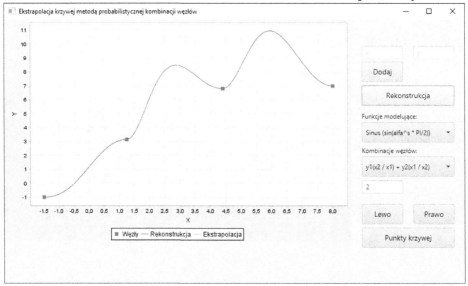

Figure 24. Left extrapolation for $F(\alpha) = sin(\alpha^2 \cdot \pi/2)$ and $h = y_1(\dfrac{x_1}{x_2}) + y_2(\dfrac{x_2}{x_1})$

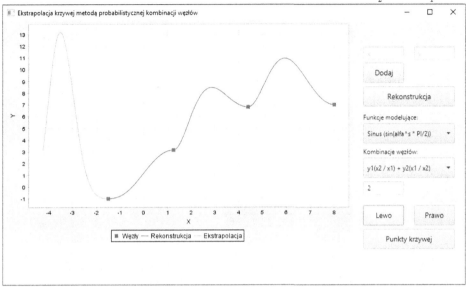

Figure 25. Right extrapolation with $F(\alpha) = sin(\alpha^2 \cdot \pi/2)$ and $h = y_1(\dfrac{x_1}{x_2}) + y_2(\dfrac{x_2}{x_1})$

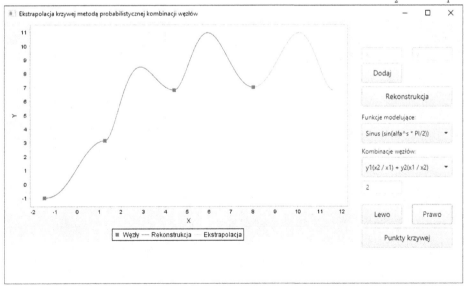

Figure 26. Interpolation for F(α) = 1-cos(α² · π/2) and h = x₁x₂ + y₁y₂

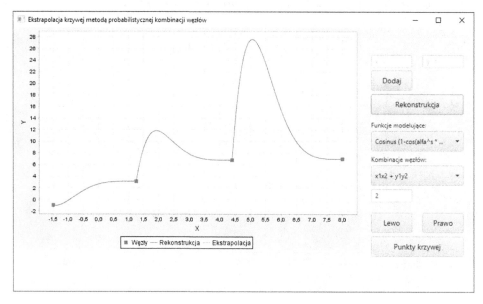

Figure 27. Left extrapolation with F(α) = 1-cos(α² · π/2) and h = x₁x₂ + y₁y₂

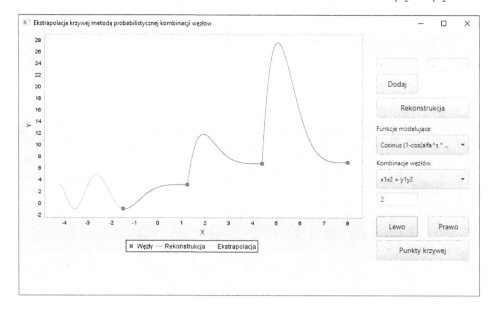

Figure 28. Right extrapolation with $F(\alpha) = 1\text{-}cos(\alpha^2 \cdot \pi/2)$ and $h = x_1x_2 + y_1y_2$

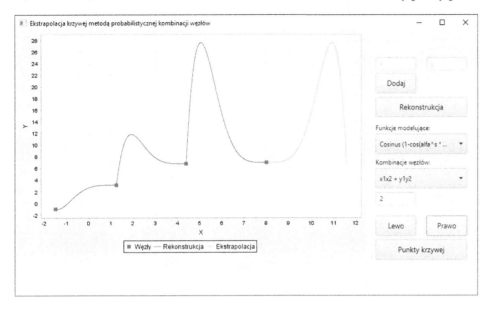

Figure 29. Interpolation for $F(\alpha) = log_2(\alpha^2 + 1)$ and $h = y_1(\dfrac{x_1}{x_2}) + y_2(\dfrac{x_2}{x_1})$

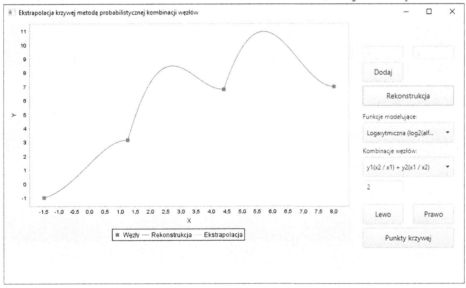

Figure 30. Left extrapolation for $F(\alpha) = log_2(\alpha^2 + 1)$ *and* $h = y_1(\dfrac{x_1}{x_2}) + y_2(\dfrac{x_2}{x_1})$

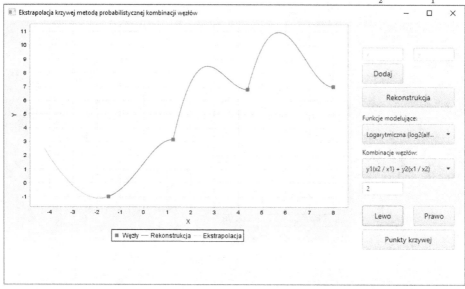

Figure 31. Right extrapolation with $F(\alpha) = log_2(\alpha^2 + 1)$ *and* $h = y_1(\dfrac{x_1}{x_2}) + y_2(\dfrac{x_2}{x_1})$

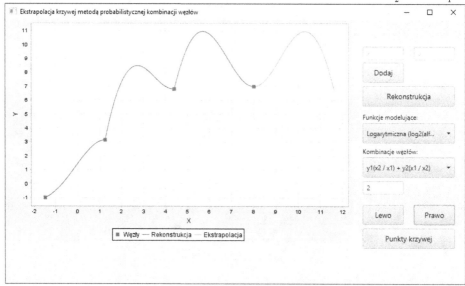

Figure 32. Interpolation with $F(\alpha) = ((a^\alpha-1)/(a-1))^2$; $h = x_1x_2 + y_1y_2$; $a=3$

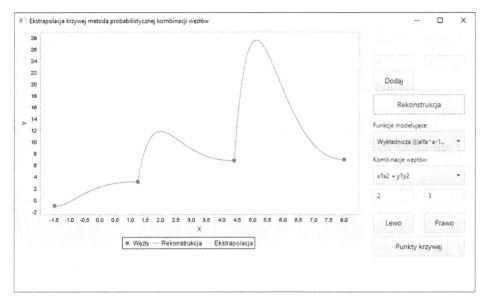

Figure 33. Left extrapolation with $F(\alpha) = ((a^\alpha-1)/(a-1))^2$; $h = x_1x_2 + y_1y_2$; $a=3$

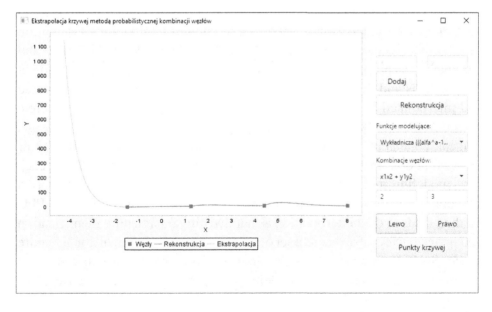

$$F(\alpha) = \log_2(\alpha^2 + 1) \text{ and } h = y_1(\frac{\pi}{2}) + y_2(\frac{x_2}{x_1})$$

Figures 32-34:

$$F(\alpha) = (\frac{x_1}{x_2})^2 \text{ and } h = x_1x_2 + y_1y_2 ; a=3;$$

Figures 35-37:

$$F(\alpha) = \frac{a^\alpha - 1}{a - 1} \cdot \arctan(\alpha^2) \text{ and } h = y_1(\frac{4}{\pi}) + y_2(\frac{x_2}{x_1})$$

Figures 38-40:

$$F(\alpha) = 2 - \frac{x_1}{x_2} \cdot arcctg(\alpha^2) \text{ and } h = x_1x_2 + y_1y_2$$

Data extrapolation is used in anticipation of trends and enables the prediction of values. Nodes are treated as characteristic points of data for modeling and analyzing. The model of data can be built by choice of probability distribution function and nodes combination. PFC modeling via nodes combination and parameter γ as probability distribution function enables value anticipation in risk analysis and decision making. Two-dimensional object is extrapolated and interpolated via nodes combination and different functions as discrete or continuous probability distribution functions: polynomial, sine, cosine, tangent, cotangent, logarithm, exponent, arc sin, arc cos, arc tan, arc cot or power function. Functions for γ calculations are chosen individually at each data modeling and it is treated as 2-dimensional probability distribution function: γ depends on initial requirements and features' specifications. PFC method leads to data interpolation as handwriting or signature identification and image retrieval via discrete set of feature vectors in 2-dimensional feature space. So PFC method makes possible the combination of two important problems: interpolation and modeling in a matter of image retrieval or writer identification. PFC interpolation develops a linear interpolation in multidimensional feature spaces into other functions as two-dimensional probability distribution functions. Future works are going to applications

Figure 34. Right extrapolation for $F(\alpha) = ((a^\alpha-1)/(a-1))^2$; $h = x_1x_2 + y_1y_2$; a=3

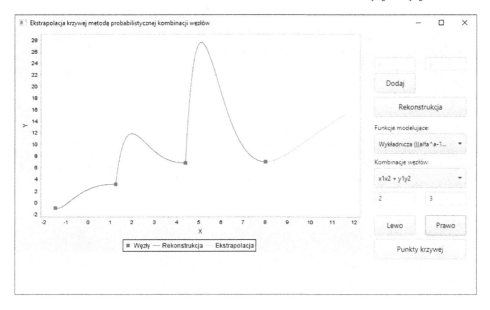

Figure 35. Interpolation with $F(\alpha) = 4/\pi \cdot arctan(\alpha^2)$ and $h = y_1(\frac{x_1}{x_2})+ y_2(\frac{x_2}{x_1})$

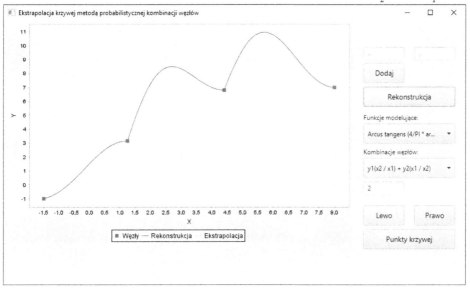

Figure 36. Left extrapolation for $F(\alpha) = 4/\pi \cdot arctan(\alpha^2)$ and $h = y_1(\dfrac{x_1}{x_2}) + y_2(\dfrac{x_2}{x_1})$

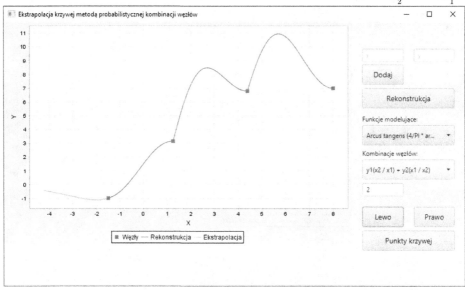

Figure 37. Right extrapolation with $F(\alpha) = 4/\pi \cdot arctan(\alpha^2)$ and $h = y_1(\dfrac{x_1}{x_2}) + y_2(\dfrac{x_2}{x_1})$

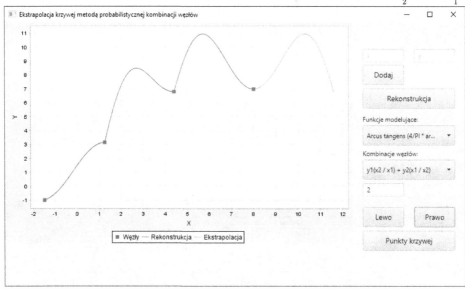

Figure 38. Interpolation for F(α) = 2-4/π · arcctg(α^2) and h = $x_1x_2 + y_1y_2$

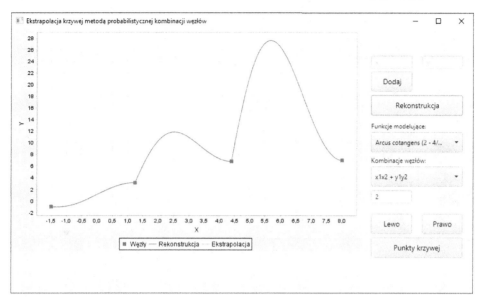

Figure 39. Left extrapolation for F(α) = 2-4/π · arcctg(α^2) and h = $x_1x_2 + y_1y_2$

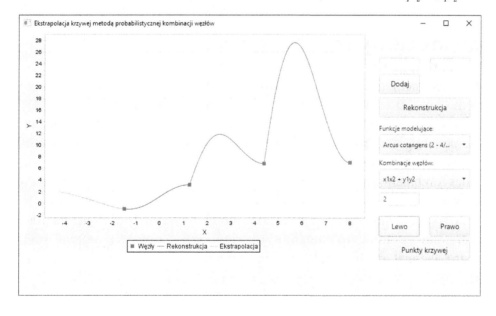

Figure 40. Right extrapolation with $F(\alpha) = 2-4/\pi \cdot arcctg(\alpha^2)$ and $h = x_1x_2 + y_1y_2$

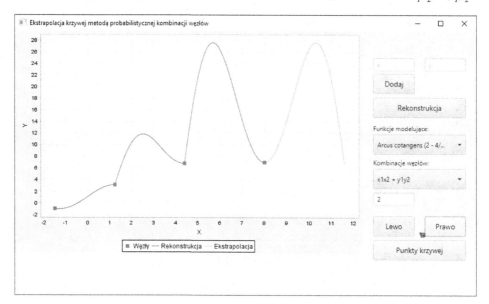

of PFC method in biometric recognition, computer vision and artificial intelligence.

SOLUTIONS AND RECOMMENDATIONS

Proposed method, called Probabilistic Features Combination (PFC), is the method of 2D curve interpolation and extrapolation using the set of key points (knots or nodes). Nodes can be treated as characteristic points of data for modeling and analyzing. The model of data can be built by choice of probability distribution function and nodes combination. PFC modeling via nodes combination and parameter γ as probability distribution function enables value anticipation in risk analysis and decision making. Two-dimensional curve is extrapolated and interpolated via nodes combination and different functions as discrete or continuous probability distribution functions: polynomial, sine, cosine, tangent, cotangent, logarithm, exponent, arc sin, arc cos, arc tan, arc cot or power function.

FUTURE RESEARCH DIRECTIONS

Future trends will go to various directions: how to fix the best probability distribution function for the nodes, how to calculate the most appropriate nodes combination and what extrapolation is the most valuable in decision making and risk analysis.

CONCLUSION

What is the most important feature of MHR and PNC methods? Interpolation methods and curve fitting represent so huge problem that each individual interpolation is exceptional and requires specific solutions. PNC method is such a novel tool with its all pros and cons. The user has to decide which interpolation method is the best in a single situation. The choice is yours if you have any choice. Presented method is such a new possibility for curve fitting and interpolation when specific data (for example handwritten symbol or character) starts up with no rules for polynomial interpolation. This book consists of two generalizations: generalization of previous MHR method with various nodes combinations and generalization of linear interpolation with different (no basic) probability distribution functions and nodes combinations. The method of Probabilistic Nodes Combination (PNC) enables interpolation and modeling of two-dimensional curves using nodes combinations and different coefficients γ: polynomial, sinusoidal, cosinusoidal, tangent, cotangent, logarithmic, exponential, arc sin, arc cos, arc tan, arc cot or power function, also inverse functions. This probabilistic view is novel approach a problem of modeling and interpolation. Computer vision and pattern recognition are interested in appropriate methods of shape representation and curve modeling. PNC method represents the possibilities of shape reconstruction and curve interpolation via the choice of nodes combination and probability distribution function for interpolated points. It seems to be quite new look at the problem of contour representation and curve modeling in artificial intelligence and computer vision. Function for γ calculations is chosen individually at each curve modeling and it is treated as probability distribution function: γ depends on initial requirements and curve specifications. PNC method leads to curve interpolation as handwriting modeling via discrete set of fixed knots. So PNC makes possible the combination of two important problems: interpolation and modeling. The method of Probabilistic Features Combination (PFC) enables interpolation and modeling of high-dimensional N data using features' combinations and different coefficients γ: polynomial, sinusoidal, cosinusoidal, tangent, cotangent, logarithmic, exponential, arc sin, arc cos, arc tan, arc cot or power function. Functions for γ calculations are chosen individually at each data modeling and it is treated as N-dimensional probability distribution function: γ depends on initial requirements and features' specifications. PFC method leads to data interpolation as handwriting or signature identification and image retrieval via discrete set of feature vectors in N-dimensional feature space. So PFC method makes possible the combination of two important problems: interpolation and modeling in a matter of image retrieval or writer identification. Main features of PFC method are: PFC interpolation develops a linear interpolation in multidimensional feature spaces into other functions as N-dimensional probability distribution functions; PFC is a generalization of MHR method and PNC method via different nodes combinations; interpolation of L points is connected with the computational cost of rank $O(L)$ as in MHR and PNC method; nodes combination and coefficients γ are crucial in the process of data probabilistic parameterization and interpolation: they are computed individually for a single feature. Future works are going to applications of PFC method in signature and handwriting biometric recognition: choice and features of nodes combinations h and coefficients γ.

Proposed method, called Probabilistic Features Combination (PFC), is the method of N-dimensional data interpolation and extrapolation using the set of key points (knots or nodes). Nodes can be treated as characteristic points of data for modeling and analyzing. The model of data can be built by choice of probability distribution function and nodes combination. PFC modeling via nodes combination and parameter γ as probability distribution function enables value anticipation in risk analysis and decision making. N-dimensional object is extrapolated and interpolated via nodes combination and different functions as discrete or continuous probability distribution functions: polynomial, sine, cosine, tangent, cotangent, logarithm, exponent, arc sin, arc cos, arc tan, arc cot or power function. The method of Probabilistic Features Combination (PFC) enables interpolation and modeling of high-dimensional data using features' combinations and different coefficients γ as modeling function. Functions for γ calculations are chosen individually at each data modeling and it is treated as N-dimensional probability distribution function: γ depends on initial requirements and features' specifications. PFC method leads to data interpolation as handwriting or signature identification and image retrieval via discrete set of feature vectors in N-dimensional feature space. So PFC method makes possible the combination of two important problems: interpolation and modeling in a matter of image retrieval or writer identification. PFC interpolation develops a linear interpolation in multidimensional feature spaces into other functions as N-dimensional probability distribution functions. Future works are going to applications of PFC method in biometric recognition, computer vision and artificial intelligence. Nodes are treated as characteristic points of data for modeling and analyzing. The model of data can be built by choice of probability distribution function and nodes combination. PFC modeling via nodes combination and parameter γ as probability distribution function enables value anticipation in risk analysis and decision making. Two-dimensional object is extrapolated and interpolated via nodes combination and different functions as discrete or continuous probability distribution functions: polynomial, sine, cosine, tangent, cotangent, logarithm, exponent, arc sin, arc cos, arc tan, arc cot or power function. Functions for γ calculations are chosen individually at each data modeling and it is treated as 2-dimensional probability distribution function: γ depends on initial requirements and features' specifications. PFC method leads to data interpolation as handwriting or signature identification and image retrieval via discrete set of feature vectors in 2-dimensional feature space. So PFC method makes possible the combination of two important problems: interpolation and modeling in a matter of image retrieval or writer identification. PFC interpolation develops a linear interpolation in multidimensional feature spaces into other functions as two-dimensional probability distribution functions.

The method of Probabilistic Features Combination (PFC) enables interpolation and modeling of high-dimensional N data using features' combinations and different coefficients γ: polynomial, sinusoidal, cosinusoidal, tangent, cotangent, logarithmic, exponential, arc sin, arc cos, arc tan, arc cot or power function. Functions for γ calculations are chosen individually at each data modeling and it is treated as N-dimensional probability distribution function: γ depends on initial requirements and features' specifications. PFC method leads to data interpolation as handwriting or signature identification and image retrieval via discrete set of feature vectors in N-dimensional feature space. So PFC method makes possible the combination of two important problems: interpolation and modeling in a matter of image retrieval or writer identification. Main features of PFC method are: PFC interpolation develops a linear interpolation in multidimensional feature spaces into other functions as N-dimensional probability distribution functions; PFC is a generalization of MHR method and PNC method via different nodes combinations; interpolation of L points is connected with the computational cost of rank $O(L)$ as in MHR and PNC method; nodes combination and coefficients γ are crucial in the process of data probabilistic parameterization and interpolation: they are computed individually for a single feature. Future works are going to applications of PFC method in signature and handwriting biometric recognition: choice and features of nodes combinations *h* and coefficients γ.

REFERENCES

Bulacu, M., & Schomaker, L. (2007). Text-independent writer identification and verification using textural and allographic features. *IEEE Transactions on Pattern Analysis and Machine Intelligence, 29*(4), 701–717. doi:10.1109/TPAMI.2007.1009 PMID:17299226

Bulacu, M., Schomaker, L., & Brink, A. (2007). Text-independent writer identification and verification on off-line Arabic handwriting. *International Conference on Document Analysis and Recognition*, 769–773.

Chapra, S. C. (2012). *Applied Numerical Methods*. McGraw-Hill.

Chen, J., Cheng, W., & Lopresti, D. (2011). Using perturbed handwriting to support writer identification in the presence of severe data constraints. Document Recognition and Retrieval, 1–10. doi:10.1117/12.876497

Chen, J., Lopresti, D., & Kavallieratou, E. (2010). The impact of ruling lines on writer identification. *International Conference on Frontiers in Handwriting Recognition*, 439–444. doi:10.1109/ICFHR.2010.75

Collins, G. W. II. (2003). *Fundamental Numerical Methods and Data Analysis*. Case Western Reserve University.

Djeddi, C., & Souici-Meslati, L. (2010). A texture based approach for Arabic writer identification and verification. *International Conference on Machine and Web Intelligence*, 115–120.

Djeddi, C., & Souici-Meslati, L. (2011). Artificial immune recognition system for Arabic writer identification. *International Symposium on Innovation in Information and Communication Technology*, 159–165. doi:10.1109/ISIICT.2011.6149612

Galloway, M. M. (1975). Texture analysis using gray level run lengths. *Computer Graphics and Image Processing, 4*(2), 172–179. doi:10.1016/S0146-664X(75)80008-6

Garain, U., & Paquet, T. (2009). Off-line multi-script writer identification using AR coefficients. *International Conference on Document Analysis and Recognition*, 991–995. doi:10.1109/ICDAR.2009.222

Ghiasi, G., & Safabakhsh, R. (2013). Offline text-independent writer identification using codebook and efficient code extraction methods. *Image and Vision Computing*, *31*(5), 379–391. doi:10.1016/j.imavis.2013.03.002

Jakóbczak, D. J. (2014). *2D Curve Modeling via the Method of Probabilistic Nodes Combination-Shape Representation, Object Modeling and Curve Interpolation-Extrapolation with the Applications*. Saarbrucken: LAP Lambert Academic Publishing.

Marti, U.-V., & Bunke, H. (2002). The IAM-database: An English sentence database for offline handwriting recognition. *Int. J. Doc. Anal. Recognit.*, *5*(1), 39–46. doi:10.1007/s100320200071

Nosary, A., Heutte, L., & Paquet, T. (2004). Unsupervised writer adaption applied to handwritten text recognition. *Pattern Recognition Letters*, *37*(2), 385–388. doi:10.1016/S0031-3203(03)00185-7

Ozaki, M., Adachi, Y., & Ishii, N. (2006). Examination of effects of character size on accuracy of writer recognition by new local arc method. *International Conference on Knowledge- Based Intelligent Information and Engineering Systems*, 1170–1175. doi:10.1007/11893004_148

Ralston, A., & Rabinowitz, P. (2001). *A First Course in Numerical Analysis* (2nd ed.). New York: Dover Publications.

Schlapbach, A., & Bunke, H. (2004). Using HMM based recognizers for writer identification and verification. *9th Int. Workshop on Frontiers in Handwriting Recognition*, 167–172. doi:10.1109/IWFHR.2004.107

Schlapbach, A., & Bunke, H. (2006). Off-line writer identification using Gaussian mixture models. *International Conference on Pattern Recognition*, 992–995.

Schlapbach, A., & Bunke, H. (2007). A writer identification and verification system using HMM based recognizers. *Pattern Analysis & Applications*, *10*(1), 33–43. doi:10.1007/s10044-006-0047-5

Schomaker, L., Franke, K., & Bulacu, M. (2007). Using codebooks of fragmented connected- component contours in forensic and historic writer identification. *Pattern Recognition Letters*, *28*(6), 719–727. doi:10.1016/j.patrec.2006.08.005

Schumaker, L. L. (2007). *Spline Functions: Basic Theory*. Cambridge Mathematical Library. doi:10.1017/CBO9780511618994

Shahabinejad, F., & Rahmati, M. (2007). A new method for writer identification and verification based on Farsi/Arabic handwritten texts. *Ninth International Conference on Document Analysis and Recognition (ICDAR 2007)*, 829–833.

Siddiqi, I., Cloppet, F., & Vincent, N. (2009). Contour based features for the classification of ancient manuscripts. Conference of the International Graphonomics Society, 226–229.

Siddiqi, I., & Vincent, N. (2010). Text independent writer recognition using redundant writing patterns with contour-based orientation and curvature features. *Pattern Recognition Letters*, *43*(11), 3853–3865. doi:10.1016/j.patcog.2010.05.019

Van, E. M., Vuurpijl, L., Franke, K., & Schomaker, L. (2005). The WANDA measurement tool for forensic document examination. *J. Forensic Doc. Exam.*, *16*, 103–118.

Zhang, D., & Lu, G. (2004). Review of Shape Representation and Description Techniques. *Pattern Recognition*, *1*(37), 1–19. doi:10.1016/j.patcog.2003.07.008

ADDITIONAL READING

Ballard, D. H. (1982). *Computer Vision*. New York, USA: Prentice Hall.

Basu, S., & Bresler, Y. (2000). $O(N^2 \log_2 N)$ filtered backprojection reconstruction algorithm for tomography. *IEEE Transactions on Image Processing*, *9*(10), 1760–1773. doi:10.1109/83.869187 PMID:18262914

Brankov, J. G., Yang, Y., & Wernick, M. N. (2004). Tomographic image reconstruction based on a Content–Adaptive Mesh Model. *IEEE Transactions on Medical Imaging*, *2*(23), 202–212. doi:10.1109/TMI.2003.822822 PMID:14964565

Brasse, D., & Defrise, M. (2004). Fast fully 3-D image reconstruction in PET using planograms. *IEEE Transactions on Medical Imaging, 4*(23), 413–425. doi:10.1109/TMI.2004.824231 PMID:15084067

Cetin, M., Karl, W. C., & Willsky, A. S. (2002, September). *Edge – preserving image reconstruction for coherent imaging application.* Paper presented at the IEEE International Conference on Image Processsing, Rochester, NY, USA. doi:10.1109/ICIP.2002.1039992

Chlebus, E., & Cholewa, M. (1999). Rapid prototyping – rapid tooling. *CADCAM Forum, 11*, 23-28.

Choraś, R. S. (2005). *Computer Vision.* Warsaw, Poland: Exit.

Cocozza-Thivent, C., Eymard, R., Mercier, S., & Roussignol, M. (2006). Characterization of the Marginal Distributions of Markov Processes Used in Dynamic Reliability. *Journal of Applied Mathematics and Stochastic Analysis. Article ID, 92156*, 1–18.

Cormen, T. H., Leiserson, C. E., & Rivest, R. L. (1996). *Introduction to algorithms.* Massachusetts, USA: the Massachusetts Institute of Technology Press and McGraw-Hill.

Dahlquist, G., & Bjoerck, A. (1974). *Numerical Methods.* New York, USA: Prentice Hall.

Defrise, M. (2001). A short readers guide to 3D tomographic reconstruction. *Computerized Medical Imaging and Graphics, 25*(2), 113–116. doi:10.1016/S0895-6111(00)00061-6 PMID:11137787

Dejdumrong, N. (2007). A Shape Preserving Verification Techniques for Parametric Curves. *Computer Graphics, Imaging and Visualization. CGIV, 2007*, 163–168.

Dryja, M., Jankowska, J., & Jankowski, M. (1982). *Survey of numerical methods and algorithms. Part II.* Warsaw, Poland: WNT.

Dyn, N., Levin, D., & Gregory, J. A. (1987). A 4-Point Interpolatory Subdivision Scheme for Curve Design. *Computer Aided Geometric Design, 4*(4), 257–268. doi:10.1016/0167-8396(87)90001-X

Eldar, Y. C. (2001). *Quantum Signal Processing.* (Unpublished doctoral dissertation). Massachusetts Institute of Technology, USA.

Eldar, Y. C., & Oppenheim, A. V. (2002). Quantum Signal Processing. *IEEE Signal Processing Magazine*, *6*(19), 12–32. doi:10.1109/MSP.2002.1043298

Fortuna, Z., Macukow, B., & Wąsowski, J. (1982). *Numerical methods*. Warsaw, Poland: WNT.

Jakóbczak, D. (2005). Hurwitz-Radon matrices and their children. *Computer Science*, *5*(8), 29–38.

Jakóbczak, D. (2007). 2D and 3D Image Modeling Using Hurwitz-Radon Matrices. *Polish Journal of Environmental Studies*, *4A*(16), 104–107.

Jakóbczak, D. (2009). Curve Interpolation Using Hurwitz-Radon Matrices. *Polish Journal of Environmental Studies*, *3B*(18), 126–130.

Jakóbczak, D. (2010). Shape Representation and Shape Coefficients via Method of Hurwitz-Radon Matrices. *Lecture Notes in Computer Science*, *6374*, 411–419. doi:10.1007/978-3-642-15910-7_47

Jakóbczak, D. (2010). Object Modeling Using Method of Hurwitz-Radon Matrices of Rank k. In W. Wolski & M. Borawski (Eds.), *Computer Graphics: Selected Issues* (pp. 79–90). Szczecin, Poland: University of Szczecin Press.

Jakóbczak, D. (2011). Curve Parameterization and Curvature via Method of Hurwitz-Radon Matrices. *Image Processing & Communications-. International Journal (Toronto, Ont.)*, *1-2*(16), 49–56.

Jakóbczak, D. (2011). Data Extrapolation and Decision Making via Method of Hurwitz-Radon Matrices. *Lecture Notes in Computer Science*, *6922*, 173–182. doi:10.1007/978-3-642-23935-9_17

Jakóbczak, D. (2011). Curve Extrapolation and Data Analysis using the Method of Hurwitz-Radon Matrices. *Folia Oeconomica Stetinensia*. 9(17)/2010, 121-138.

Jakóbczak, D. (2013). Probabilistic Modeling of Signature using the Method of Hurwitz-Radon Matrices. *Global Perspectives on Artificial Intelligence*, *1*(1), 1–7.

Jankowska, J., & Jankowski, M. (1981). *Survey of numerical methods and algorithms. Part I*. Warsaw, Poland: WNT.

Kontaxakis, G., & Strauss, L. G. (1998). Maximum likelihood algorithms for image reconstruction in Positron Emission Tomography. *Radionuclides for Oncology – Current Status and Future Aspects, 1998,* 73-106.

Kowalczuk, Z., & Wiszniewski, B. (Eds.). (2007). *Intelligent data mining in diagnostic purposes: Automatics and informatics*. Gdansk, Poland: PWNT.

Kozera, R. (2004). *Curve Modeling via Interpolation Based on Multidimensional Reduced Data*. Gliwice, Poland: Silesian University of Technology Press.

Kundur, D., & Hatzinakos, D. (1998). A novel blind deconvolution scheme for image restoration using recursive filtering. *IEEE Transactions on Signal Processing*, 2(46), 375–390. doi:10.1109/78.655423

Laine, A., & Zong, X. (1996). *Border identification of echocardiograms via multiscale edge detection and shape modeling*. Paper presented at the IEEE International Conference on Image Processsing, Lausanne, Switzerland. doi:10.1109/ICIP.1996.560486

Lang, S. (1970). *Algebra*. Reading, Massachusetts, USA: Addison-Wesley Publishing Company.

Le Buhan Jordan, C., Bossen, F., & Ebrahimi, T. (1997). *Scalable shape representation for content based visual data compression*. Paper presented at the International Conference on Image Processing, Santa Barbara, CA, USA. doi:10.1109/ICIP.1997.647962

Liu, T., & Geiger, D. (1999). Approximate tree matching and shape similarity. *Int. Conf. Computer Vision*. Corfu, Greece.

Lorton, A., Fouladirad, M., & Grall, A. (2013). A Methodology for Probabilistic Model-based Prognosis. *European Journal of Operational Research*, 225(3), 443–454. doi:10.1016/j.ejor.2012.10.025

Marker, J., Braude, I., Museth, K., & Breen, D. (2006). Contour-based surface reconstruction using implicit curve fitting, and distance field filtering and interpolation. *Volume Graphics*, 2006, 1–9.

Meyer, Y. (1993). *Wavelets: algorithms & applications*. Philadelphia, USA: Society for Industrial and Applied Mathematics.

Pergler, M., & Freeman, A. (2008). Probabilistic Modeling as an Exploratory Decision-Making Tool. *McKinsey Working Papers on Risk*. 6, 1-18.

Poggio, T., & Smale, S. (2003). The mathematics of learning: Dealing with data. *Notices of the American Mathematical Society*, 5(50), 537–544.

Przelaskowski, A. (2005). *Data compression*. Warsaw, Poland: BTC.

Rogers, D. F. (2001). *An Introduction to NURBS with Historical Perspective.* Morgan Kaufmann Publishers.

Rutkowski, L., Siekmann, J., Tadeusiewicz, R., & Zadeh, A. (Eds.). (2004). *Lecture notes on artificial intelligence: Artificial intelligence and soft computing.* Berlin-Heidelberg, Germany: Springer-Verlag.

Saber, E., Xu, Y., & Murat Tekalp, A. (2005). Partial shape recognition by sub-matrix matching for partial matching guided image labeling. *Pattern Recognition*, *38*(10), 1560–1573. doi:10.1016/j.patcog.2005.03.027

Sebastian, T. B., Klein, P. N., & Kimia, B. B. (2003). On aligning curves. *IEEE Transactions on Pattern Analysis and Machine Intelligence*, *25*(1), 116–124. doi:10.1109/TPAMI.2003.1159951

Siddiqi, I., & Vincent, N. (2010). Text independent writer recognition using redundant writing patterns with contour-based orientation and curvature features. *Pattern Recognition Letters*, *43*(11), 3853–3865. doi:10.1016/j.patcog.2010.05.019

Tadeusiewicz, R., & Flasiński, M. (1991). *Image Recognition.* Warsaw, Poland: PWN.

Vakhania, N. (1993). Orthogonal random vectors and the Hurwitz – Radon-Eckmann theorem. *Proc. of the Georgian Academy of Sciences-Mathematics*, *1(1)*, 109-125.

Willis, M. (2000). *Algebraic reconstruction algorithms for remote sensing image enhancement.* Unpublished doctoral dissertation, Department of Electrical and Computer Engineering, Brigham Young University.

Xu, Fang, & Mueller, K. (2005). Accelerating popular tomographic reconstruction algorithms on commodity PC graphics hardware. *IEEE Transactions on Nuclear Science*, *3*(52), 654–661.

Zaletelj, J., & Tasic, J. F. (2003). *Optimization and tracking of polygon vertices for shape coding.* Berlin-Heidelberg, Germany: Springer-Verlag. doi:10.1007/978-3-540-45179-2_52

Zhang, J. K., Davidson, T., & Wong, K. M. (2004). Efficient design of orthonormal wavelet bases for signal representation. *IEEE Transactions on Signal Processing*, *7*(52), 1983–1996. doi:10.1109/TSP.2004.828923

KEY TERMS AND DEFINITIONS

Curve Interpolation: Computing new and unknown points of a curve and creating a graph of a curve using existing data points – interpolation nodes.

Data Extrapolation: Calculation of unknown values for the points situated outside the ranges of nodes.

Hurwitz – Radon Matrices: A family of skew – symmetric and orthogonal matrices with columns and rows that create, together with identical matrix, the base in vector spaces of dimensions $N = 2$, 4 or 8.

MHR Method: The method of curve interpolation and extrapolation using linear (convex) combinations of OHR operators.

OHR Operator: Matrix operator of Hurwitz – Radon built from coordinates of interpolation nodes.

Value Anticipation: Foreseeing next value when last value is known.

Chapter 4
Contour Reconstruction:
2D Object Modeling

ABSTRACT

The method of Probabilistic Features Combination (PFC) enables interpolation and modeling of high-dimensional N data using features' combinations and different coefficients γ: polynomial, sinusoidal, cosinusoidal, tangent, cotangent, logarithmic, exponential, arc sin, arc cos, arc tan, arc cot or power function. Functions for γ calculations are chosen individually at each data modeling and it is treated as N-dimensional probability distribution function: γ depends on initial requirements and features' specifications. PFC method leads to data interpolation as handwriting or signature identification and image retrieval via discrete set of feature vectors in N-dimensional feature space. So PFC method makes possible the combination of two important problems: interpolation and modeling in a matter of image retrieval or writer identification. Main features of PFC method are: PFC interpolation develops a linear interpolation in multidimensional feature spaces into other functions as N-dimensional probability distribution functions.

INTRODUCTION

Probabilistic modeling is still developing branch of the computer science: operational research (for example probabilistic model-based prognosis) (Lorton, Fouladirad & Grall, 2013), decision making techniques and probabilistic modeling (Pergler & Freeman, 2008), artificial intelligence and

DOI: 10.4018/978-1-5225-2531-8.ch004

machine learning. There are used different aspects of probabilistic methods: stochastic processes and stochastic model-based techniques, Markov processes (Cocozza-Thivent, Eymard, Mercier & Roussignol, 2006), Poisson processes, Gamma processes, a Monte Carlo method, Bayes rule, conditional probability and many probability distributions. In this chapter the goal of probability distribution function is to describe the position of unknown points between given interpolation nodes. Two-dimensional curve (opened or closed) is used to represent the data points.

So problem statement of this chapter is: how to reconstruct (interpolate) missing points of 2D curve having the set of interpolation nodes (key points) and using the information about probabilistic distribution of unknown points. For example the simplest basic distribution leads to the easiest interpolation – linear interpolation. Apart from probability distribution, additionally there is the second factor of proposed interpolation method: nodes combination. The simplest nodes combination is zero. Thus proposed curve modeling is based on two agents: probability distribution and nodes combination.

Curve interpolation (Collins, 2003) represents one of the most important problems in mathematics and computer science: how to model the curve (Chapra, 2012) via discrete set of two-dimensional points (Ralston & Rabinowitz, 2001)? Also the matter of shape representation (as closed curve-contour) and curve parameterization is still opened (Zhang & Lu, 2004). For example pattern recognition, signature verification or handwriting identification problems are based on curve modeling via the choice of key points. So interpolation is not only a pure mathematical problem but important task in computer vision and artificial intelligence. The chapter wants to approach a problem of curve modeling by characteristic points. Proposed method relies on nodes combination and functional modeling of curve points situated between the basic set of key points. The functions that are used in calculations represent whole family of elementary functions with inverse functions: polynomials, trigonometric, cyclometric, logarithmic, exponential and power function. These functions are treated as probability distribution functions in the range [0;1]. Curve interpolation represents one of the most important problems in mathematics and computer science: how to model the curve via discrete set of two-dimensional points? Also the matter of shape representation (as closed curve-contour) and curve parameterization is still opened. For example pattern recognition, signature verification or handwriting identification problems are based on curve modeling via the choice of key points. So interpolation is not only a pure mathematical problem but important task in computer vision and artificial intelligence. The monograph wants to approach a problem of curve modeling by characteristic points. Proposed method relies on nodes combination and functional modeling of curve points situated between the basic set of key points. The functions that are used in calculations represent whole family of elementary functions with inverse functions: polynomials, trigonometric, cyclometric, logarithmic, exponential and power function. These functions are treated as probability distribution functions in the range [0;1]. Significant problem in machine vision and computer vision is that of appropriate 2D shape representation and reconstruction. Classical discussion about shape representation is based on the problem: contour versus skeleton. This monograph is voting for contour which forms boundary of the object. Contour of the object, represented by successive contour points, consists of information which allows us to describe many important features of the object as shape coefficients. 2D curve modeling and generation is a basic subject in many branches of industry and computer science, for example in the cad/cam software. The representation of shape can have a great impact on the accuracy and effectiveness of object recognition. In the literature, shape has been represented by many options including curves, graph-based algorithms and medial axis to enable shape-based object recognition. Digital 2D curve (open or closed) can be represented by chain code (Freeman's code). Chain code depends on selection of the started point and transformations of the object. So Freeman's code is one of the method how to describe and to find contour of the object. Analog (continuous) version of Freeman's code is the curve α-*s*. Another contour representation and reconstruction is based on Fourier coefficients calculated in discrete Fourier transformation (DFT). These coefficients are used to fix similarity of the contours with different sizes or directions. If we assume that contour is built from segments of a line and fragments of circles or ellipses, hough transformation is applied to detect contour lines. Also geometrical moments of the object are used during the process of object shape representation. Contour is also applied in shape decomposition. Many branches of medicine, industry and manufacturing are looking for methods connected with geometry of the contour. Why and when should we use MHR and PNC methods? Interpolation methods and curve fitting represent so huge problem that each individual interpolation is exceptional and requires specific solutions. PNC method is such a novel tool with its all pros and cons. The user has to decide which interpolation method is the best in a single situation. The choice is yours if you have any choice. Presented method is such a new possibility for curve fitting and interpolation when specific data (for example handwritten symbol or character) starts up with no rules for polynomial interpolation. This book consists of two generalizations: generalization of previous MHR method with various nodes combinations and generalization of linear interpolation with different (no basic) probability distribution functions and nodes combinations. The method of Probabilistic Nodes Combination (PNC) enables interpolation and modeling of two-dimensional curves using nodes combinations and different coefficients γ: polynomial, sinusoidal, cosinusoidal, tangent, cotangent, logarithmic, exponential, arc sin, arc cos, arc tan, arc cot or power function, also inverse functions. This probabilistic view is novel approach a problem of modeling and interpolation. Computer vision and pattern recognition are interested in appropriate methods of shape representation and curve modeling. PNC method represents the possibilities of shape reconstruction and curve interpolation via the choice of nodes combination and probability distribution function for interpolated points. It seems to be quite new look at the problem of contour representation and curve modeling in artificial intelligence and computer vision. Function for γ calculations is chosen individually at each curve modeling and it is treated as probability distribution function: γ depends on initial requirements and curve specifications. PNC method leads to curve interpolation as handwriting modeling via discrete set of fixed knots. So PNC makes possible the combination of two important problems: interpolation and modeling. Nodes are treated as characteristic points of data for modeling and analyzing. The model of data can be built by choice of probability distribution function and nodes combination. PFC modeling via nodes combination and parameter γ as probability distribution function enables value anticipation in risk analysis and decision making. Two-dimensional object is extrapolated and interpolated via nodes combination and different functions as discrete or continuous probability distribution functions: polynomial, sine, cosine, tangent, cotangent, logarithm, exponent, arc sin, arc cos, arc tan, arc cot or power function. Functions for γ calculations are chosen individually at each data modeling and it is treated as 2-dimensional probability distribution function: γ depends on initial requirements and features' specifications. PFC method leads to data interpolation as handwriting or signature identification and image retrieval via discrete set of feature vectors in 2-dimensional feature space. So PFC method makes possible the combination of two important problems: interpolation and modeling in a matter of image retrieval or writer identification. PFC interpolation develops a linear interpolation in multidimensional feature spaces into other functions as two-dimensional probability distribution functions. Future works are going to applications of PFC method in biometric recognition, computer vision and artificial intelligence.

BACKGROUND

Shape Representation and Curve Reconstruction

An important problem in machine vision and computer vision (Ballard, 1982) is that of appropriate shape representation and reconstruction. Classical discussion about shape representation is based on the problem: contour versus skeleton. This chapter is voting for contour which forms boundary of the object. Contour of the object, represented by contour points, consists of information which allows us to describe many important features of the object as shape coefficients (Tadeusiewicz & Flasiński, 1991). In the chapter contour is dealing with a set of curves. Curve modeling and generation is a basic subject in many branches of industry and computer science, for example in the CAD/CAM software.

The representation of shape has a great impact on the accuracy and effectiveness of object recognition (Saber, Yaowu & Murat Tekalp, 2005). In the literature, shape has been represented by many options including curves (Sebastian & Klein, 2003), graph-based algorithms and medial axis (Liu & Geiger, 1999) to enable shape-based object recognition. Digital curve (open or closed) can be represented by chain code (Freeman's code). Chain code depends on selection of the started point and transformations of the object. So Freeman's code is one of the method how to describe and to find contour of the object. An analog (continuous) version of Freeman's code is the curve α-s. Another contour representation and reconstruction is based on Fourier coefficients calculated in Discrete Fourier Transformation (DFT). These coefficients are used to fix similarity of the contours with different sizes or directions. If we assume that contour is built from segments of a line and fragments of circles or ellipses, Hough transformation is applied to detect contour lines. Also geometrical moments of the object are used during the process of object shape representation (Choraś, 2005).

Nowadays methods apply mainly polynomial functions, for example Bernstein polynomials in Bezier curves, splines (Schumaker, 2007) and NURBS (Rogers, 2001). But Bezier curves don't represent the interpolation method and cannot be used for example in handwriting modeling with key points (interpolation nodes). In comparison PNC method with Bézier curves, Hermite curves and B-curves (*B-splines*) or NURBS one unpleasant feature of these curves has to be mentioned: small change of one characteristic point can result in unwanted change of whole reconstructed curve. Such a feature does not appear in proposed PNC method. Numerical methods for data interpolation are based on polynomial or trigonometric functions, for example Lagrange, Newton, Aitken and Hermite methods. These methods have many weak sides (Dahlquist & Bjoerck, 1974) and are not sufficient for curve interpolation in the situations when the curve cannot be build by polynomials or trigonometric functions. Also there exists several well established methods of curve modeling, for example shape-preserving techniques (Dejdumrong, 2007), subdivision algorithms (Dyn, Levin & Gregory, 1987) and others (Kozera, 2004) to overcome difficulties of polynomial interpolation, but probabilistic interpolation with nodes combination seems to be quite novel in the area of shape modeling. Proposed 2D curve interpolation is the functional modeling via any elementary functions and it helps us to fit the curve during the computations.

This chapter presents novel Probabilistic Nodes Combination (PNC) method of curve interpolation. This chapter takes up new PNC method of two-dimensional curve modeling via the examples using the family of Hurwitz-Radon matrices (MHR method) (Jakóbczak, 2007), but not only (other nodes combinations). The method of PNC requires minimal assumptions: the only information about a curve is the set of at least two nodes. Proposed PNC method is applied in curve modeling via different coefficients: polynomial, sinusoidal, cosinusoidal, tangent, cotangent, logarithmic, exponential, arc sin, arc cos, arc tan, arc cot or power. Function for PNC calculations is chosen individually at each interpolation and it represents probability distribution function of parameter $\alpha \in [0;1]$ for every point situated between two interpolation knots. PNC method uses two-dimensional vectors (x,y) for curve modeling-knots $p_i = (x_i, y_i) \in R^2$ in PNC method, $i = 1,2,...n$:

1. PNC needs 2 knots or more ($n \geq 2$);
2. If first node and last node are the same ($p_1 = p_n$), then curve is closed (contour);
3. For more precise modeling knots ought to be settled at key points of the curve, for example local minimum or maximum and at least one node between two successive local extrema.

Condition 3 means for example the highest point of the curve in a particular orientation, convexity changing or curvature extrema. So this chapter wants to answer the question: how to interpolate the curve by a set of knots (Jakóbczak, 2010)?

Algorithm of PNC interpolation and modeling (1) looks as follows:

Step 1: Choice of knots p_i at key points.
Step 2: Choice of nodes combination $h(p_1, p_2, ..., p_m)$.
Step 3: Choice of distribution $\gamma = F(\alpha)$ (continuous or discrete).
Step 4: Determining values of α: $\alpha = 0.1, 0.2...0.9$ (nine points) or 0.01, 0.02...0.99 (99 points) or others.
Step 5: The computations.

These five steps can be treated as the algorithm of PNC method of curve modeling and interpolation. Without knowledge about the formula of curve or function, PNC interpolation has to implement the coefficients γ, but PNC is not limited only to these coefficients. Each strictly monotonic function F between points (0;0) and (1;1) can be used in PNC modeling.

HANDWRITTEN CHARACTER AND SHAPE MODELING

Issues

Curve knots $p_1 = (0.1;10)$, $p_2 = (0.2;5)$, $p_3 = (0.4;2.5)$, $p_4 = (1;1)$ and $p_5 = (2;5)$ are used in some examples of PNC method in handwritten character modeling. Figures 1-8 represent PNC as MHR interpolation (Jakóbczak, 2011) with different γ. Points of the curve are calculated with no matrices ($N = 1$) and $\gamma = \alpha$ in example 1 and with matrices of dimension $N = 2$ in examples 2-8 for $\alpha = 0.1, 0.2,...,0.9$.

Example 1

PNC curve interpolation for $\gamma = \alpha$ and

$$h(p_1, p_2) = \frac{y_1}{x_1} x_2 + \frac{y_2}{x_2} x_1.$$

Figure 1. PNC character modeling for nine reconstructed points between nodes

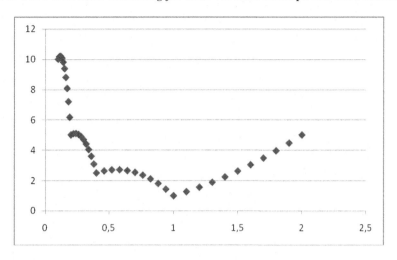

See Figure 1.

For $N = 2$ (examples $2 - 8$) MHR version (Jakóbczak, 2011) as PNC method gives us:

$$h(p_1, p_2, p_3, p_4) = \frac{1}{x_1^2 + x_3^2}(x_1 x_2 y_1 + x_2 x_3 y_3 + x_3 x_4 y_1 - x_1 x_4 y_3) +$$

$$\frac{1}{x_2^2 + x_4^2}(x_1 x_2 y_2 + x_1 x_4 y_4 + x_3 x_4 y_2 - x_2 x_3 y_4)$$

Figure 2. Sinusoidal modeling with nine reconstructed curve points between nodes

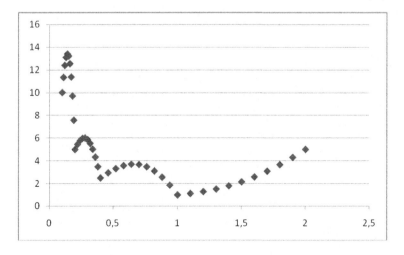

Figure 3. Tangent character modeling with nine interpolated points between nodes

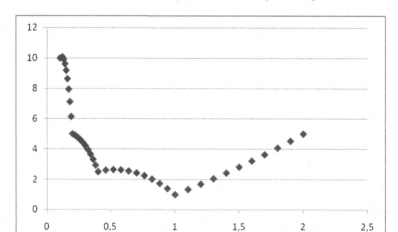

Example 2

PNC sinusoidal interpolation with $\gamma = sin(\alpha \cdot \pi/2)$.

Example 3

PNC tangent interpolation for $\gamma = tan(\alpha \cdot \pi/4)$.

Figure 4. Tangent curve modeling with nine recovered points between nodes

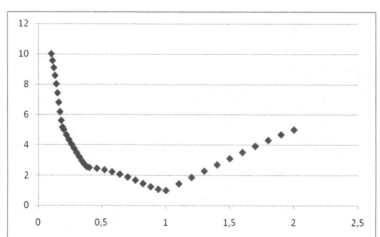

Example 4

PNC tangent interpolation with $\gamma = tan(\alpha^s \cdot \pi/4)$ and $s = 1.5$.

Proposed method, called Probabilistic Nodes Combination (PNC), is the method of 2D curve interpolation and extrapolation using the set of key points (knots or nodes). Nodes can be treated as characteristic points of data for modeling and analyzing. The model of data can be built by choice of probability distribution function and nodes combination. PNC modeling via nodes combination and parameter γ as probability distribution function enables value anticipation in risk analysis and decision making. Two-dimensional curve is extrapolated and interpolated via nodes combination and different functions as discrete or continuous probability distribution functions: polynomial, sine, cosine, tangent, cotangent, logarithm, exponent, arc sin, arc cos, arc tan, arc cot or power function. Novelty of this book consists of two generalizations: generalization of previous MHR method with various nodes combinations and generalization of linear interpolation with different (no basic) probability distribution functions and nodes combinations. Computer vision needs suitable methods of shape representation and contour reconstruction. One of them, invented by the author and called method of Hurwitz-Radon Matrices (MHR), can be used in representation and reconstruction of shapes of the objects in the plane. Proposed method is based on a family of Hurwitz-Radon (HR) matrices. The matrices are skew-symmetric and possess columns composed of orthogonal vectors. 2D shape is represented by the set of successive nodes.

Figure 5. Tangent symbol modeling with nine reconstructed points between nodes

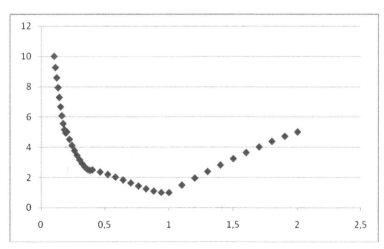

Figure 6. Sinusoidal modeling with nine interpolated curve points between nodes

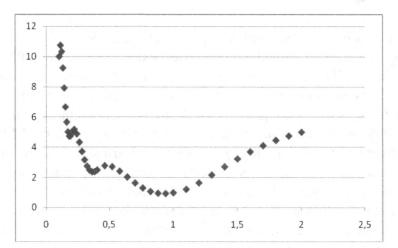

It is shown how to create the orthogonal and discrete OHR operator and how to use it in a process of shape representation and reconstruction. Then MHR method is generalized to Probabilistic Nodes Combination (PNC) method.

Example 5

PNC tangent curve interpolation for $\gamma = tan(\alpha^s \cdot \pi/4)$ and $s = 1.797$.

Example 6

PNC sinusoidal interpolation with $\gamma = sin(\alpha^s \cdot \pi/2)$ and $s = 2.759$.

Example 7

PNC power function modeling for $\gamma = \alpha^s$ and $s = 2.1205$.

Example 8

PNC logarithmic curve modeling with $\gamma = log_2(\alpha^s + 1)$ and $s = 2.533$.

These eight examples demonstrate possibilities of PNC curve interpolation and handwritten character modeling for key nodes in MHR version. And here are other examples of PNC modeling (but not MHR):

Figure 7. Power function curve modeling with nine recovered points between nodes

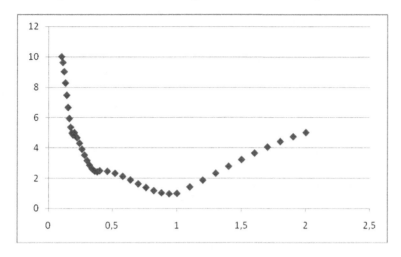

Figure 8. Logarithmic character modeling with nine reconstructed points between nodes

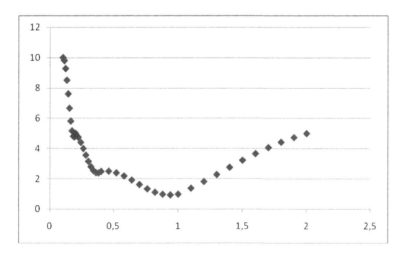

Example 9

PNC for $\gamma = \alpha^2$ and $h(p_1, p_2) = x_1 y_1 + x_2 y_2$:

Curve interpolation represents one of the most important problems in mathematics and computer science: how to model the curve via discrete set of two-dimensional points? Also the matter of shape representation (as closed curve-contour) and curve parameterization is still opened. For example pattern

Figure 9. Quadratic symbol modeling with nine reconstructed points between nodes

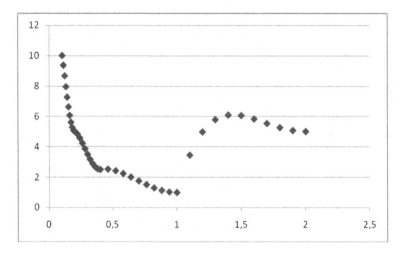

Figure 10. Cubic character modeling with nine reconstructed points between nodes

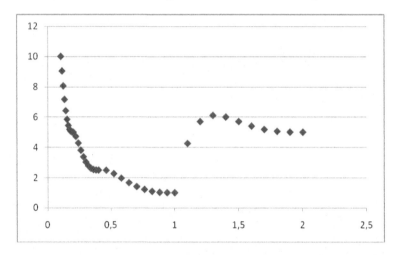

recognition, signature verification or handwriting identification problems are based on curve modeling via the choice of key points. So interpolation is not only a pure mathematical problem but important task in computer vision and artificial intelligence. The monograph wants to approach a problem of curve modeling by characteristic points. Proposed method relies on nodes combination and functional modeling of curve points situated between the basic set of key points. The functions that are used in calculations represent whole family of elementary functions with inverse functions: polynomials, trigonometric, cyclometric, logarithmic, exponential and power function. These functions are treated as probability distribution functions in the range [0;1].

Example 10

PNC for $\gamma = \alpha^3$ and $h(p_1, p_2) = x_1 y_1 + x_2 y_2$:

If we consider Figure 1 as closed curve (contour) with the node $p_6 = p_1$ = (0.1;10) then examples 8 and 9 give the shapes:

Example 11

PNC for $\gamma = \alpha^2$ and $h(p_1, p_2) = x_1 y_1 + x_2 y_2$:

Example 12

PNC for $\gamma = \alpha^3$ and $h(p_1, p_2) = x_1 y_1 + x_2 y_2$:

Every man has individual style of handwriting. Recognition of handwritten letter or symbol need modeling and the model of each individual symbol or character can be built by choice of γ and h. PNC modeling via nodes combinations h and parameter γ as probability distribution function enables curve interpolation for each specific letter or symbol.

Figure 11. Quadratic contour modeling with nine reconstructed points between nodes

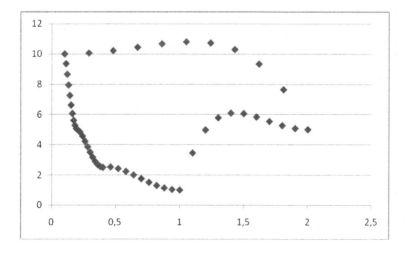

Figure 12. Cubic shape modeling with nine reconstructed points between nodes

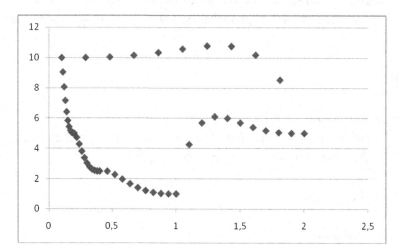

Number of reconstructed points depends on a user by value α. If for example $\alpha = 0.01, 0.02,\ldots,0.99$ then 99 points are interpolated for each pair of nodes. Reconstructed values and interpolated points, calculated by PNC method, are applied in the process of curve modeling. Every curve can be interpolated by some distribution function as parameter γ and nodes combination h. Parameter γ is treated as probability distribution function for each curve.

Beta Distribution

Basic distribution ($\gamma = \alpha$) with nodes combination $h = 0$ turns PNC interpolation (1) to linear interpolation. What about PNC in the case of yet another distribution on the range [0;1]: beta distribution? Power functions as γ used in examples 1, 7 and 9-12 are also connected with beta distribution. Here are the examples of PNC modeling for beta distribution with nodes combination $h = 0$.

Example 13

PNC for $\gamma = 3\alpha^2 - 2\alpha^3$ and $h(p_1, p_2) = 0$:

Example 14

PNC for $\gamma = 4\alpha^3 - 3\alpha^4$ and $h(p_1, p_2) = 0$:

Figure 13. Beta distribution in handwritten character modeling

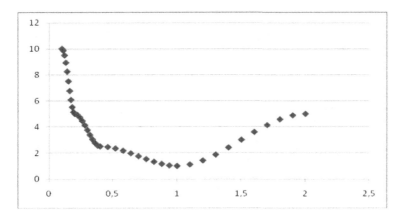

Figure 14. Beta distribution in handwritten symbol modeling

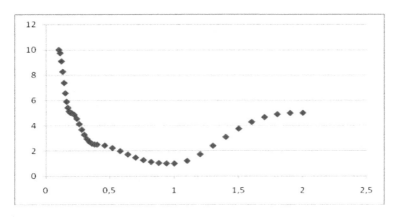

Example 15

PNC for $\gamma = 2\alpha\text{-}\alpha^2$ and $h(p_1, p_2) = 0$:

Examples 9-12 represent beta distribution with $h(p_1, p_2) = x_1 y_1 + x_2 y_2$.

Exponential Distribution

Exponential distribution is dealing with random variable ≥ 0, but in PNC interpolation random variable $\alpha \in [0;1]$. Then exponential distribution is represented by distribution function:

Figure 15. Beta distribution in handwritten letter modeling

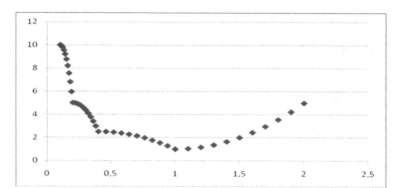

Figure 16. Exponential distribution in handwritten character modeling

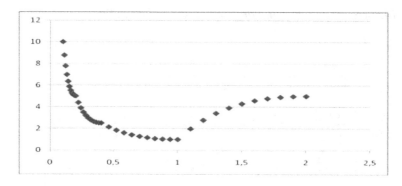

$$\gamma = F(\alpha) = 1 - (1 - \alpha)e^{\alpha}.$$

Example 16

PNC for $\gamma = 1\text{-}(1\text{-}\alpha)e^{\alpha}$ and $h(p_1, p_2) = 0$:

Example 17

PNC for $\gamma = 1\text{-}(1\text{-}\alpha)e^{\alpha}$ and $h(p_1, p_2) = \dfrac{y_2}{y_1} + \dfrac{x_2}{x_1}$:

These examples show the variety of possibilities in curve modeling via the choice of nodes combination and probability distribution function for interpolated points.

Figure 17. Exponential distribution in handwritten symbol modeling

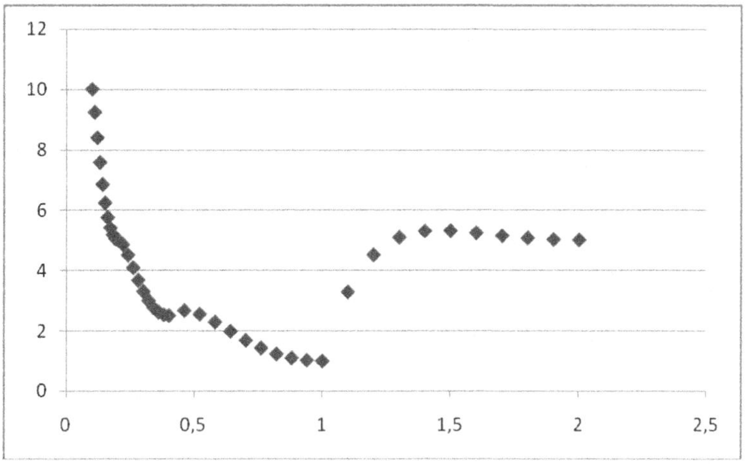

2D OBJECT MODELING

What about contours – closed curves? The only assumption is that first node and last node are the same. The simplest way is the linear interpolation for $h = 0$ and $\gamma = \alpha$. (Figure 18).

Proposed method, called Probabilistic Nodes Combination (PNC), is the method of 2D curve interpolation and extrapolation using the set of key points (knots or nodes). Nodes can be treated as characteristic points of data for modeling and analyzing. The model of data can be built by choice of probability distribution function and nodes combination. PNC modeling via nodes combination and parameter γ as probability distribution function enables value anticipation in risk analysis and decision making. Two-dimensional curve is extrapolated and interpolated via nodes combination and different functions as discrete or continuous probability distribution functions: polynomial, sine, cosine, tangent, cotangent, logarithm, exponent, arc sin, arc cos, arc tan, arc cot or power function. Novelty of this book consists of two generalizations: generalization of previous MHR method with various nodes combinations and generalization of linear interpolation with different (no basic) probability distribution functions and nodes combinations. Here are examples of shape modeling for five (or rather six) nodes:

Significant problem in machine vision and computer vision is that of appropriate 2D shape representation and reconstruction. Classical discussion about shape representation is based on the problem: contour versus skeleton.

Figure 18. Contour reconstructed 1for $h = 0$ *and* $\gamma = \alpha$

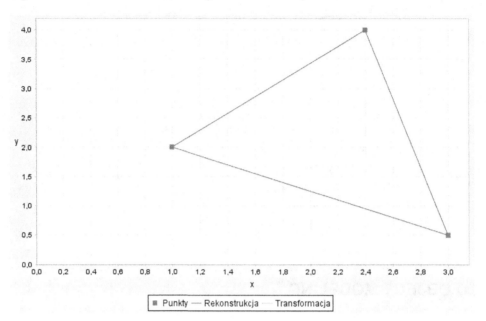

Table 1. Shape modeling for nodes

Lp.	x	y
1	1	2.5
2	1.7	4
3	2.6	3
4	2.3	0.5
5	1.5	1

This monograph is voting for contour which forms boundary of the object. Contour of the object, represented by successive contour points, consists of information which allows us to describe many important features of the object as shape coefficients. 2D curve modeling and generation is a basic subject in many branches of industry and computer science, for example in the cad/cam software. The representation of shape can have a great impact on the accuracy and effectiveness of object recognition.

The method of Probabilistic Nodes Combination (PNC) enables interpolation and modeling of two-dimensional curves using nodes combinations and different coefficients γ: polynomial, sinusoidal, cosinusoidal,

Figure 19. PFC 2D modeling for $s = 1, h = 0, \gamma = \alpha^s$ *(linear modeling)*

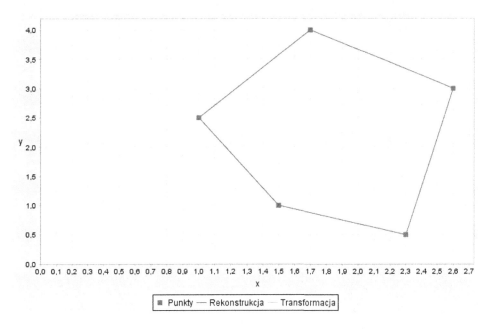

Figure 20. PFC 2D modeling for $s = 1, h = x_1 x_2 + y_1 y_2, \gamma = \alpha^s$

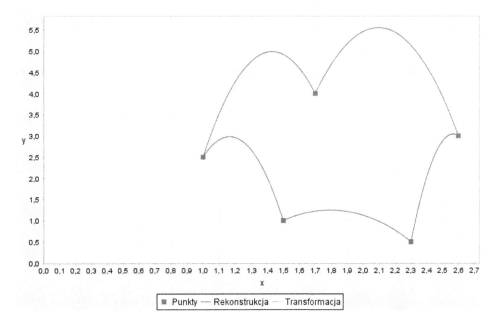

Figure 21. PFC 2D modeling for $s = 0,7, h = 0, \gamma = \alpha^s$

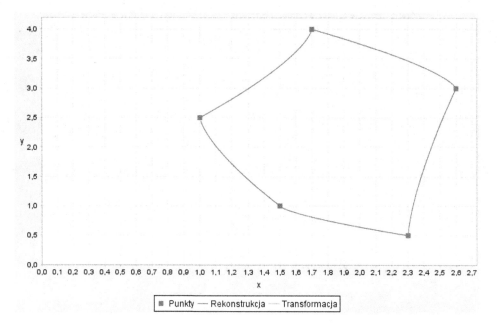

Figure 22. PFC 2D modeling for $s = 1, h = 0, \gamma = \sin\left(\alpha^s \cdot \dfrac{\pi}{2}\right)$

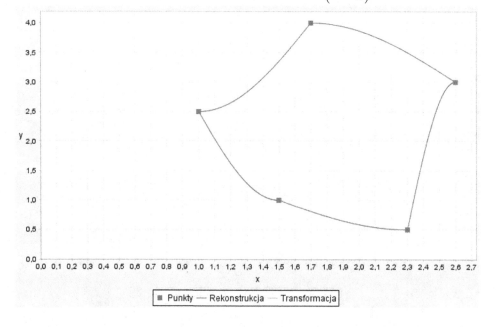

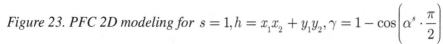

Figure 23. PFC 2D modeling for $s = 1, h = x_1 x_2 + y_1 y_2, \gamma = 1 - \cos\left(\alpha^s \cdot \dfrac{\pi}{2}\right)$

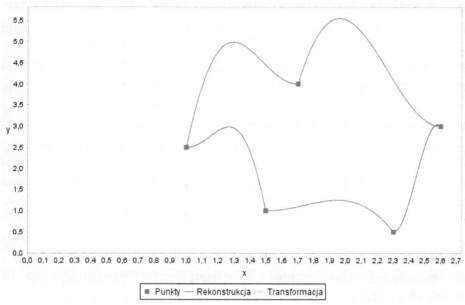

Figure 24. PFC 2D modeling for $s = 0.6, h = 0, \gamma = \dfrac{2}{\pi} \cdot \arcsin\left(\alpha^s\right)$

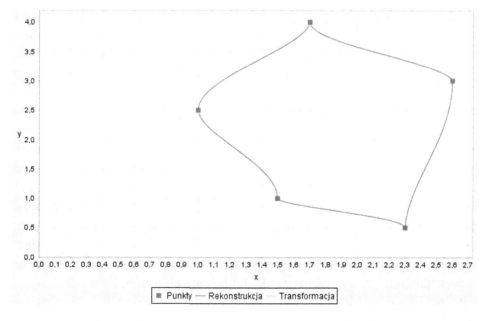

tangent, cotangent, logarithmic, exponential, arc sin, arc cos, arc tan, arc cot or power function, also inverse functions. This probabilistic view is novel approach a problem of modeling and interpolation. Computer vision and pattern recognition are interested in appropriate methods of shape representation and curve modeling. PNC method represents the possibilities of shape reconstruction and curve interpolation via the choice of nodes combination and probability distribution function for interpolated points. It seems to be quite new look at the problem of contour representation and curve modeling in artificial intelligence and computer vision.

Function for γ calculations is chosen individually at each curve modeling and it is treated as probability distribution function: γ depends on initial requirements and curve specifications. PNC method leads to curve interpolation as handwriting modeling via discrete set of fixed knots. So PNC makes possible the combination of two important problems: interpolation and modeling.

For the same set of nodes above contours are reconstructed via modeling functions γ and parameters s, h. Minimal set of characteristic points in contour reconstruction consists of three nodes. Here are PNC shape modeling for nodes: (1;1), (10;10), (20;5).

Significant problem in machine vision and computer vision is that of appropriate 2D shape representation and reconstruction. Classical discussion about shape representation is based on the problem: contour versus skeleton. This monograph is voting for contour which forms boundary of the object. Contour of the object, represented by successive contour points, consists of information which allows us to describe many important features of the object as shape coefficients. 2D curve modeling and generation is a basic subject in many branches of industry and computer science, for example in the cad/cam software. The representation of shape can have a great impact on the accuracy and effectiveness of object recognition.

Nodes are treated as characteristic points of data for modeling and analyzing. The model of data can be built by choice of probability distribution function and nodes combination. PFC modeling via nodes combination and parameter γ as probability distribution function enables value anticipation in risk analysis and decision making. Two-dimensional object is extrapolated and interpolated via nodes combination and different functions as discrete or continuous probability distribution functions: polynomial, sine, cosine, tangent, cotangent, logarithm, exponent, arc sin, arc cos, arc tan, arc cot or power function. Functions for γ calculations are chosen individually at each data modeling and it is treated as 2-dimensional probability distribution function: γ depends on initial requirements and features' specifications. PFC

Figure 25. Contour interpolation for: $2\,s = 0.6, h = x_1 x_2 + y_1 y_2, \gamma = \dfrac{2}{\pi} \cdot \arcsin\left(\alpha^s\right)$

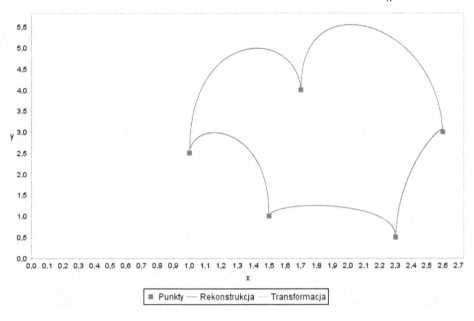

Figure 26. Shape reconstruction for: $s = 1, h = 0, \gamma = 1 - \dfrac{2}{\pi} \cdot \arccos\left(\alpha^s\right)$

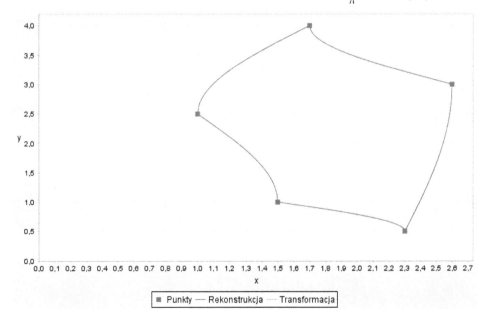

Figure 27. Contour modeling for: $s = 1, h = x_1 x_2 + y_1 y_2, \gamma = 1 - \dfrac{2}{\pi} \cdot \arccos\left(\alpha^s\right)$

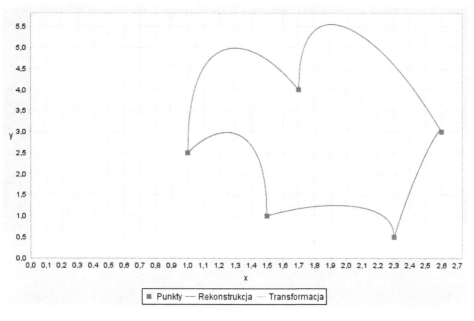

Figure 28. Object reconstruction for: $s = 1.3, h = 0, \gamma = 1 - \dfrac{2}{\pi} \cdot \arccos\left(\alpha^s\right)$

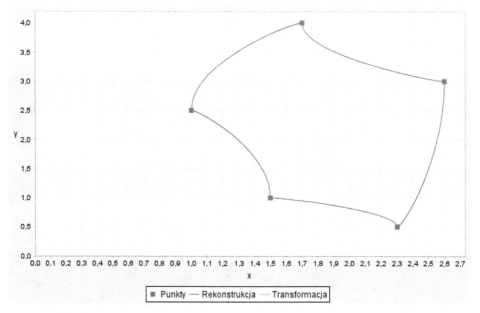

Figure 29. Shape interpolation for: $s = 1.3, h = x_1x_2 + y_1y_2, \gamma = 1 - \dfrac{2}{\pi} \cdot \arccos\left(\alpha^s\right)$

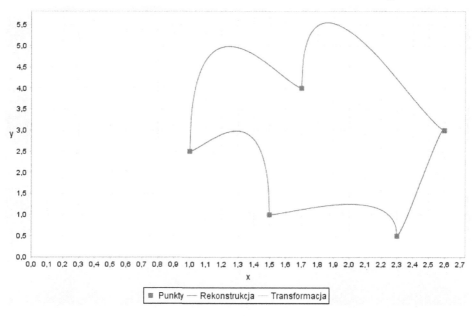

Figure 30. Contour reconstruction for s = 1.2, h = 0, $\gamma = \sin\left(\alpha^s * \dfrac{\pi}{2}\right)$

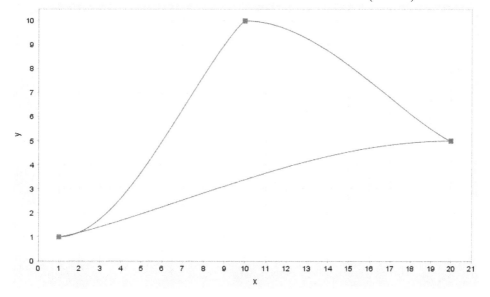

Figure 31. Shape interpolation for s = 1.2, h = 0, $\gamma = \log_2\left(\alpha^s + 1\right)$

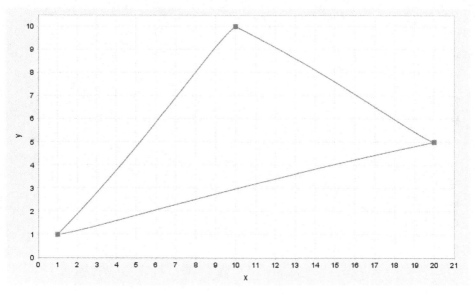

Figure 32. Object modeling for s = 1.2, h = 0, $\gamma = \dfrac{2}{\pi} * \arcsin\left(\alpha^s\right)$

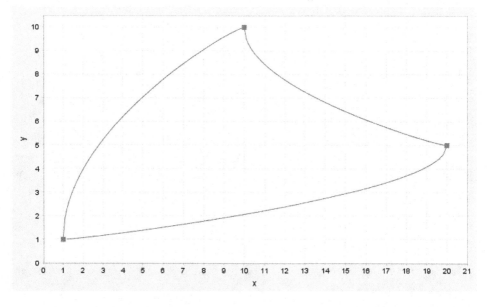

Figure 33. Shape reconstruction for s = 1.4, h = $y_1\left(\dfrac{x_2}{x_1}\right) + y_2\left(\dfrac{x_1}{x_2}\right)$, $\gamma = 1 - \cos\left(\alpha^s * \dfrac{\pi}{2}\right)$

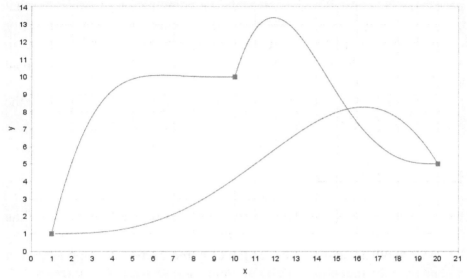

Figure 34. Contour interpolation for s = 1.4, h = $y_1\left(\dfrac{x_2}{x_1}\right) + y_2\left(\dfrac{x_1}{x_2}\right)$, $\gamma = ctg\left(\dfrac{\pi}{2} - \alpha^s * \dfrac{\pi}{4}\right)$

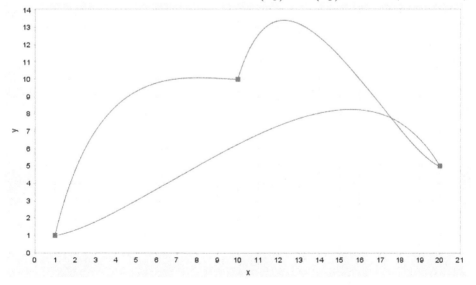

method leads to data interpolation as handwriting or signature identification and image retrieval via discrete set of feature vectors in 2-dimensional feature space. So PFC method makes possible the combination of two important problems: interpolation and modeling in a matter of image retrieval or writer identification. PFC interpolation develops a linear interpolation in multidimensional feature spaces into other functions as two-dimensional probability distribution functions.

These examples of shape modeling and contour reconstruction show the variety of PNC interpolations via chosen parameters and set of nodes.

RESULT ANALYSIS

PFC method is interpolating a curve between each pair of nodes using modeling function $\gamma = F(\alpha)$ and nodes combination h. The simplest way of comparing PFC with another method is to see the example. Here is the application of PFC method for function $f(x)=1/x$ and nine nodes: $y = 0.2, 0.4, 0.6, 0.8, 1, 1.2, 1.4, 1.6, 1.8$. PFC represents (Figure 42) much more precise interpolation than Lagrange or Newton polynomial interpolation (Figure 43).

Figure 35. Object modeling with $s=1.4$, $h = y_1\left(\dfrac{x_2}{x_1}\right) + y_2\left(\dfrac{x_1}{x_2}\right)$, $\gamma = 1 - \dfrac{2}{\pi} * \arccos\left(\alpha^s\right)$

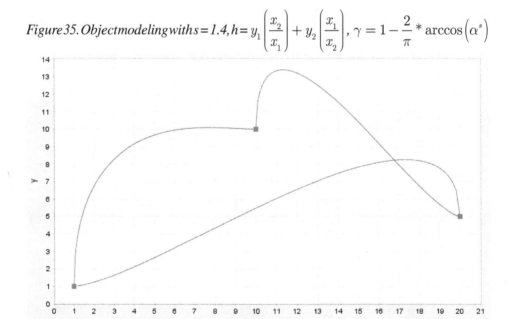

Figure 36. Shape interpolation with s = 1.1, $h = x_1x_2 + y_1y_2$, $\gamma = \sin\left(\alpha^s * \dfrac{\pi}{2}\right)$

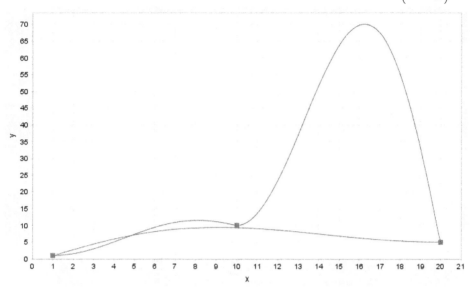

Figure 37. Object reconstruction with s = 1.1, $h = x_1x_2 + y_1y_2$, $\gamma = ctg\left(\dfrac{\pi}{2} - \alpha^s * \dfrac{\pi}{4}\right)$

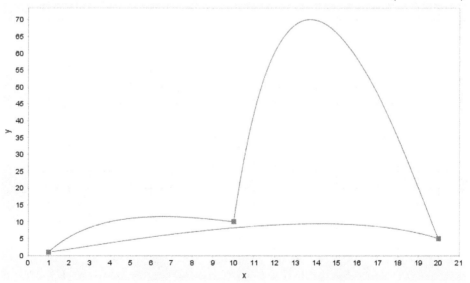

161

Figure 38. Contour modeling with s = 1.1, $h = x_1 x_2 + y_1 y_2$, $\gamma = \dfrac{4}{\pi} * \arctan\left(\alpha^s\right)$

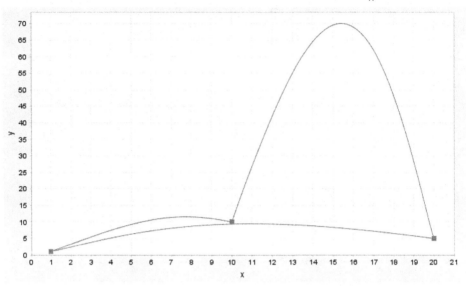

Figure 39. Shape modeling with s = 1.3, $h = x_1 x_2 + y_1 y_2$, $\gamma = 1 - \cos\left(\alpha^s * \dfrac{\pi}{2}\right)$

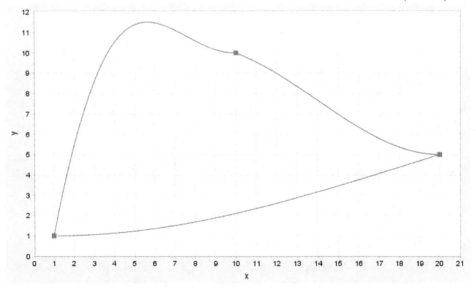

Figure 40. Object interpolation with s = 1.3, $h = \left(\dfrac{x_2}{x_1}\right) + \left(\dfrac{y_2}{y_1}\right)$, $\gamma = ctg\left(\dfrac{\pi}{2} - \alpha^s * \dfrac{\pi}{4}\right)$

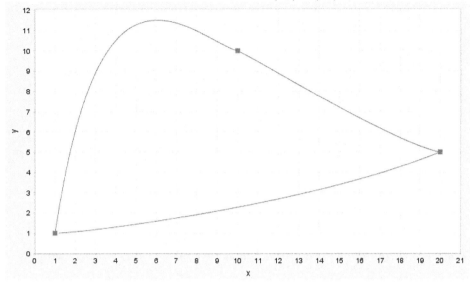

Figure 41. Contour reconstruction with s = 1.3, $h = \left(\dfrac{x_2}{x_1}\right) + \left(\dfrac{y_2}{y_1}\right)$, $\gamma = \dfrac{2}{\pi} * \arcsin\left(\alpha^s\right)$

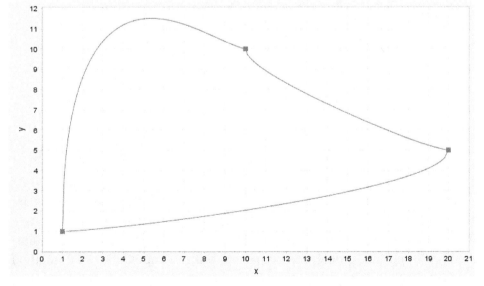

Figure 42. Points of function f(x) = 1/x using PFC method with 9 nodes – better than polynomial interpolation

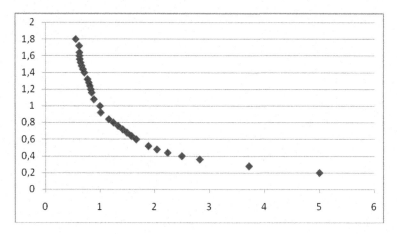

Figure 43. Interpolation polynomial of function f(x) = 1/x is completely wrong

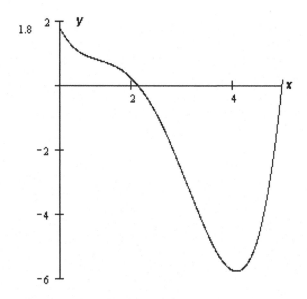

PFC interpolation is more accurate than polynomial interpolation by Newton or Lagrange. Very important matter is dealing with closed curves. PFC reconstruction of the contour or shape is done with the same formulas. Another important problem is connected with extrapolation. PFC method gives the tool of data anticipation or prediction.

Figure 44. Extrapolation of data right of the last node

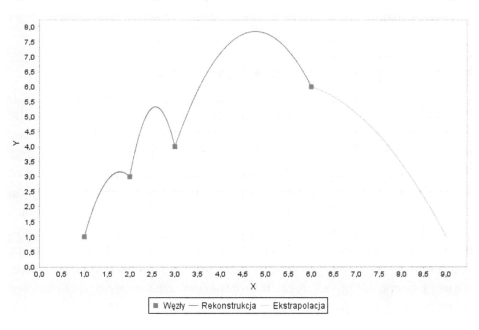

Figure 45. Prediction of values left of first node

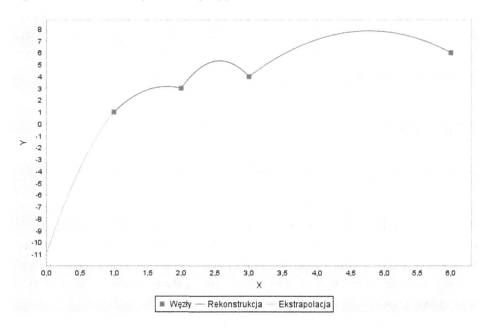

PFC is a novel approach to the matter of data modeling, reconstruction and extrapolation.

SOLUTIONS AND RECOMMENDATIONS

Proposed method, called Probabilistic Features Combination (PFC), is the method of 2D curve interpolation and extrapolation using the set of key points (knots or nodes). Nodes can be treated as characteristic points of data for modeling and analyzing. The model of data can be built by choice of probability distribution function and nodes combination. PFC modeling via nodes combination and parameter γ as probability distribution function enables value anticipation in risk analysis and decision making. Two-dimensional curve is extrapolated and interpolated via nodes combination and different functions as discrete or continuous probability distribution functions: polynomial, sine, cosine, tangent, cotangent, logarithm, exponent, arc sin, arc cos, arc tan, arc cot or power function.

FUTURE RESEARCH DIRECTIONS

Future trends will go to various directions: how to fix the best probability distribution function for the nodes, how to calculate the most appropriate nodes combination and what extrapolation is the most valuable in decision making and risk analysis.

CONCLUSION

The method of Probabilistic Nodes Combination (PNC) enables interpolation and modeling of two-dimensional curves using nodes combinations and different coefficients γ: polynomial, sinusoidal, cosinusoidal, tangent, cotangent, logarithmic, exponential, arc sin, arc cos, arc tan, arc cot or power function, also inverse functions. This probabilistic view is novel approach a problem of modeling and interpolation. Computer vision and pattern recognition are interested in appropriate methods of shape representation and curve modeling. PNC method represents the possibilities of shape reconstruction and curve interpolation via the choice of nodes combination and probability distribution function for interpolated points. It seems to be quite new look at the problem of contour representation and curve modeling in artificial intelligence and computer vision. Function for γ calculations is chosen individually at each curve modeling and it is treated as probability distribution function: γ depends on initial requirements and curve specifications. PNC method leads to curve interpolation as handwriting modeling via discrete set of fixed knots. So PNC makes possible the combination of two important problems: interpolation and modeling. Main features of PNC method are:

1. The smaller distance between knots the better;
2. Calculations for coordinates close to zero and near by extremum require more attention because of importance of these points;
3. PNC interpolation develops a linear interpolation into other functions as probability distribution functions;
4. PNC is a generalization of MHR method via different nodes combinations;
5. Interpolation of L points is connected with the computational cost of rank $O(L)$ as in MHR method;
6. Nodes combination and coefficient γ are crucial in the process of curve probabilistic parameterization and interpolation: they are computed individually for a single curve.

What is the most important feature of MHR and PNC methods? Interpolation methods and curve fitting represent so huge problem that each individual interpolation is exceptional and requires specific solutions. PNC method is such a novel tool with its all pros and cons. The user has to decide which interpolation method is the best in a single situation. The choice is yours if you have any choice. Presented method is such a new possibility for curve fitting and interpolation when specific data (for example handwritten symbol or character) starts up with no rules for polynomial interpolation. This book consists of two generalizations: generalization of previous MHR method with various nodes combinations and generalization of linear interpolation with different (no basic) probability distribution functions and nodes combinations. The method of Probabilistic Nodes Combination (PNC) enables interpolation and modeling of two-dimensional curves using nodes combinations and different coefficients γ: polynomial, sinusoidal, cosinusoidal, tangent, cotangent, logarithmic, exponential, arc sin, arc cos, arc tan, arc cot or power function, also inverse functions. This probabilistic view is novel approach a problem of modeling and interpolation. Computer vision and pattern recognition are interested in appropriate methods of shape representation and curve modeling. PNC method represents the possibilities of shape reconstruction and curve interpolation via the choice of nodes combination and probability distribution function for interpolated points. It seems to be quite new look at the problem of contour representation and curve modeling in artificial intelligence and computer vision. Function for γ calculations is chosen individually at each curve modeling and it is treated as probability distribution function: γ depends on initial requirements and curve specifications. PNC method leads to curve interpolation as handwriting modeling via discrete set of fixed knots. So PNC makes possible the combination of two important problems: interpolation and modeling. The method of Probabilistic Features Combination (PFC) enables interpolation and modeling of high-dimensional *N* data using features' combinations and different coefficients γ: polynomial, sinusoidal, cosinusoidal, tangent, cotangent, logarithmic, exponential, arc sin, arc cos, arc tan, arc cot or power function. Functions for γ calculations are chosen individually at each data modeling and it is treated as *N*-dimensional probability distribution function: γ depends on initial requirements and features' specifications. PFC method leads to data interpolation as handwriting or signature identification and image retrieval via discrete set of feature vectors in N-dimensional feature space. So PFC method makes possible the combination of two important problems: interpolation and modeling in a matter of image retrieval or writer identification. Main features of PFC method are: PFC interpolation develops a linear interpolation in multidimensional feature spaces into other functions as *N*-dimensional probability distribution functions; PFC is a generalization of MHR method and PNC method via different nodes combinations; interpolation of *L* points is connected with the computational cost of rank $O(L)$ as in MHR and PNC method; nodes combination and coefficients γ are crucial in the process of data probabilistic parameterization and interpolation: they are computed individually for a single feature. Future works are going to applications of PFC method in signature and handwriting biometric recognition: choice and features of nodes combinations *h* and coefficients γ.

Proposed method, called Probabilistic Features Combination (PFC), is the method of *N*-dimensional data interpolation and extrapolation using the set of key points (knots or nodes). Nodes can be treated as characteristic points of data for modeling and analyzing. The model of data can be built by choice of probability distribution function and nodes combination. PFC modeling via nodes combination and parameter γ as probability distribution function enables value anticipation in risk analysis and decision making. *N*-dimensional object is extrapolated and interpolated via nodes combination and different functions as discrete or continuous probability distribution functions: polynomial, sine, cosine, tangent, cotangent, logarithm, exponent, arc sin, arc cos, arc tan, arc cot or power function. The method of Probabilistic Features Combination (PFC) enables interpolation and modeling of high-dimensional data using features' combinations and different coefficients γ as modeling function. Functions for γ calculations are chosen individually at each data modeling and it is treated as N-dimensional probability distribution function: γ depends on initial requirements and features' specifications. PFC method leads to data interpolation as handwriting or signature identification and image retrieval via discrete set of feature vectors in N-dimensional feature space. So PFC method makes possible the combination of two important problems: interpolation and modeling in a matter of image retrieval or writer identification. PFC interpolation develops a linear interpolation in multidimensional feature spaces into other functions as N-dimensional probability distribution functions. Future works are going to applications of PFC method in biometric recognition, computer vision and artificial intelligence. Nodes are treated as characteristic points of data for modeling and analyzing. The model of data can be built by choice of probability distribution function and nodes combination. PFC modeling via nodes combination and parameter γ as probability distribution function enables value anticipation in risk analysis and decision making. Two-dimensional object is extrapolated and interpolated via nodes combination and different functions as discrete or continuous probability distribution functions: polynomial, sine, cosine, tangent, cotangent, logarithm, exponent, arc sin, arc cos, arc tan, arc cot or power function. Functions for γ calculations are chosen individually at each data modeling and it is treated as 2-dimensional probability distribution function: γ depends on initial requirements and features' specifications. PFC method leads to data interpolation as handwriting or signature identification and image retrieval via discrete set of feature vectors in 2-dimensional feature space. So PFC method makes possible the combination of two important problems: interpolation and modeling in a matter of image retrieval or writer identification. PFC interpolation develops a linear interpolation in multidimensional feature spaces into other functions as two-dimensional probability distribution functions.

Future works are going to: application of PNC method in signature and handwriting recognition, choice and features of nodes combinations and coefficient γ, implementation of PNC in computer vision and artificial intelligence: shape geometry, contour modelling, object recognition and curve parameterization.

REFERENCES

Ballard, D. H. (1982). *Computer Vision*. New York: Prentice Hall.

Chapra, S. C. (2012). *Applied Numerical Methods*. McGraw-Hill.

Choraś, R. S. (2005). *Computer Vision*. Warsaw, Poland: Exit.

Cocozza-Thivent, C., Eymard, R., Mercier, S., & Roussignol, M. (2006). Characterization of the Marginal Distributions of Markov Processes Used in Dynamic Reliability. *Journal of Applied Mathematics and Stochastic Analysis*, 1–18.

Collins, G. W. II. (2003). *Fundamental Numerical Methods and Data Analysis*. Case Western Reserve University.

Dahlquist, G., & Bjoerck, A. (1974). *Numerical Methods*. New York: Prentice Hall.

Dejdumrong, N. (2007). A Shape Preserving Verification Techniques for Parametric Curves. *Computer Graphics, Imaging and Visualization*, 163–168.

Dyn, N., Levin, D., & Gregory, J. A. (1987). A 4-Point Interpolatory Subdivision Scheme for Curve Design. *Computer Aided Geometric Design*, *4*(4), 257–268. doi:10.1016/0167-8396(87)90001-X

Jakóbczak, D. (2007). 2D and 3D Image Modeling Using Hurwitz-Radon Matrices. *Polish Journal of Environmental Studies*, *4A*(16), 104–107.

Jakóbczak, D. (2009). Curve Interpolation Using Hurwitz-Radon Matrices. *Polish Journal of Environmental Studies*, *3B*(18), 126–130.

Jakóbczak, D. (2010a). Shape Representation and Shape Coefficients via Method of Hurwitz-Radon Matrices. *Lecture Notes in Computer Science*, *6374*, 411–419. doi:10.1007/978-3-642-15910-7_47

Jakóbczak, D. (2010b). Object Modeling Using Method of Hurwitz-Radon Matrices of Rank k. In W. Wolski & M. Borawski (Eds.), *Computer Graphics: Selected Issues* (pp. 79–90). Szczecin, Poland: University of Szczecin Press.

Jakóbczak, D. (2011a). Curve Parameterization and Curvature via Method of Hurwitz-Radon Matrices. *Image Processing & Communications- International Journal (Toronto, Ont.)*, *1-2*(16), 49–56.

Jakóbczak, D. (2011b). Data Extrapolation and Decision Making via Method of Hurwitz-Radon Matrices. *Lecture Notes in Computer Science, 6922,* 173–182. doi:10.1007/978-3-642-23935-9_17

Jakóbczak, D. (2011c). Curve Extrapolation and Data Analysis using the Method of Hurwitz-Radon Matrices. *Folia Oeconomica Stetinensia, 9*(17), 121-138.

Jakóbczak, D. (2013). Probabilistic Modeling of Signature using the Method of Hurwitz-Radon Matrices. *Global Perspectives on Artificial Intelligence, 1*(1), 1–7.

Kozera, R. (2004). *Curve Modeling via Interpolation Based on Multidimensional Reduced Data.* Gliwice, Poland: Silesian University of Technology Press.

Liu, T., & Geiger, D. (1999). Approximate tree matching and shape similarity. *Int. Conf. Computer Vision,* Corfu, Greece.

Lorton, A., Fouladirad, M., & Grall, A. (2013). A Methodology for Probabilistic Model-based Prognosis. *European Journal of Operational Research, 225*(3), 443–454. doi:10.1016/j.ejor.2012.10.025

Pergler, M., & Freeman, A. (2008). Probabilistic Modeling as an Exploratory Decision-Making Tool. *McKinsey Working Papers on Risk, 6,* 1-18.

Ralston, A., & Rabinowitz, P. (2001). *A First Course in Numerical Analysis* (2nd ed.). New York: Dover Publications.

Rogers, D. F. (2001). *An Introduction to NURBS with Historical Perspective.* Morgan Kaufmann Publishers.

Saber, E., Xu, Y., & Murat Tekalp, A. (2005). Partial shape recognition by sub-matrix matching for partial matching guided image labeling. *Pattern Recognition, 38*(10), 1560–1573. doi:10.1016/j.patcog.2005.03.027

Schumaker, L. L. (2007). *Spline Functions: Basic Theory.* Cambridge Mathematical Library. doi:10.1017/CBO9780511618994

Sebastian, T. B., Klein, P. N., & Kimia, B. B. (2003). On aligning curves. *IEEE Transactions on Pattern Analysis and Machine Intelligence, 25*(1), 116–124. doi:10.1109/TPAMI.2003.1159951

Tadeusiewicz, R., & Flasiński, M. (1991). *Image Recognition.* Warsaw, Poland: PWN.

Zhang, D., & Lu, G. (2004). Review of Shape Representation and Description Techniques. *Pattern Recognition, 1*(37), 1–19. doi:10.1016/j.patcog.2003.07.008

ADDITIONAL READING

Basu, S., & Bresler, Y. (2000). O(N^2log$_2$N) filtered backprojection reconstruction algorithm for tomography. *IEEE Transactions on Image Processing, 9*(10), 1760–1773. doi:10.1109/83.869187 PMID:18262914

Brankov, J. G., Yang, Y., & Wernick, M. N. (2004). Tomographic image reconstruction based on a Content – Adaptive Mesh Model. *IEEE Transactions on Medical Imaging, 2*(23), 202–212. doi:10.1109/TMI.2003.822822 PMID:14964565

Brasse, D., & Defrise, M. (2004). Fast fully 3-D image reconstruction in PET using planograms. *IEEE Transactions on Medical Imaging, 4*(23), 413–425. doi:10.1109/TMI.2004.824231 PMID:15084067

Bulacu, M., & Schomaker, L. (2007). Text-independent writer identification and verification using textural and allographic features. *IEEE Transactions on Pattern Analysis and Machine Intelligence, 29*(4), 701–717. doi:10.1109/TPAMI.2007.1009 PMID:17299226

Bulacu, M., Schomaker, L., & Brink, A. (2007). *Text-independent writer identification and verification on off-line Arabic handwriting.* In: *International Conference on Document Analysis and Recognition.* 769–773.

Cetin, M., Karl, W. C., & Willsky, A. S. (2002, September). *Edge – preserving image reconstruction for coherent imaging application.* Paper presented at the IEEE International Conference on Image Processsing, Rochester, NY, USA. doi:10.1109/ICIP.2002.1039992

Chen, J., Cheng, W., & Lopresti, D. (2011). Using perturbed handwriting to support writer identification in the presence of severe data constraints. In: Document Recognition and Retrieval. 1–10. doi:10.1117/12.876497

Chen, J., Lopresti, D., & Kavallieratou, E. (2010). *The impact of ruling lines on writer identification.* In: *International Conference on Frontiers in Handwriting Recognition.* 439–444. doi:10.1109/ICFHR.2010.75

Chlebus, E., & Cholewa, M. (1999). Rapid prototyping – rapid tooling. *CADCAM Forum, 11*, 23-28.

Cormen, T. H., Leiserson, C. E., & Rivest, R. L. (1996). *Introduction to algorithms*. Massachusetts, USA: the Massachusetts Institute of Technology Press and McGraw-Hill.

Defrise, M. (2001). A short readers guide to 3D tomographic reconstruction. *Computerized Medical Imaging and Graphics, 25*(2), 113–116. doi:10.1016/S0895-6111(00)00061-6 PMID:11137787

Djeddi, C., & Souici-Meslati, L. (2010). *A texture based approach for Arabic writer identification and verification*. In: *International Conference on Machine and Web Intelligence*. 115–120.

Djeddi, C., & Souici-Meslati, L. (2011). *Artificial immune recognition system for Arabic writer identification*. In: *International Symposium on Innovation in Information and Communication Technology*. 159–165. doi:10.1109/ISIICT.2011.6149612

Dryja, M., Jankowska, J., & Jankowski, M. (1982). *Survey of numerical methods and algorithms. Part II*. Warsaw, Poland: WNT.

Eldar, Y. C. (2001). *Quantum Signal Processing*. (Unpublished doctoral dissertation). Massachusetts Institute of Technology, USA.

Eldar, Y. C., & Oppenheim, A. V. (2002). Quantum Signal Processing. *IEEE Signal Processing Magazine, 6*(19), 12–32. doi:10.1109/MSP.2002.1043298

Fortuna, Z., Macukow, B., & Wąsowski, J. (1982). *Numerical methods*. Warsaw, Poland: WNT.

Galloway, M. M. (1975). Texture analysis using gray level run lengths. *Computer Graphics and Image Processing, 4*(2), 172–179. doi:10.1016/S0146-664X(75)80008-6

Garain, U., & Paquet, T. (2009). *Off-line multi-script writer identification using AR coefficients*. In: *International Conference on Document Analysis and Recognition*. 991–995. doi:10.1109/ICDAR.2009.222

Ghiasi, G., & Safabakhsh, R. (2013). Offline text-independent writer identification using codebook and efficient code extraction methods. *Image and Vision Computing, 31*(5), 379–391. doi:10.1016/j.imavis.2013.03.002

Jakóbczak, D. (2005). Hurwitz-Radon matrices and their children. *Computer Science*, *5*(8), 29–38.

Jakóbczak, D. J. (2014). *2D Curve Modeling via the Method of Probabilistic Nodes Combination-Shape Representation, Object Modeling and Curve Interpolation-Extrapolation with the Applications*. Saarbrucken: LAP Lambert Academic Publishing.

Jankowska, J., & Jankowski, M. (1981). *Survey of numerical methods and algorithms. Part I*. Warsaw, Poland: WNT.

Kontaxakis, G., & Strauss, L. G. (1998). Maximum likelihood algorithms for image reconstruction in Positron Emission Tomography. *Radionuclides for Oncology – Current Status and Future Aspects, 1998,* 73-106.

Kowalczuk, Z., & Wiszniewski, B. (Eds.). (2007). *Intelligent data mining in diagnostic purposes: Automatics and informatics*. Gdansk, Poland: PWNT.

Kundur, D., & Hatzinakos, D. (1998). A novel blind deconvolution scheme for image restoration using recursive filtering. *IEEE Transactions on Signal Processing*, *2*(46), 375–390. doi:10.1109/78.655423

Laine, A., & Zong, X. (1996). *Border identification of echocardiograms via multiscale edge detection and shape modeling*. Paper presented at the IEEE International Conference on Image Processsing, Lausanne, Switzerland. doi:10.1109/ICIP.1996.560486

Lang, S. (1970). *Algebra*. Reading, Massachusetts, USA: Addison-Wesley Publishing Company.

Le Buhan Jordan, C., Bossen, F., & Ebrahimi, T. (1997). *Scalable shape representation for content based visual data compression*. Paper presented at the International Conference on Image Processing, Santa Barbara, CA, USA. doi:10.1109/ICIP.1997.647962

Marker, J., Braude, I., Museth, K., & Breen, D. (2006). Contour-based surface reconstruction using implicit curve fitting, and distance field filtering and interpolation. *Volume Graphics*, *2006*, 1–9.

Marti, U.-V., & Bunke, H. (2002). The IAM-database: An English sentence database for offline handwriting recognition. *Int. J. Doc. Anal. Recognit.*, *5*(1), 39–46. doi:10.1007/s100320200071

Meyer, Y. (1993). *Wavelets: algorithms & applications*. Philadelphia, USA: Society for Industrial and Applied Mathematics.

Nosary, A., Heutte, L., & Paquet, T. (2004). Unsupervised writer adaption applied to handwritten text recognition. *Pattern Recognition Letters, 37*(2), 385–388. doi:10.1016/S0031-3203(03)00185-7

Ozaki, M., Adachi, Y., & Ishii, N. (2006). *Examination of effects of character size on accuracy of writer recognition by new local arc method.* In: International Conference on Knowledge- Based Intelligent Information and Engineering Systems. 1170–1175. doi:10.1007/11893004_148

Poggio, T., & Smale, S. (2003). The mathematics of learning: Dealing with data. *Notices of the American Mathematical Society, 5*(50), 537–544.

Przelaskowski, A. (2005). *Data compression*. Warsaw, Poland: BTC.

Rutkowski, L., Siekmann, J., Tadeusiewicz, R., & Zadeh, A. (Eds.). (2004). *Lecture notes on artificial intelligence: Artificial intelligence and soft computing*. Berlin-Heidelberg, Germany: Springer-Verlag.

Schlapbach, A., & Bunke, H. (2004). *Using HMM based recognizers for writer identification and verification. 9th Int. Workshop on Frontiers in Handwriting Recognition.* 167–172. doi:10.1109/IWFHR.2004.107

Schlapbach, A., & Bunke, H. (2006). *Off-line writer identification using Gaussian mixture models.* In: *International Conference on Pattern Recognition.* 992–995.

Schlapbach, A., & Bunke, H. (2007). A writer identification and verification system using HMM based recognizers. *Pattern Analysis & Applications, 10*(1), 33–43. doi:10.1007/s10044-006-0047-5

Schomaker, L., Franke, K., & Bulacu, M. (2007). Using codebooks of fragmented connected- component contours in forensic and historic writer identification. *Pattern Recognition Letters, 28*(6), 719–727. doi:10.1016/j.patrec.2006.08.005

Shahabinejad, F., & Rahmati, M. (2007). A new method for writer identification and verification based on Farsi/Arabic handwritten texts, *Ninth International Conference on Document Analysis and Recognition (ICDAR 2007).* 829–833.

Siddiqi, I., Cloppet, F., & Vincent, N. (2009). Contour based features for the classification of ancient manuscripts. In: Conference of the International Graphonomics Society. 226–229.

Siddiqi, I., & Vincent, N. (2010). Text independent writer recognition using redundant writing patterns with contour-based orientation and curvature features. *Pattern Recognition Letters*, *43*(11), 3853–3865. doi:10.1016/j. patcog.2010.05.019

Vakhania, N. (1993). Orthogonal random vectors and the Hurwitz – Radon-Eckmann theorem. *Proc. of the Georgian Academy of Sciences-Mathematics, 1(1)*, 109-125.

Van, E. M., Vuurpijl, L., Franke, K., & Schomaker, L. (2005). The WANDA measurement tool for forensic document examination. *J. Forensic Doc. Exam.*, *16*, 103–118.

Willis, M. (2000). *Algebraic reconstruction algorithms for remote sensing image enhancement*. Unpublished doctoral dissertation, Department of Electrical and Computer Engineering, Brigham Young University.

Xu, Fang, & Mueller, K. (2005). Accelerating popular tomographic reconstruction algorithms on commodity PC graphics hardware. *IEEE Transactions on Nuclear Science*, *3*(52), 654–661.

Zaletelj, J., & Tasic, J. F. (2003). *Optimization and tracking of polygon vertices for shape coding*. Berlin-Heidelberg, Germany: Springer-Verlag. doi:10.1007/978-3-540-45179-2_52

Zhang, J. K., Davidson, T., & Wong, K. M. (2004). Efficient design of orthonormal wavelet bases for signal representation. *IEEE Transactions on Signal Processing*, *7*(52), 1983–1996. doi:10.1109/TSP.2004.828923

KEY TERMS AND DEFINITIONS

Contour: Closed curve.

Curve Interpolation: Computing new and unknown points of a curve and creating a graph of a curve using existing data points – interpolation nodes.

Data Extrapolation: Calculation of unknown values for the points situated outside the ranges of nodes.

Hurwitz – Radon Matrices: A family of skew – symmetric and orthogonal matrices with columns and rows that create, together with identical matrix, the base in vector spaces of dimensions $N = 2$, 4 or 8.

MHR Method: The method of curve interpolation and extrapolation using linear (convex) combinations of OHR operators.

OHR Operator: Matrix operator of Hurwitz – Radon built from coordinates of interpolation nodes.

Shape Representation: Data that are used in shape reconstruction.

Value Anticipation: Foreseeing next value when last value is known.

Chapter 5
PNC in 3D Surface Modeling

ABSTRACT

The model of data can be built by choice of probability distribution function and nodes combination. PFC modeling via nodes combination and parameter γ as probability distribution function enables value anticipation in risk analysis and decision making. Two-dimensional curve is extrapolated and interpolated via nodes combination and different functions as discrete or continuous probability distribution functions: polynomial, sine, cosine, tangent, cotangent, logarithm, exponent, arc sin, arc cos, arc tan, arc cot or power function. The method of Probabilistic Features Combination (PFC) enables interpolation and modeling of high-dimensional data using features' combinations and different coefficients γ as modeling function. Functions for γ calculations are chosen individually at each data modeling and it is treated as N-dimensional probability distribution function: γ depends on initial requirements and features' specifications. PFC method leads to data interpolation as handwriting or signature identification and image retrieval via discrete set of feature vectors in N-dimensional feature space.

INTRODUCTION

Three-dimensional data modeling appears in science and industry. Image retrieval, data reconstruction, object identification or pattern recognition are still the open questions. The chapter is dealing with these questions via modeling of high-dimensional data for applications of image segmentation in image retrieval and recognition tasks. This chapter is concerned with two parts: image retrieval and recognition tasks. Image retrieval is based on

DOI: 10.4018/978-1-5225-2531-8.ch005

probabilistic modeling of unknown features via combination of 3-dimensional probability distribution function for each feature treated as random variable. The sketch of proposed Probabilistic Features Combination (PFC) method consists of three steps: first handwritten letter or symbol must be modeled by a vector of features (*N*-dimensional data, for example $N = 3$), then compared with unknown letter and finally there is a decision of identification. Author recognition of handwriting and signature is based on the choice of feature vectors and modeling functions. So high-dimensional data interpolation in handwriting identification (Marti & Bunke, 2002) is not only a pure mathematical problem but important task in pattern recognition and artificial intelligence such as: biometric recognition (Nosary, Heutte & Paquet, 2004), personalized handwriting recognition (Djeddi & Souici-Meslati, 2010 & 2011), automatic forensic document examination (Van, Vuurpijl, Franke & Schomaker, 2005) (Schomaker, Franke & Bulacu, 2007), classification of ancient manuscripts (Siddiqi, Cloppet & Vincent, 2009). Also writer recognition (Garain & Paquet, 2009) in monolingual handwritten texts (Ozaki, Adachi & Ishii, 2006) is an extensive area of study (Chen, Lopresti & Kavallieratou, 2010) and the methods independent from the language (Chen, Cheng & Lopresti, 2011) are well-seen (Bulacu, Schomaker & Brink, 2007). No method is dealing with writer identification via 3-dimensional data modeling or interpolation and multidimensional points comparing as it is presented in this chapter. The chapter wants to approach a problem of curve interpolation and shape modeling by characteristic points in handwriting identification. The method of Probabilistic Features Combination (PFC) enables interpolation and modeling of high-dimensional data using features' combinations and different coefficients γ as modeling function. Functions for γ calculations are chosen individually at each data modeling and it is treated as *3*-dimensional probability distribution function: γ depends on initial requirements and features' specifications. PFC method leads to data interpolation as handwriting or signature identification and image retrieval via discrete set of feature vectors in N-dimensional feature space. So PFC method makes possible the combination of two important problems: interpolation and modeling in a matter of image retrieval or writer identification. PFC interpolation develops a linear interpolation in multidimensional feature spaces into other functions as *N*-dimensional probability distribution functions. Future works are going to applications of PFC method in biometric recognition, computer vision and artificial intelligence.

BACKGROUND

Current methods apply mainly polynomial functions, for example Bernstein polynomials in Bezier curves, splines (Schumaker, 2007) and NURBS. But Bezier curves don't represent the interpolation method and cannot be used for example in signature and handwriting modeling with characteristic points (nodes). Numerical methods (Collins, 2003) for data interpolation are based on polynomial or trigonometric functions (Chapra, 2012), for example Lagrange, Newton, Aitken and Hermite methods (Ralston & Rabinowitz, 2001). These methods have some weak sides and are not sufficient for curve interpolation in the situations when the curve cannot be build by polynomials or trigonometric functions (Zhang & Lu, 2004).

Writer recognition methods in the recent years are going to various directions (Galloway, 1975): writer recognition using multi-script handwritten texts, introduction of new features (Ghiasi & Safabakhsh, 2013), combining different types of features (Siddiqi & Vincent, 2010), studying the sensitivity of character size on writer identification, investigating writer identification in multi-script environments (Shahabinejad & Rahmati, 2007), impact of ruling lines on writer identification, model perturbed handwriting, methods based on run-length features, the edge-direction and edge-hinge features, a combination of codebook and visual features extracted from chain code and polygonized representation of contours, the autoregressive coefficients, codebook and efficient code extraction methods, texture analysis with Gabor filters and extracting features (Schlapbach & Bunke, 2007), using Hidden Markov Model (Schlapbach & Bunke, 2004) or Gaussian Mixture Model (Schlapbach & Bunke, 2006). So hybrid soft computing is essential: no method is dealing with writer identification via N-dimensional data modeling or interpolation and multidimensional points comparing as it is presented in this chapter. The chapter wants to approach a problem of curve interpolation and shape modeling by characteristic points in handwriting identification (Bulacu & Schomaker, 2007). Proposed method relies on nodes combination and functional modeling of curve points situated between the basic set of key points. The functions that are used in calculations represent whole family of elementary functions with inverse functions: polynomials, trigonometric, cyclometric, logarithmic, exponential and power function. These functions are treated as probability distribution functions in the range [0;1]. Nodes are treated as characteristic points of data for modeling and analyzing. The model of data can be built by choice of probability distribution function and nodes combination. PFC modeling via nodes combination and parameter γ as probability distribution function enables value anticipation in risk analysis and decision making. Two-dimensional object is extrapolated and interpolated via nodes combination and different functions as discrete or continuous probability distribution functions: polynomial, sine, cosine, tangent, cotangent, logarithm, exponent, arc sin, arc cos, arc tan, arc cot or power function. Functions for γ calculations are chosen individually at each data modeling and it is treated as 3-dimensional probability distribution function: γ depends on initial requirements and features' specifications. PFC method leads to data interpolation as handwriting or signature identification and image retrieval via discrete set of feature vectors in 3-dimensional feature space. So PFC method makes possible the combination of two important problems: interpolation and modeling in a matter of image retrieval or writer identification. PFC interpolation develops a linear interpolation in multidimensional feature spaces into other functions as two-dimensional probability distribution functions. Future works are going to applications of PFC method in biometric recognition, computer vision and artificial intelligence.

This chapter presents novel Probabilistic Features Combination (PFC) method of high-dimensional interpolation in hybrid soft computing and takes up PFC method of multidimensional data modeling. The method of PFC requires information about data (image, object, curve) as the set of N-dimensional feature vectors (for example $N = 3$). Proposed PFC method is applied in image retrieval and recognition tasks via different coefficients for each feature as random variable: polynomial, sinusoidal, cosinusoidal, tangent, cotangent, logarithmic, exponential, arc sin, arc cos, arc tan, arc cot or power. Modeling functions for PFC calculations are chosen individually for every task and they represent probability distribution functions of random variable $\alpha_i \in [0;1]$ for every feature $i = 1,2$. So this chapter wants to answer the question: how to retrieve the image using 3-dimensional feature vectors and to recognize a handwritten letter or symbol by a set of 3-dimensional nodes?

THREE-DIMENSIONAL MODELING OF DATA

Issues

The method of PFC is computing (interpolating) unknown (unclear, noised or destroyed) values of features between two successive nodes (3-dimensional vectors of features) using hybridization of probabilistic methods and numerical methods. Calculated values (unknown or noised features such as coordinates, colors, textures or any coefficients of pixels, voxels and doxels or image parameters) are interpolated and parameterized for real number α_i $\in [0;1]$ ($i = 1,2$) between two successive values of feature. PFC method uses the combinations of nodes (N-dimensional feature vectors in the case of $N = 3$): $p_1=(x_1,y_1,z_1)$, $p_2=(x_2,y_2,z_2)$,..., $p_n=(x_n,y_n,z_n)$ as $h(p_1,p_2,...,p_m)$ and $m = 1,2,...n$ to interpolate unknown value of feature (for example y) for the rest of coordinates:

$$c_1 = \alpha_1 \cdot x_k + (1-\alpha_1) \cdot x_{k+1},\ c_2 = \alpha_2 \cdot z_k + (1-\alpha_2) \cdot z_{k+1},\ k = 1,2,...n-1,$$

$$c = (c_1,c_2),\ \alpha = (\alpha_1,\alpha_2),\ \gamma_i = F_i(\alpha_i) \in [0;1],\ i = 1,2$$

$$y(c) = \gamma \cdot y_k + (1 - \gamma)y_{k+1} + \gamma(1 - \gamma) \cdot h(p_1, p_2, ..., p_m),\ \ \ \ \ \ \ \ (1)$$

$$\alpha_i \in [0;1],\ \gamma = F(\alpha) = F(\alpha_1,\alpha_2) \in [0;1].$$

The basic structure of eq. (1) is built on modeling function $\gamma = F(\alpha)$ which is used for points' interpolation between the nodes. Additionally for better reconstruction and modeling there is a factor with function $\gamma = F(\alpha)$ and nodes combination h.

Then two features c_1,c_2 are parameterized by α_1,α_2 between two nodes and the last feature (for example y) is interpolated via formula (1). Of course there can be calculated $x(c)$ or $z(c)$ using (1). Two examples of h (when $N = 2$) computed for MHR method (Jakóbczak, 2014) with good features because of orthogonal rows and columns at Hurwitz-Radon family of matrices that origins from some calculations with orthogonal matrices:

$$h(p_1, p_2) = \frac{y_1}{x_1} x_2 + \frac{y_2}{x_2} x_1 \ \ \ \ \ \ \ \ (2)$$

or

$$h(p_1, p_2, p_3, p_4) = \frac{1}{x_1^2 + x_3^2}(x_1 x_2 y_1 + x_2 x_3 y_3 + x_3 x_4 y_1 - x_1 x_4 y_3)$$
$$+ \frac{1}{x_2^2 + x_4^2}(x_1 x_2 y_2 + x_1 x_4 y_4 + x_3 x_4 y_2 - x_2 x_3 y_4) .$$

The simplest nodes combination is

$$h(p_1, p_2, ..., p_m) = 0 \tag{3}$$

and then there is a formula of interpolation:

$$y(c) = \gamma \cdot y_i + (1 - \gamma)y_{i+1}.$$

Formula (1) gives the infinite number of calculations for unknown feature (determined by choice of F and h) as there is the infinite number of objects to recognize or the infinite number of images to retrieve. Nodes combination is the individual feature of each modeled data. Coefficient $\gamma = F(\alpha)$ and nodes combination h are key factors in PFC data interpolation and object modeling.

Three-Dimensional Probability Distribution Functions in PFC Modeling

Unknown values of features, settled between the nodes, are computed using PFC method as in (1). The simplest way of PFC calculation means $h = 0$ and $\gamma_i = \alpha_i$ (uniform probability distribution for each random variable α_i). Then PFC represents a linear interpolation.

MHR method (Jakóbczak, 2014) is the example of PFC modeling for feature vector of dimension $N=2$. Each interpolation requires specific distributions of random variables α_i and γ in (1) depends on parameters $\alpha_i \in [0;1]$:

$$\gamma = F(\alpha), \ F:[0;1]^2 \rightarrow [0;1], \ F(0,0) = 0, \ F(1,1) = 1$$

and F is strictly monotonic for each random variable α_i separately. Coefficient γ_i are calculated using appropriate function and choice of function is connected with initial requirements and data specifications. Different values of coefficients γ_i are connected with applied functions $F_i(\alpha_i)$. These functions $\gamma_i = F_i(\alpha_i)$ represent the examples of probability distribution functions for random variable $\alpha_i \in [0;1]$ and real number $s>0$, $i = 1,2$:

$$\gamma_i = \alpha_i^s,$$

$$\gamma_i = sin(\alpha_i^s \cdot \pi/2),$$

$$\gamma_i = sin^s(\alpha_i \cdot \pi/2),$$

$$\gamma_i = 1 - \cos(\alpha_i^s \cdot \pi/2),$$

$$\gamma_i = 1 - \cos^s(\alpha_i \cdot \pi/2),$$

$$\gamma_i = \tan(\alpha_i^s \cdot \pi/4),$$

$$\gamma_i = \tan^s(\alpha_i \cdot \pi/4),$$

$$\gamma_i = \log_2(\alpha_i^s + 1),$$

$$\gamma_i = \log_2^s(\alpha_i + 1),$$

$$\gamma_i = (2^\alpha - 1)^s,$$

$$\gamma_i = 2/\pi \cdot \arcsin(\alpha_i^s),$$

$$\gamma_i = (2/\pi \cdot \arcsin\alpha_i)^s,$$

$$\gamma_i = 1 - 2/\pi \cdot \arccos(\alpha_i^s),$$

$$\gamma_i = 1 - (2/\pi \cdot \arccos\alpha_i)^s,$$

$$\gamma_i = 4/\pi \cdot \arctan(\alpha_i^s),$$

$$\gamma_i = (4/\pi \cdot \arctan\alpha_i)^s,$$

$$\gamma_i = ctg(\pi/2 - \alpha_i^s \cdot \pi/4),$$

$$\gamma_i = ctg^s(\pi/2 - \alpha_i \cdot \pi/4),$$

$$\gamma_i = 2 - 4/\pi \cdot arcctg(\alpha_i^s),$$

$$\gamma_i = (2 - 4/\pi \cdot arcctg\alpha_i)^s$$

or any strictly monotonic function between points $(0;0;0)$ and $(1;1;1)$ – for example combinations of these functions.

Main advantage and superiority of PFC method comparing with known approaches are that there is no method connecting all these ten points below together:

1. Interpolation of some complicated formulas using combinations of a simple function;
2. Only local changes of data if one node is exchanged;
3. No matter if the curve or surface is opened or closed;
4. Data extrapolation is computed via the same formulas as interpolation;
5. Object modeling in any dimension N;
6. Curve and surface parameterization;
7. Modeling of specific and non-typical curves or surfaces: signatures, fonts, symbols, characters or handwriting;
8. Reconstruction of irregular shapes;
9. Applications in numerical analysis because of very precise interpolation of unknown values;
10. Even for only two nodes a curve or surfacecan be modeled.

Functions γ_i are strictly monotonic for each random variable $\alpha_i \in [0;1]$ as $\gamma = F(\alpha)$ is 3-dimensional probability distribution function, for example:

$$\gamma = \frac{1}{2}\sum_{i-1}^{2}\gamma_i, \ \gamma = \prod_{i=1}^{2}\gamma_i$$

and every monotonic combination of γ_i such as

$$\gamma = F(\alpha), \ F:[0;1]^2 \rightarrow [0;1], \ F(0,0) = 0, \ F(1,1) = 1.$$

For example when $N = 3$ there is a bilinear interpolation:

$$\gamma_1 = \alpha_1, \gamma_2 = \alpha_2, \gamma = \tfrac{1}{2}(\alpha_1 + \alpha_2) \tag{4}$$

or a bi-quadratic interpolation:

$$\gamma_1 = \alpha_1^2, \gamma_2 = \alpha_2^2, \gamma = \tfrac{1}{2}(\alpha_1^2 + \alpha_2^2) \tag{5}$$

or a bi-cubic interpolation:

$$\gamma_1 = \alpha_1^3, \gamma_2 = \alpha_2^3, \gamma = \tfrac{1}{2}(\alpha_1^3 + \alpha_2^3) \tag{6}$$

or others modeling functions γ. Choice of functions γ_i and value s depends on the specifications of feature vectors. What is very important in PFC method:

two data sets (for example a handwritten letter or signature) may have the same set of nodes (feature vectors: pixel coordinates, pressure, speed, angles) but different h or γ results in different interpolations. Formula of 2D curve or 3D surface is not given.

Algorithm of PFC retrieval, interpolation and modeling consists of five steps: first choice of nodes p_i (feature vectors), then choice of nodes combination $h(p_1, p_2, \ldots, p_m)$, choice of distribution (modeling function) $\gamma = F(\alpha)$, determining values of $\alpha_i \in [0;1]$ and finally the computations (1).

Discussion Over PFC Approach

What are the unique features of PFC method comparing with other methods of function interpolation, curve modeling and data extrapolation? This paragraph is answer this question.

Interpolation of Some Complicated Formulas Using Combinations of a Simple Function

Some mathematical formulas of functions are very complicated and have very high complexity of calculations. Then there is necessity of modeling via any simple function. Of course one can take a linear function between two nodes but this is non-effective approach. The idea of PFC formula

$$y(c) = \gamma \cdot y_k + (1 - \gamma)y_{k+1} + \gamma(1 - \gamma) \cdot h(p_1, p_2, \ldots, p_m)$$

is to calculate unknown value or coordinate as follows: take another modeling function (not linear) between two nodes. This function $\gamma = F(\alpha)$ is a probability distribution function of random variable $\alpha \in [0;1]$: for example uniform distribution means linear interpolation when $\gamma = \alpha$. Random variable $\alpha \in [0;1]$ is a parameter for known coordinate or value between two nodes:

$$c = \alpha \cdot x_k + (1-\alpha) \cdot x_{k+1}.$$

Additionally there is nodes combination h for better modeling. The simplest nodes combination is $h = 0$ and then PFC formula is

$$y(c) = \gamma \cdot y_i + (1 - \gamma)y_{i+1}. \tag{7}$$

Only Local Changes of Data If One Node is Exchanged

Nodes combination h is responsible for the range of changes if one node is exchanged. For example $h = 0$ means changes between two nodes whereas

$$h(p_1, p_2, p_3, p_4) = \frac{1}{x_1^2 + x_3^2}(x_1 x_2 y_1 + x_2 x_3 y_3 + x_3 x_4 y_1 - x_1 x_4 y_3)$$
$$+ \frac{1}{x_2^2 + x_4^2}(x_1 x_2 y_2 + x_1 x_4 y_4 + x_3 x_4 y_2 - x_2 x_3 y_4)$$

means changes between four nodes.

No Matter If the Curve Or surface is Opened or Closed

PFC formulas require the order and numbering of nodes exactly like on the curve, for example a graph of function. The only assumption for closed curve is that first node and last node are the same.

Data Extrapolation Is Computed Via the Same Formulas as Interpolation

Extrapolation is computed for real parameter $\alpha \notin [0;1]$. Then modeling function $\gamma = F(\alpha)$ has to be chosen for the situation when $\alpha < 0$ or $\alpha > 1$. Sometimes one can take a parallel (alternative) version of PFC formulas:

$$y(c) = \gamma \cdot y_{k+1} + (1 - \gamma)y_k + \gamma(1 - \gamma) \cdot h(p_1, p_2, ..., p_m),$$

$$c = \alpha \cdot x_{k+1} + (1-\alpha) \cdot x_k.$$

when for example calculations with $\alpha < 0$ are impossible and they are replaced by alternative calculations with $\alpha > 1$.

Object Modeling in Any Dimension N

Chapter six is dealing with this subject.

Surface or Curve Parameterization

Parameterization of the curve or surface between each pair of nodes is connected with random variable α.

Modeling of Specific and Non-Typical Curves or Surfaces: Signatures, Fonts, Symbols, Characters, or Handwriting

Figures in chapters 1-4 show the examples of PFC modeling. In the individual cases one can take for each pair of nodes different functions $\gamma = F(\alpha)$ and different nodes combinations h.

Reconstruction of Irregular Shapes

Chapter 3 is dealing with this subject.

Applications in Numerical Analysis Because of Very Precise Interpolation of Unknown Values

All numerical methods for numerical analysis (quadratures, derivatives, non-linear equations etc.) are based on the values of function given in the table. PFC method enables precise interpolation of the function. Chapter 7 is dealing with this subject.

Even for Only Two Nodes a Curve or Surface Can Be Modeled

Thankfully that PFC is modeling the curve or surface between each pair of nodes, even two nodes are enough in some cases for interpolation and reconstruction.

Above ten points are concerned on some aspects and features of PFC approach from mathematical and computational points of view.

IMAGE RETRIEVAL VIA PFC 3-DIMENSIONAL FEATURE RECONSTRUCTION

After the process of image segmentation and during the next steps of retrieval, recognition or identification, there is a huge number of features included in

3-dimensional feature vector. These vectors can be treated as "points" in three-dimensional feature space. For example in artificial intelligence there is a high-dimensional search space (the set of states that can be reached in a search problem) or hypothesis space (the set of hypothesis that can be generated by a machine learning algorithm). This chapter is dealing with 3-dimensional feature spaces that are used in computer vision, image processing and machine learning.

Having monochromatic (binary) image which consists of some objects, there is only 2-dimensional feature space (x_i, y_i) – coordinates of black pixels or coordinates of white pixels. No other parameters are needed. Thus any object can be described by a contour (closed binary curve). Binary images are attractive in processing (fast and easy) but don't include important information. If the image has grey shades, there is 3-dimensional feature space (x_i, y_i, z_i) with grey shade z_i. For example most of medical images are written in grey shades to get quite fast processing.

Voxel Reconstruction-Grey Scale Image Retrieval Using PFC 3D Method

Binary images are just the case of 2D points (x, y): 0 or 1, black or white, so retrieval of monochromatic images is done for the closed curves (first and last node are the same) as the contours of the objects for $N = 2$. Grey scale images are the case of 3D points (x, y, s) with s as the shade of grey. So the grey scale between the nodes $p_1 = (x_1, y_1, s_1)$ and $p_2 = (x_2, y_2, s_2)$ is computed with $\gamma = F(\alpha) = F(\alpha_1, \alpha_2)$ as (1) and for example (4)-(6) or others modeling functions γ_i. As the simple example two successive nodes of the image are: left upper corner with coordinates $p_1 = (x_1, y_1, 2)$ and right down corner $p_2 = (x_2, y_2, 10)$. The image retrieval with the grey scale 2-10 between p_1 and p_2 looks as shown in Table 1 for a bilinear interpolation (4).

Or for other modeling functions γ_i as shown in Table 2.

The feature vector of dimension $N = 3$ is called a voxel.

Recognition Tasks via Three-Dimensional Feature Vectors' Interpolation

The process of biometric recognition and identification consists of three parts: pre-processing, image segmentation with feature extraction and recognition or verification. Pre-processing is a common stage for all methods with

Table 1. Reconstructed grey scale numbered at each pixel

2	3	4	5	6	7	8	9	10
2	3	4	5	6	7	8	9	10
2	3	4	5	6	7	8	9	10
2	3	4	5	6	7	8	9	10
2	3	4	5	6	7	8	9	10
2	3	4	5	6	7	8	9	10
2	3	4	5	6	7	8	9	10
2	3	4	5	6	7	8	9	10
2	3	4	5	6	7	8	9	10

Table 2. Grey scale image with shades of grey retrieved at each pixel

2	2	2	2	2	2	2	2	2
2	3	3	3	3	3	3	3	3
2	3	4	4	4	4	4	4	4
2	3	4	5	5	5	5	5	5
2	3	4	5	6	6	6	6	6
2	3	4	5	6	7	7	7	7
2	3	4	5	6	7	8	8	8
2	3	4	5	6	7	8	9	9
2	3	4	5	6	7	8	9	10

binarization, thinning, size standardization. Proposed approach is based on 2D curve modeling and multi-dimensional feature vectors' interpolation. Feature extraction gives the key points (nodes as 3-dimensional feature vectors) that are used in PFC curve reconstruction and identification. PFC method enables signature and handwriting recognition, which is used for biometric purposes, because human signature or handwriting consists of non-typical curves and irregular shapes. This process of recognition consists of three parts:

1. **Before Recognition – The Data Basis:** Patterns' modeling – choice of nodes combination, probabilistic distribution function (1) and values of features (pen pressure, speed, pen angle etc.) appearing in high dimensional feature vectors for known signature or handwritten letters of some persons in the basis;

2. **Feature Extraction:** Unknown author – fixing the values in feature vectors for unknown signature or handwritten words: *N*-dimensional feature vectors $(x,y,p,s,a,t,...)$ limited to 3-dimensional feature vectors with x,y-points' coordinates, p-pen pressure, s-speed of writing, a- pen angle or any other features t;

3. **The Result:** Recognition or identification-comparing the results of PFC interpolation for known patterns from the data basis with features of unknown object.

Signature Modeling and Three-Dimensional Recognition

Human signature or handwriting consists mainly of non-typical curves and irregular shapes. So how to model two-dimensional handwritten characters via PFC method? Each model has to be described (1) by the set of nodes, nodes combination h and a function $\gamma=F(\alpha)$ for each letter. Other features in multi-dimensional feature space are not visible but used in recognition process (for example p-pen pressure, s-speed of writing, a- pen angle). Curves on the plane are two-dimensional subspace of N-dimensional feature space, for example (x,y,p,s,a,t) when $N = 6$. If the recognition process is working "offline" and features p-pen pressure, s-speed of writing, a- pen angle or another feature t are not given, the only information before recognition is situated in x,y-points' coordinates.

After pre-processing (binarization, thinning, size standarization), feature extraction is second part of biometric identification. The range of coefficients x has to be the same like the x range in the basis of patterns. When the nodes are fixed, each coordinate of every chosen point on the curve $(x_0{}^c,y_0{}^c)$, $(x_1{}^c,y_1{}^c),...,$ $(x_M{}^c,y_M{}^c)$ is accessible to be used for comparing with the models. Then function $\gamma = F(\alpha)$ and nodes combination h have to be taken from the basis of modeled letters to calculate appropriate second coordinates $y_i{}^{(j)}$ of the pattern S_j for first coordinates $x_i{}^c$, $i = 0,1,...,M$. After interpolation it is possible to compare given handwritten symbol with a letter in the basis of patterns. Comparing the results of PFC interpolation for required second coordinates of a model in the basis of patterns with points on the curve $(x_0{}^c,y_0{}^c)$, $(x_1{}^c,y_1{}^c),...,(x_M{}^c,y_M{}^c)$, one can say if the letter or symbol is written by person P1, P2 or another. The comparison and decision of recognition (Jakóbczak, 2014) is done via minimal distance criterion. Curve points of unknown handwritten symbol are: $(x_0{}^c,y_0{}^c)$, $(x_1{}^c,y_1{}^c),...,(x_M{}^c,y_M{}^c)$. The criterion of recognition for models S_j $= \{(x_0{}^c,y_0{}^{(j)})$, $(x_1{}^c,y_1{}^{(j)}),...,(x_M{}^c,y_M{}^{(j)})$, $j=0,1,2,3...K\}$ is given as:

$$\sum_{i=0}^{M} \left| y_i^c - y_i^{(j)} \right| \to \min \text{ or } \sqrt{\sum_{i=0}^{M} \left| y_i^c - y_i^{(j)} \right|^2} \to \min . \tag{8}$$

Minimal distance criterion helps us to fix a candidate for unknown writer as a person from the model S_j in the basis.

If the recognition process is "online" and features p-pen pressure, s-speed of writing, a- pen angle or some feature t are given, then there is more information in the process of author recognition, identification or verification in a feature space (x,y,p,s,a,t) of dimension $N = 6$ or others. Some person may know how the signature of another man looks like, but other extremely important features p,s,a,t are not visible. Dimension N of a feature space may be very high, but this is no problem. The problem connected with the curse of dimensionality with feature selection does not matter. There is no need to fix which feature is less important and can be eliminated. Every feature is very important and each of them can be interpolated between the nodes using PFC high-dimensional interpolation. For example pressure of the pen p differs during the signature writing and p is changing for particular letters or fragments of the signature. Then feature vector (x,y,p) of dimension $N_1 = 3$ is dealing with p interpolation at the point (x,y) via modeling functions (4)-(6) or others. If angle of the pen a differs during the signature writing and a is changing for particular letters or fragments of the signature, then feature vector (x,y,a) of dimension $N_1 = 3$ is dealing with a interpolation at the point (x,y) via modeling functions (4)-(6) or others. If speed of the writing s differs during the signature writing and s is changing for particular letters or fragments of the signature, then feature vector (x,y,s) of dimension $N_1 = 3$ is dealing with s interpolation at the point (x,y) via modeling functions (4)-(6) or others. This PFC 3D interpolation is the same like grey scale image retrieval but for selected pairs (α_1, α_2) – only for the points of signature between $(x_1,y_1,2)$ and $(x_2,y_2,10)$.

Tables 3-5 are the examples of denotation for the features that are not visible during the signing or handwriting but very important in the process of "online" recognition, identification or verification.

Even if from technical reason or other reasons only some points of signature or handwriting (feature nodes) are given in the process of "online" recognition, identification or verification, the values of features between nodes are computed via 3-dimensional PFC interpolation like for example between $(x_1,y_1,2)$ and $(x_2,y_2,10)$ on Table 3, between $(x_1,y_1,1)$ and $(x_2,y_2,9)$ on Table 4 or between $(x_1,y_1,30)$ and $(x_2,y_2,60)$ on Table 5. Reconstructed features are

Table 3. Reconstructed speed of the writing s at the pixels of signature

2	3	0	0	0	0	0	0	0
0	0	4	5	0	0	0	0	0
0	0	0	0	6	0	0	0	0
0	0	0	0	0	7	0	0	0
0	0	0	0	0	0	8	0	0
0	0	0	0	0	0	0	9	0
0	0	0	0	0	0	0	0	10
0	0	0	0	0	0	0	0	10
0	0	0	0	0	0	0	0	10

Table 4. Reconstructed pen pressure p at the pixels of signature

1	1	0	0	0	0	0	0	0
0	0	2	2	0	0	0	0	0
0	0	0	0	3	0	0	0	0
0	0	0	0	0	4	0	0	0
0	0	0	0	0	0	5	0	0
0	0	0	0	0	0	0	6	0
0	0	0	0	0	0	0	0	7
0	0	0	0	0	0	0	0	8
0	0	0	0	0	0	0	0	9

Table 5. Reconstructed angle a at the pixels of signature

30	30	0	0	0	0	0	0	0
0	0	32	34	0	0	0	0	0
0	0	0	0	37	0	0	0	0
0	0	0	0	0	43	0	0	0
0	0	0	0	0	0	45	0	0
0	0	0	0	0	0	0	46	0
0	0	0	0	0	0	0	0	53
0	0	0	0	0	0	0	0	56
0	0	0	0	0	0	0	0	60

compared with the features in the basis of patterns like parameter y in (8) and appropriate criterion gives the result.

So persons with the parameters of their signatures are allocated in the basis of patterns. Every letter or a part of signature is modeled by PFC via three factors: the set of high-dimensional feature nodes, probability distribution function $\gamma = F(\alpha)$ and nodes combination h. These three factors are chosen individually for each letter or a part of signature therefore this information about modeled curves seems to be enough for specific PFC 3-dimensional curve interpolation and handwriting identification. What is very important, PFC three-dimensional modeling is independent of the language or a kind of symbol (letters, numbers, characters or others). Summarize: every person has the basis of patterns for each handwritten letter or symbol, described by the set of feature nodes, modeling function $\gamma = F(\alpha)$ and nodes combination h. Whole basis of patterns consists of models S_j for $j = 0,1,2,3...K$.

Some 3D models can be visualized by proper choice of the parameters for PNC 2D interpolation. This approach is extremely important because of 3D visualization on the plane (Figures 1-5): here are the examples of 2D PNC reconstruction as 3D visualization with only three nodes.

Figure 1. Surface reconstruction for $s = 1.4, h = y_1 \left(\dfrac{x_2}{x_1} \right) + y_2 \left(\dfrac{x_1}{x_2} \right), \gamma = 1 - \cos\left(\alpha^s * \dfrac{\pi}{2} \right)$

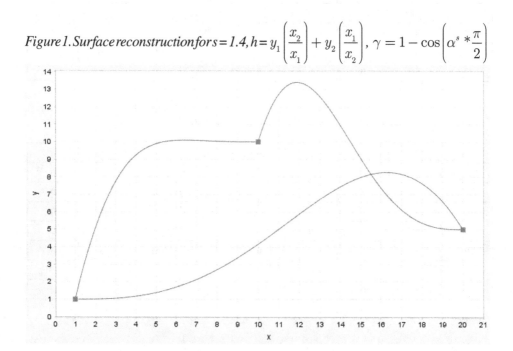

Figure 2. 3D object interpolation for s = 1.4, $h = y_1\left(\dfrac{x_2}{x_1}\right) + y_2\left(\dfrac{x_1}{x_2}\right)$,

$$\gamma = ctg\left(\dfrac{\pi}{2} - \alpha^s * \dfrac{\pi}{4}\right)$$

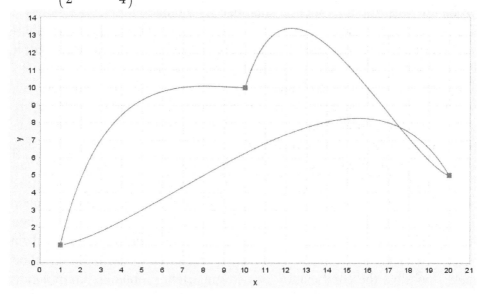

Figure 3. Surface modeling with s = 1.4, $h = y_1\left(\dfrac{x_2}{x_1}\right) + y_2\left(\dfrac{x_1}{x_2}\right)$, $\gamma = 1 - \dfrac{2}{\pi} * \arccos\left(\alpha^s\right)$

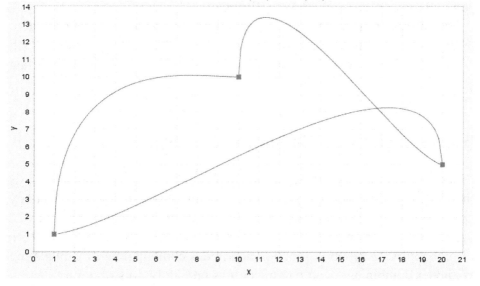

Proposed method, called Probabilistic Features Combination (PFC), is the method of N-dimensional data interpolation and extrapolation using the set of key points (knots or nodes). Nodes can be treated as characteristic points of data for modeling and analyzing. The model of data can be built by choice of probability distribution function and nodes combination. PFC modeling via nodes combination and parameter γ as probability distribution function enables value anticipation in risk analysis and decision making. N-dimensional object is extrapolated and interpolated via nodes combination and different functions as discrete or continuous probability distribution functions: polynomial, sine, cosine, tangent, cotangent, logarithm, exponent, arc sin, arc cos, arc tan, arc cot or power function. The method of Probabilistic Features Combination (PFC) enables interpolation and modeling of high-dimensional data using features' combinations and different coefficients γ as modeling function. Functions for γ calculations are chosen individually at each data modeling and it is treated as N-dimensional probability distribution function: γ depends on initial requirements and features' specifications. PFC method leads to data interpolation as handwriting or signature identification and image retrieval via discrete set of feature vectors in N-dimensional feature space. So PFC method makes possible the combination of two important problems: interpolation and modeling in a matter of image retrieval or writer identification. PFC interpolation develops a linear interpolation in multidimensional feature spaces into other functions as N-dimensional probability distribution functions. Future works are going to applications of PFC method in biometric recognition, computer vision and artificial intelligence.

3D modeling of surface on the plane is extremely important problem in computer science and applied mathematics. PNC method enables such a modeling using two-dimensional nodes and 2D curves via appropriate parameters in PNC modeling.

SOLUTIONS AND RECOMMENDATIONS

Proposed method, called Probabilistic Features Combination (PFC), is the method of 3D data interpolation and extrapolation using the set of key points (knots or nodes). Nodes can be treated as characteristic points of data for modeling and analyzing. The model of data can be built by choice of probability distribution function and nodes combination. PFC modeling via nodes combination and parameter γ as probability distribution function enables value anticipation in risk analysis and decision making. Three-

Figure 4. Three-dimensional object achieved after geometrical operations

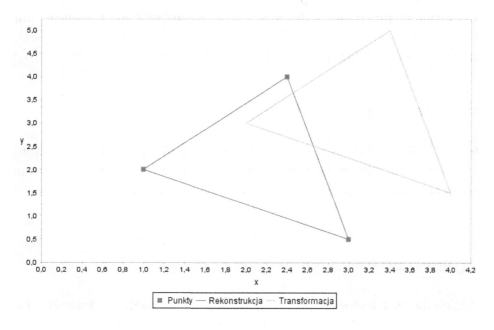

Figure 5. 3-dimensional object visualized after geometrical operations

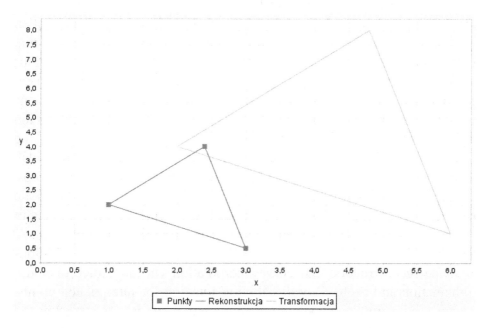

dimensional surface is extrapolated and interpolated via nodes combination and different functions as discrete or continuous probability distribution functions: polynomial, sine, cosine, tangent, cotangent, logarithm, exponent, arc sin, arc cos, arc tan, arc cot or power function.

FUTURE RESEARCH DIRECTIONS

Future trends will go to various directions: how to fix the best probability distribution function for the nodes, how to calculate the most appropriate nodes combination and what extrapolation is the most valuable in decision making and risk analysis.

CONCLUSION

What is the most important feature of MHR and PNC methods? Interpolation methods and curve fitting represent so huge problem that each individual interpolation is exceptional and requires specific solutions. PNC method is such a novel tool with its all pros and cons. The user has to decide which interpolation method is the best in a single situation. The choice is yours if you have any choice. Presented method is such a new possibility for curve fitting and interpolation when specific data (for example handwritten symbol or character) starts up with no rules for polynomial interpolation. This chapter consists of two generalizations: generalization of previous MHR method with various nodes combinations and generalization of linear interpolation with different (no basic) probability distribution functions and nodes combinations. The method of Probabilistic Nodes Combination (PNC) enables interpolation and modeling of two-dimensional curves using nodes combinations and different coefficients γ: polynomial, sinusoidal, cosinusoidal, tangent, cotangent, logarithmic, exponential, arc sin, arc cos, arc tan, arc cot or power function, also inverse functions. This probabilistic view is novel approach a problem of modeling and interpolation. Computer vision and pattern recognition are interested in appropriate methods of shape representation and curve modeling. PNC method represents the possibilities of shape reconstruction and curve interpolation via the choice of nodes combination and probability distribution function for interpolated points. It seems to be quite new look at the problem of contour representation and curve modeling in artificial intelligence and computer vision. Function for γ calculations is chosen individually at each curve modeling and it is treated as probability distribution function: γ depends on initial requirements and curve specifications. PNC method leads to curve interpolation as handwriting modeling via discrete set of fixed knots. So PNC makes possible the combination of two important problems: interpolation and modeling. The method of Probabilistic Features Combination (PFC) enables interpolation and modeling of high-dimensional N data using features' combinations and different coefficients γ: polynomial, sinusoidal, cosinusoidal, tangent, cotangent, logarithmic, exponential, arc sin, arc cos, arc tan, arc cot or power function. Functions for γ calculations are chosen individually at each data modeling and it is treated as N-dimensional probability distribution function: γ depends on initial requirements and features' specifications. PFC method leads to data interpolation as handwriting or signature identification and image retrieval via discrete set of feature vectors in N-dimensional feature space. So PFC method makes possible the combination of two important problems: interpolation and modeling in a matter of image retrieval or writer identification. Main features of PFC method are: PFC interpolation develops a linear interpolation in multidimensional feature spaces into other functions as N-dimensional probability distribution functions; PFC is a generalization of MHR method and PNC method via different nodes combinations; interpolation of L points is connected with the computational cost of rank $O(L)$ as in MHR and PNC method; nodes combination and coefficients γ are crucial in the process of data probabilistic parameterization and interpolation: they are computed individually for a single feature. Future works are going to applications of PFC method in signature and handwriting biometric recognition: choice and features of nodes combinations h and coefficients γ.

Proposed method, called Probabilistic Features Combination (PFC), is the method of N-dimensional data interpolation and extrapolation using the set of key points (knots or nodes). Nodes can be treated as characteristic points of data for modeling and analyzing. The model of data can be built by choice of probability distribution function and nodes combination. PFC modeling via nodes combination and parameter γ as probability distribution function enables value anticipation in risk analysis and decision making. N-dimensional object is extrapolated and interpolated via nodes combination and different functions as discrete or continuous probability distribution functions: polynomial, sine, cosine, tangent, cotangent, logarithm, exponent, arc sin, arc cos, arc tan, arc cot or power function. The method of Probabilistic Features Combination (PFC) enables interpolation and modeling of high-dimensional data using features' combinations and different coefficients γ as modeling function.

Functions for γ calculations are chosen individually at each data modeling and it is treated as N-dimensional probability distribution function: γ depends on initial requirements and features' specifications. PFC method leads to data interpolation as handwriting or signature identification and image retrieval via discrete set of feature vectors in N-dimensional feature space. So PFC method makes possible the combination of two important problems: interpolation and modeling in a matter of image retrieval or writer identification. PFC interpolation develops a linear interpolation in multidimensional feature spaces into other functions as N-dimensional probability distribution functions. Future works are going to applications of PFC method in biometric recognition, computer vision and artificial intelligence. Nodes are treated as characteristic points of data for modeling and analyzing. The model of data can be built by choice of probability distribution function and nodes combination. PFC modeling via nodes combination and parameter γ as probability distribution function enables value anticipation in risk analysis and decision making. Two-dimensional object is extrapolated and interpolated via nodes combination and different functions as discrete or continuous probability distribution functions: polynomial, sine, cosine, tangent, cotangent, logarithm, exponent, arc sin, arc cos, arc tan, arc cot or power function. Functions for γ calculations are chosen individually at each data modeling and it is treated as 2-dimensional probability distribution function: γ depends on initial requirements and features' specifications. PFC method leads to data interpolation as handwriting or signature identification and image retrieval via discrete set of feature vectors in 2-dimensional feature space. So PFC method makes possible the combination of two important problems: interpolation and modeling in a matter of image retrieval or writer identification. PFC interpolation develops a linear interpolation in multidimensional feature spaces into other functions as two-dimensional probability distribution functions.

The method of Probabilistic Features Combination (PFC) enables interpolation and modeling of three-dimensional data using features' combinations and different coefficients γ as modeling function. Functions for γ calculations are chosen individually at each data modeling and it is treated as 3-dimensional probability distribution function: γ depends on initial requirements and features' specifications. PFC method leads to data interpolation as handwriting or signature identification and image retrieval via discrete set of feature vectors in 3-dimensional feature space. So PFC method makes possible the combination of two important problems: interpolation and modeling in a matter of image retrieval or writer identification. PFC interpolation develops a linear interpolation in multidimensional feature spaces into other functions as three-dimensional probability distribution functions. Future works are going to applications of PFC method in biometric recognition, computer vision and artificial intelligence.

REFERENCES

Bulacu, M., & Schomaker, L. (2007). Text-independent writer identification and verification using textural and allographic features. *IEEE Transactions on Pattern Analysis and Machine Intelligence, 29*(4), 701–717. doi:10.1109/TPAMI.2007.1009 PMID:17299226

Bulacu, M., Schomaker, L., & Brink, A. (2007). Text-independent writer identification and verification on off-line Arabic handwriting. *International Conference on Document Analysis and Recognition*, 769–773.

Chapra, S. C. (2012). *Applied Numerical Methods*. McGraw-Hill.

Chen, J., Cheng, W., & Lopresti, D. (2011). Using perturbed handwriting to support writer identification in the presence of severe data constraints. Document Recognition and Retrieval, 1–10. doi:10.1117/12.876497

Chen, J., Lopresti, D., & Kavallieratou, E. (2010). The impact of ruling lines on writer identification. *International Conference on Frontiers in Handwriting Recognition*, 439–444. doi:10.1109/ICFHR.2010.75

Collins, G. W. II. (2003). *Fundamental Numerical Methods and Data Analysis*. Case Western Reserve University.

Djeddi, C., & Souici-Meslati, L. (2010). A texture based approach for Arabic writer identification and verification. *International Conference on Machine and Web Intelligence*, 115–120.

Djeddi, C., & Souici-Meslati, L. (2011). Artificial immune recognition system for Arabic writer identification. *International Symposium on Innovation in Information and Communication Technology*, 159–165. doi:10.1109/ISIICT.2011.6149612

Galloway, M. M. (1975). Texture analysis using gray level run lengths. *Computer Graphics and Image Processing, 4*(2), 172–179. doi:10.1016/S0146-664X(75)80008-6

Garain, U., & Paquet, T. (2009). Off-line multi-script writer identification using AR coefficients. *International Conference on Document Analysis and Recognition*, 991–995. doi:10.1109/ICDAR.2009.222

Ghiasi, G., & Safabakhsh, R. (2013). Offline text-independent writer identification using codebook and efficient code extraction methods. *Image and Vision Computing*, *31*(5), 379–391. doi:10.1016/j.imavis.2013.03.002

Jakóbczak, D. J. (2014). *2D Curve Modeling via the Method of Probabilistic Nodes Combination-Shape Representation, Object Modeling and Curve Interpolation-Extrapolation with the Applications*. Saarbrucken: LAP Lambert Academic Publishing.

Marti, U.-V., & Bunke, H. (2002). The IAM-database: An English sentence database for offline handwriting recognition. *Int. J. Doc. Anal. Recognit.*, *5*(1), 39–46. doi:10.1007/s100320200071

Nosary, A., Heutte, L., & Paquet, T. (2004). Unsupervised writer adaption applied to handwritten text recognition. *Pattern Recognition Letters*, *37*(2), 385–388. doi:10.1016/S0031-3203(03)00185-7

Ozaki, M., Adachi, Y., & Ishii, N. (2006). Examination of effects of character size on accuracy of writer recognition by new local arc method. *International Conference on Knowledge-Based Intelligent Information and Engineering Systems*, 1170–1175. doi:10.1007/11893004_148

Ralston, A., & Rabinowitz, P. (2001). *A First Course in Numerical Analysis* (2nd ed.). New York: Dover Publications.

Schlapbach, A., & Bunke, H. (2004). Using HMM based recognizers for writer identification and verification. *9th Int. Workshop on Frontiers in Handwriting Recognition*, 167–172. doi:10.1109/IWFHR.2004.107

Schlapbach, A., & Bunke, H. (2006). Off-line writer identification using Gaussian mixture models. *International Conference on Pattern Recognition*, 992–995.

Schlapbach, A., & Bunke, H. (2007). A writer identification and verification system using HMM based recognizers. *Pattern Analysis & Applications*, *10*(1), 33–43. doi:10.1007/s10044-006-0047-5

Schomaker, L., Franke, K., & Bulacu, M. (2007). Using codebooks of fragmented connected-component contours in forensic and historic writer identification. *Pattern Recognition Letters, 28*(6), 719–727. doi:10.1016/j. patrec.2006.08.005

Schumaker, L. L. (2007). *Spline Functions: Basic Theory*. Cambridge Mathematical Library. doi:10.1017/CBO9780511618994

Shahabinejad, F., & Rahmati, M. (2007). A new method for writer identification and verification based on Farsi/Arabic handwritten texts. *Ninth International Conference on Document Analysis and Recognition (ICDAR 2007)*, 829–833.

Siddiqi, I., Cloppet, F., & Vincent, N. (2009). Contour based features for the classification of ancient manuscripts. Conference of the International Graphonomics Society, 226–229.

Siddiqi, I., & Vincent, N. (2010). Text independent writer recognition using redundant writing patterns with contour-based orientation and curvature features. *Pattern Recognition Letters, 43*(11), 3853–3865. doi:10.1016/j. patcog.2010.05.019

Van, E. M., Vuurpijl, L., Franke, K., & Schomaker, L. (2005). The WANDA measurement tool for forensic document examination. *J. Forensic Doc. Exam., 16*, 103–118.

Zhang, D., & Lu, G. (2004). Review of Shape Representation and Description Techniques. *Pattern Recognition, 1*(37), 1–19. doi:10.1016/j. patcog.2003.07.008

ADDITIONAL READING

Ballard, D. H. (1982). *Computer Vision*. New York, USA: Prentice Hall.

Basu, S., & Bresler, Y. (2000). $O(N^2\log_2 N)$ filtered backprojection reconstruction algorithm for tomography. *IEEE Transactions on Image Processing, 9*(10), 1760–1773. doi:10.1109/83.869187 PMID:18262914

Brankov, J. G., Yang, Y., & Wernick, M. N. (2004). Tomographic image reconstruction based on a Content–Adaptive Mesh Model. *IEEE Transactions on Medical Imaging, 2*(23), 202–212. doi:10.1109/TMI.2003.822822 PMID:14964565

Brasse, D., & Defrise, M. (2004). Fast fully 3-D image reconstruction in PET using planograms. *IEEE Transactions on Medical Imaging*, *4*(23), 413–425. doi:10.1109/TMI.2004.824231 PMID:15084067

Cetin, M., Karl, W. C., & Willsky, A. S. (2002, September). *Edge – preserving image reconstruction for coherent imaging application*. Paper presented at the IEEE International Conference on Image Processsing, Rochester, NY, USA. doi:10.1109/ICIP.2002.1039992

Chlebus, E., & Cholewa, M. (1999). Rapid prototyping – rapid tooling. *CADCAM Forum, 11*, 23-28.

Choraś, R. S. (2005). *Computer Vision*. Warsaw, Poland: Exit.

Cocozza-Thivent, C., Eymard, R., Mercier, S., & Roussignol, M. (2006). Characterization of the Marginal Distributions of Markov Processes Used in Dynamic Reliability. *Journal of Applied Mathematics and Stochastic Analysis. Article ID, 92156*, 1–18.

Cormen, T. H., Leiserson, C. E., & Rivest, R. L. (1996). *Introduction to algorithms*. Massachusetts, USA: the Massachusetts Institute of Technology Press and McGraw-Hill.

Dahlquist, G., & Bjoerck, A. (1974). *Numerical Methods*. New York, USA: Prentice Hall.

Defrise, M. (2001). A short readers guide to 3D tomographic reconstruction. *Computerized Medical Imaging and Graphics*, *25*(2), 113–116. doi:10.1016/S0895-6111(00)00061-6 PMID:11137787

Dejdumrong, N. (2007). A Shape Preserving Verification Techniques for Parametric Curves. *Computer Graphics, Imaging and Visualization. CGIV, 2007*, 163–168.

Dryja, M., Jankowska, J., & Jankowski, M. (1982). *Survey of numerical methods and algorithms. Part II*. Warsaw, Poland: WNT.

Dyn, N., Levin, D., & Gregory, J. A. (1987). A 4-Point Interpolatory Subdivision Scheme for Curve Design. *Computer Aided Geometric Design*, *4*(4), 257–268. doi:10.1016/0167-8396(87)90001-X

Eldar, Y. C. (2001). *Quantum Signal Processing*. (Unpublished doctoral dissertation). Massachusetts Institute of Technology, USA.

Eldar, Y. C., & Oppenheim, A. V. (2002). Quantum Signal Processing. *IEEE Signal Processing Magazine*, *6*(19), 12–32. doi:10.1109/MSP.2002.1043298

Fortuna, Z., Macukow, B., & Wąsowski, J. (1982). *Numerical methods*. Warsaw, Poland: WNT.

Jakóbczak, D. (2005). Hurwitz-Radon matrices and their children. *Computer Science*, *5*(8), 29–38.

Jakóbczak, D. (2007). 2D and 3D Image Modeling Using Hurwitz-Radon Matrices. *Polish Journal of Environmental Studies*, *4A*(16), 104–107.

Jakóbczak, D. (2009). Curve Interpolation Using Hurwitz-Radon Matrices. *Polish Journal of Environmental Studies*, *3B*(18), 126–130.

Jakóbczak, D. (2010). Shape Representation and Shape Coefficients via Method of Hurwitz-Radon Matrices. *Lecture Notes in Computer Science*, *6374*, 411–419. doi:10.1007/978-3-642-15910-7_47

Jakóbczak, D. (2010). Object Modeling Using Method of Hurwitz-Radon Matrices of Rank k. In W. Wolski & M. Borawski (Eds.), *Computer Graphics: Selected Issues* (pp. 79–90). Szczecin, Poland: University of Szczecin Press.

Jakóbczak, D. (2011). Curve Parameterization and Curvature via Method of Hurwitz-Radon Matrices. *Image Processing & Communications-. International Journal (Toronto, Ont.)*, *1-2*(16), 49–56.

Jakóbczak, D. (2011). Data Extrapolation and Decision Making via Method of Hurwitz-Radon Matrices. *Lecture Notes in Computer Science*, *6922*, 173–182. doi:10.1007/978-3-642-23935-9_17

Jakóbczak, D. (2011). Curve Extrapolation and Data Analysis using the Method of Hurwitz-Radon Matrices. *Folia Oeconomica Stetinensia*. 9(17)/2010, 121-138.

Jakóbczak, D. (2013). Probabilistic Modeling of Signature using the Method of Hurwitz-Radon Matrices. *Global Perspectives on Artificial Intelligence*, *1*(1), 1–7.

Jankowska, J., & Jankowski, M. (1981). *Survey of numerical methods and algorithms. Part I*. Warsaw, Poland: WNT.

Kontaxakis, G., & Strauss, L. G. (1998). Maximum likelihood algorithms for image reconstruction in Positron Emission Tomography. *Radionuclides for Oncology – Current Status and Future Aspects, 1998,* 73-106.

Kowalczuk, Z., & Wiszniewski, B. (Eds.). (2007). *Intelligent data mining in diagnostic purposes: Automatics and informatics*. Gdansk, Poland: PWNT.

Kozera, R. (2004). *Curve Modeling via Interpolation Based on Multidimensional Reduced Data*. Gliwice, Poland: Silesian University of Technology Press.

Kundur, D., & Hatzinakos, D. (1998). A novel blind deconvolution scheme for image restoration using recursive filtering. *IEEE Transactions on Signal Processing, 2*(46), 375–390. doi:10.1109/78.655423

Laine, A., & Zong, X. (1996). *Border identification of echocardiograms via multiscale edge detection and shape modeling*. Paper presented at the IEEE International Conference on Image Processsing, Lausanne, Switzerland. doi:10.1109/ICIP.1996.560486

Lang, S. (1970). *Algebra*. Reading, Massachusetts, USA: Addison-Wesley Publishing Company.

Le Buhan Jordan, C., Bossen, F., & Ebrahimi, T. (1997). *Scalable shape representation for content based visual data compression*. Paper presented at the International Conference on Image Processing, Santa Barbara, CA, USA. doi:10.1109/ICIP.1997.647962

Liu, T., & Geiger, D. (1999). Approximate tree matching and shape similarity. *Int. Conf. Computer Vision*. Corfu, Greece.

Lorton, A., Fouladirad, M., & Grall, A. (2013). A Methodology for Probabilistic Model-based Prognosis. *European Journal of Operational Research, 225*(3), 443–454. doi:10.1016/j.ejor.2012.10.025

Marker, J., Braude, I., Museth, K., & Breen, D. (2006). Contour-based surface reconstruction using implicit curve fitting, and distance field filtering and interpolation. *Volume Graphics, 2006*, 1–9.

Meyer, Y. (1993). *Wavelets: algorithms & applications*. Philadelphia, USA: Society for Industrial and Applied Mathematics.

Pergler, M., & Freeman, A. (2008). Probabilistic Modeling as an Exploratory Decision-Making Tool. *McKinsey Working Papers on Risk*. 6, 1-18.

Poggio, T., & Smale, S. (2003). The mathematics of learning: Dealing with data. *Notices of the American Mathematical Society, 5*(50), 537–544.

Przelaskowski, A. (2005). *Data compression*. Warsaw, Poland: BTC.

Rogers, D. F. (2001). *An Introduction to NURBS with Historical Perspective.* Morgan Kaufmann Publishers.

Rutkowski, L., Siekmann, J., Tadeusiewicz, R., & Zadeh, A. (Eds.). (2004). *Lecture notes on artificial intelligence: Artificial intelligence and soft computing.* Berlin-Heidelberg, Germany: Springer-Verlag.

Saber, E., Xu, Y., & Murat Tekalp, A. (2005). Partial shape recognition by sub-matrix matching for partial matching guided image labeling. *Pattern Recognition, 38*(10), 1560–1573. doi:10.1016/j.patcog.2005.03.027

Sebastian, T. B., Klein, P. N., & Kimia, B. B. (2003). On aligning curves. *IEEE Transactions on Pattern Analysis and Machine Intelligence, 25*(1), 116–124. doi:10.1109/TPAMI.2003.1159951

Tadeusiewicz, R., & Flasiński, M. (1991). *Image Recognition.* Warsaw, Poland: PWN.

Vakhania, N. (1993). Orthogonal random vectors and the Hurwitz – Radon-Eckmann theorem. *Proc. of the Georgian Academy of Sciences-Mathematics, 1(1),* 109-125.

Willis, M. (2000). *Algebraic reconstruction algorithms for remote sensing image enhancement.* Unpublished doctoral dissertation, Department of Electrical and Computer Engineering, Brigham Young University.

Xu, Fang, & Mueller, K. (2005). Accelerating popular tomographic reconstruction algorithms on commodity PC graphics hardware. *IEEE Transactions on Nuclear Science, 3*(52), 654–661.

Zaletelj, J., & Tasic, J. F. (2003). *Optimization and tracking of polygon vertices for shape coding.* Berlin-Heidelberg, Germany: Springer-Verlag. doi:10.1007/978-3-540-45179-2_52

Zhang, J. K., Davidson, T., & Wong, K. M. (2004). Efficient design of orthonormal wavelet bases for signal representation. *IEEE Transactions on Signal Processing, 7*(52), 1983–1996. doi:10.1109/TSP.2004.828923

KEY TERMS AND DEFINITIONS

3D Visualization: 2D object is playing role as a 3D figure.

Contour Modeling: Calculation of unknown points of the object contour having information about some points of the object contour.

Curve Interpolation: Computing new and unknown points of a curve and creating a graph of a curve using existing data points – interpolation nodes.

Data Extrapolation: Calculation of unknown values for the points situated outside the ranges of nodes.

Hurwitz – Radon Matrices: A family of skew – symmetric and orthogonal matrices with columns and rows that create, together with identical matrix, the base in vector spaces of dimensions $N = 2, 4$ or 8.

MHR Method: The method of curve interpolation and extrapolation using linear (convex) combinations of OHR operators.

OHR Operator: Matrix operator of Hurwitz – Radon built from coordinates of interpolation nodes.

Surface Interpolation: Computing new and unknown points of a surface and creating a graph using existing data points – interpolation nodes.

Value Anticipation: Foreseeing next value when last value is known.

Chapter 6
PNC in 4D Object and Multi-Dimensional Data Modeling

ABSTRACT

Proposed method, called Probabilistic Features Combination (PFC), is the method of N-dimensional data interpolation and extrapolation using the set of key points (knots or nodes). The method of Probabilistic Features Combination (PFC) enables interpolation and modeling of high-dimensional data using features' combinations and different coefficients γ as modeling function. Functions for γ calculations are chosen individually at each data modeling and it is treated as N-dimensional probability distribution function: γ depends on initial requirements and features' specifications. PFC method leads to data interpolation as handwriting or signature identification and image retrieval via discrete set of feature vectors in N-dimensional feature space. So PFC method makes possible the combination of two important problems: interpolation and modeling in a matter of image retrieval or writer identification. PFC interpolation develops a linear interpolation in multidimensional feature spaces into other functions as N-dimensional probability distribution functions.

INTRODUCTION AND BACKGROUND

Multidimensional data modeling appears in many branches of science and industry. Image retrieval, data reconstruction, object identification or pattern recognition are still the open problems in artificial intelligence and computer

DOI: 10.4018/978-1-5225-2531-8.ch006

vision. The chapter is dealing with these questions via modeling of high-dimensional data for applications of image segmentation in image retrieval and recognition tasks. Handwriting based author recognition offers a huge number of significant implementations which make it an important research area in pattern recognition. There are so many possibilities and applications of the recognition algorithms that implemented methods have to be concerned on a single problem: retrieval, identification, verification or recognition. This chapter is concerned with two parts: image retrieval and recognition tasks. Image retrieval is based on probabilistic modeling of unknown features via combination of N-dimensional probability distribution function for each feature treated as random variable. Handwriting and signature recognition and identification represents a significant problem. In the case of biometric writer recognition, each person is represented by the set of modeled letters or symbols. The sketch of proposed Probabilistic Features Combination (PFC) method consists of three steps: first handwritten letter or symbol must be modeled by a vector of features (N-dimensional data), then compared with unknown letter and finally there is a decision of identification. Author recognition of handwriting and signature is based on the choice of feature vectors and modeling functions. So high-dimensional data interpolation in handwriting identification (Marti & Bunke, 2002) is not only a pure mathematical problem but important task in pattern recognition and artificial intelligence such as: biometric recognition (Nosary, Heutte & Paquet, 2004), personalized handwriting recognition (Djeddi & Souici-Meslati, 2010 & 2011), automatic forensic document examination (Van, Vuurpijl, Franke & Schomaker, 2005; Schomaker, Franke & Bulacu, 2007), classification of ancient manuscripts (Siddiqi, Cloppet & Vincent, 2009). Also writer recognition (Garain & Paquet, 2009) in monolingual handwritten texts (Ozaki, Adachi & Ishii, 2006) is an extensive area of study (Chen, Lopresti & Kavallieratou, 2010) and the methods independent from the language (Chen, Cheng & Lopresti, 2011) are well-seen (Bulacu, Schomaker & Brink, 2007).

This chapter presents novel Probabilistic Features Combination (PFC) method of high-dimensional interpolation in hybrid soft computing and takes up PFC method of multidimensional data modeling. The method of PFC requires information about data (image, object, curve) as the set of N-dimensional feature vectors. Proposed PFC method is applied in image retrieval and recognition tasks via different coefficients for each feature as random variable: polynomial, sinusoidal, cosinusoidal, tangent, cotangent, logarithmic, exponential, arc sin, arc cos, arc tan, arc cot or power. Modeling functions for PFC calculations are chosen individually for every task and they represent probability distribution functions of random variable $\alpha_i \in [0;1]$ for every feature $i=1,2,\ldots N\text{-}1$. So this chapter wants to answer the question: how to retrieve the image using N-dimensional feature vectors and to recognize a handwritten letter or symbol by a set of high-dimensional nodes via hybrid soft computing? The method of Probabilistic Features Combination (PFC) enables interpolation and modeling of high-dimensional data using features' combinations and different coefficients γ as modeling function. Functions for γ calculations are chosen individually at each data modeling and it is treated as N-dimensional probability distribution function: γ depends on initial requirements and features' specifications. PFC method leads to data interpolation as handwriting or signature identification and image retrieval via discrete set of feature vectors in N-dimensional feature space. So PFC method makes possible the combination of two important problems: interpolation and modeling in a matter of image retrieval or writer identification. PFC interpolation develops a linear interpolation in multidimensional feature spaces into other functions as N-dimensional probability distribution functions. Future works are going to applications of PFC method in biometric recognition, computer vision and artificial intelligence. Nodes are treated as characteristic points of data for modeling and analyzing. The model of data can be built by choice of probability distribution function and nodes combination. PFC modeling via nodes combination and parameter γ as probability distribution function enables value anticipation in risk analysis and decision making. Two-dimensional object is extrapolated and interpolated via nodes combination and different functions as discrete or continuous probability distribution functions: polynomial, sine, cosine, tangent, cotangent, logarithm, exponent, arc sin, arc cos, arc tan, arc cot or power function.

REPRESENTATION OF N-DIMENSIONAL DATA AND MULTIDIMENSIONAL MODELING OF FEATURE VECTORS

Issues

The method of PFC is computing (interpolating) unknown (unclear, noised or destroyed) values of features between two successive nodes (N-dimensional vectors of features) using hybridization of probabilistic methods and numerical methods. Calculated values (unknown or noised features such as coordinates, colors, textures or any coefficients of pixels, voxels and doxels or image parameters) are interpolated and parameterized for real number $\alpha_i \in [0;1]$ ($i = 1,2,...N$-1) between two successive values of feature. PFC method uses the combinations of nodes (N-dimensional feature vectors): $p_1 = (x_1, y_1, ..., z_1)$, $p_2 = (x_2, y_2, ... z_2)$,..., $p_n = (x_n, y_n, ... z_n)$ as $h(p_1, p_2, ..., p_m)$ and $m = 1,2,...n$ to interpolate unknown value of feature (for example y) for the rest of coordinates:

$$c_1 = \alpha_1 \cdot x_k + (1-\alpha_1) \cdot x_{k+1}, \ldots\ldots c_{N-1} = \alpha_{N-1} \cdot z_k + (1-\alpha_{N-1}) \cdot z_{k+1}, k = 1,2,...n\text{-}1,$$

$$c = (c_1, ..., c_{N-1}), \alpha = (\alpha_1, ..., \alpha_{N-1}), \gamma_i = F_i(\alpha_i) \in [0;1], i = 1,2,...N\text{-}1$$

$$y(c) = \gamma \cdot y_k + (1 - \gamma)y_{k+1} + \gamma(1 - \gamma) \cdot h(p_1, p_2, ..., p_m), \tag{1}$$

$$\alpha_i \in [0;1], \gamma = F(\alpha) = F(\alpha_1, ..., \alpha_{N-1}) \in [0;1].$$

The basic structure of eq. (1) is built on modeling function $\gamma = F(\alpha)$ which is used for points' interpolation between the nodes. Additionally for better reconstruction and modeling there is a factor with function $\gamma = F(\alpha)$ and nodes combination h.

Then N-1 features $c_1, ..., c_{N-1}$ are parameterized by $\alpha_1, ..., \alpha_{N-1}$ between two nodes and the last feature (for example y) is interpolated via formula (1). Of course there can be calculated $x(c)$ or $z(c)$ using (1). Two examples of h (when $N = 2$) computed for MHR method (Jakóbczak, 2014) with good features because of orthogonal rows and columns at Hurwitz-Radon family of matrices that origins from some calculations with orthogonal matrices:

$$h(p_1, p_2) = \frac{y_1}{x_1} x_2 + \frac{y_2}{x_2} x_1 \tag{2}$$

or

$$h(p_1, p_2, p_3, p_4) = \frac{1}{x_1^2 + x_3^2}(x_1 x_2 y_1 + x_2 x_3 y_3 + x_3 x_4 y_1 - x_1 x_4 y_3)$$

$$+ \frac{1}{x_2^2 + x_4^2}(x_1 x_2 y_2 + x_1 x_4 y_4 + x_3 x_4 y_2 - x_2 x_3 y_4) \; .$$

The simplest nodes combination is

$$h(p_1, p_2, ..., p_m) = 0 \tag{3}$$

and then there is a formula of interpolation:

$$y(c) = \gamma \cdot y_i + (1 - \gamma)y_{i+1}.$$

Formula (1) gives the infinite number of calculations for unknown feature (determined by choice of F and h) as there is the infinite number of objects to recognize or the infinite number of images to retrieve. Nodes combination is the individual feature of each modeled data. Coefficient $\gamma = F(\alpha)$ and nodes combination h are key factors in PFC data interpolation and object modeling.

High-Dimensional Object Reconstruction via *N*-Dimensional Probability Distribution Functions in PFC Modeling

Unknown values of features, settled between the nodes, are computed using PFC method. Each interpolation requires specific distributions of random variables α_i and γ in (1) depends on parameters $\alpha_i \in [0;1]$:

$$\gamma = F(\alpha), \; F:[0;1]^{N-1} \rightarrow [0;1], \; F(0,\ldots,0) = 0, \; F(1,\ldots,1) = 1$$

and F is strictly monotonic for each random variable α_i separately. Coefficient γ_i are calculated using appropriate function and choice of function is connected with initial requirements and data specifications. Different values of coefficients γ_i are connected with applied functions $F_i(\alpha_i)$. These functions $\gamma_i = F_i(\alpha_i)$ represent the examples of probability distribution functions for random variable $\alpha_i \in [0;1]$ and real number $s>0$, $i = 1,2,\ldots N-1$:

$\gamma_i = \alpha_i^s,$

$\gamma_i = sin(\alpha_i^s \cdot \pi/2),$

$\gamma_i = sin^s(\alpha_i \cdot \pi/2),$

$\gamma_i = 1 - cos(\alpha_i^s \cdot \pi/2),$

$\gamma_i = 1 - cos^s(\alpha_i \cdot \pi/2),$

$\gamma_i = tan(\alpha_i^s \cdot \pi/4),$

$\gamma_i = tan^s(\alpha_i \cdot \pi/4)$,

$\gamma_i = log_2(\alpha_i^s + 1)$,

$\gamma_i = log_2^s(\alpha_i + 1)$,

$\gamma_i = (2^{\alpha_i} - 1)^s$,

$\gamma_i = 2/\pi \cdot arcsin(\alpha_i^s)$,

$\gamma_i = (2/\pi \cdot arcsin\alpha_i)^s$,

$\gamma_i = 1 - 2/\pi \cdot arccos(\alpha_i^s)$,

$\gamma_i = 1 - (2/\pi \cdot arccos\alpha_i)^s$,

$\gamma_i = 4/\pi \cdot arctan(\alpha_i^s)$,

$\gamma_i = (4/\pi \cdot arctan\alpha_i)^s$,

$\gamma_i = ctg(\pi/2 - \alpha_i^s \cdot \pi/4)$,

$\gamma_i = ctg^s(\pi/2 - \alpha_i \cdot \pi/4)$,

$\gamma_i = 2 - 4/\pi \cdot arcctg(\alpha_i^s)$,

$\gamma_i = (2 - 4/\pi \cdot arcctg\alpha_i)^s$

or any strictly monotonic function between points (0;0) and (1;1) – for example combinations of these functions. Also monotonic functions between points (0;1) and (1;0), it means opposite to *F*:

$$\gamma = 1 - F(\alpha)$$

are possible for calculations in the alternative version of PNC.

Functions γ_i are strictly monotonic for each random variable $\alpha_i \in [0;1]$ as $\gamma = F(\alpha)$ is *N*-dimensional probability distribution function, for example:

$$\gamma = \frac{1}{N-1}\sum_{i-1}^{N-1}\gamma_i \, , \; \gamma = \prod_{i=1}^{N-1}\gamma_i$$

and every monotonic combination of γ_i such as

$$\gamma = F(\alpha), \; F:[0;1]^{N-1}\rightarrow[0;1], \; F(0,\ldots,0) = 0, \; F(1,\ldots,1) = 1.$$

For example when $N = 3$ there is a bilinear interpolation:

$$\gamma_1 = \alpha_1, \; \gamma_2 = \alpha_2, \; \gamma = \tfrac{1}{2}(\alpha_1 + \alpha_2) \tag{4}$$

or a bi-quadratic interpolation:

$$\gamma_1 = \alpha_1^2, \; \gamma_2 = \alpha_2^2, \; \gamma = \tfrac{1}{2}(\alpha_1^2 + \alpha_2^2) \tag{5}$$

or a bi-cubic interpolation:

$$\gamma_1 = \alpha_1^3, \; \gamma_2 = \alpha_2^3, \; \gamma = \tfrac{1}{2}(\alpha_1^3 + \alpha_2^3) \tag{6}$$

or others modeling functions γ. Choice of functions γ_i and value s depends on the specifications of feature vectors. What is very important in PFC method: two data sets (for example a handwritten letter or signature) may have the same set of nodes (feature vectors: pixel coordinates, pressure, speed, angles) but different h or γ results in different interpolations.

Algorithm of PFC retrieval, interpolation and modeling consists of five steps: first choice of nodes p_i (feature vectors), then choice of nodes combination $h(p_1,p_2,\ldots,p_m)$, choice of distribution (modeling function) $\gamma = F(\alpha)$, determining values of $\alpha_i \in [0;1]$ and finally the computations (1).

IMAGE RETRIEVAL VIA PFC HIGH-DIMENSIONAL FEATURE RECONSTRUCTION

After the process of image segmentation and during the next steps of retrieval, recognition or identification, there is a huge number of features included in N-dimensional feature vector. These vectors can be treated as "points" in N-dimensional feature space. For example in artificial intelligence there is a high-dimensional search space (the set of states that can be reached in a search problem) or hypothesis space (the set of hypothesis that can be generated by a machine learning algorithm). This chapter is dealing with multidimensional feature spaces that are used in computer vision, image processing and machine learning.

Having monochromatic (binary) image which consists of some objects, there is only 2-dimensional feature space (x_i, y_i) – coordinates of black pixels or coordinates of white pixels. No other parameters are needed. Thus any object can be described by a contour (closed binary curve). Binary images are attractive in processing (fast and easy) but don't include important information. If the image has grey shades, there is 3-dimensional feature space (x_i, y_i, z_i) with grey shade z_i. For example most of medical images are written in grey shades to get quite fast processing. But when there are color images (three parameters for RGB or other color systems) with textures or medical data or some parameters, then it is N-dimensional feature space. Dealing with the problem of classification learning for high-dimensional feature spaces in artificial intelligence and machine learning (for example text classification and recognition), there are some methods: decision trees, k-nearest neighbors, perceptrons, naïve Bayes or neural networks methods. All of these methods are struggling with the curse of dimensionality: the problem of having too many features. And there are many approaches to get less number of features and to reduce the dimension of feature space for faster and less expensive calculations.

Writer recognition methods in the recent years are going to various directions (Galloway, 1975): writer recognition using multi-script handwritten texts, introduction of new features (Ghiasi & Safabakhsh, 2013), combining different types of features (Siddiqi & Vincent, 2010), studying the sensitivity of character size on writer identification, investigating writer identification in multi-script environments (Shahabinejad & Rahmati, 2007), impact of ruling lines on writer identification, model perturbed handwriting, methods based on run-length features, the edge-direction and edge-hinge features, a combination of codebook and visual features extracted from chain code and polygonized representation of contours, the autoregressive coefficients, codebook and efficient code extraction methods, texture analysis with Gabor filters and extracting features (Schlapbach & Bunke, 2007), using Hidden Markov Model (Schlapbach & Bunke, 2004) or Gaussian Mixture Model (Schlapbach & Bunke, 2006). So hybrid soft computing is essential: no method is dealing with writer identification via N-dimensional data modeling or interpolation and multidimensional points comparing as it is presented in this chapter. The chapter wants to approach a problem of curve interpolation and shape modeling by characteristic points in handwriting identification (Bulacu & Schomaker, 2007). Proposed method relies on nodes combination and functional modeling of curve points situated between the basic set of key points. The functions that are used in calculations represent whole family of elementary functions with inverse functions: polynomials, trigonometric, cyclometric, logarithmic, exponential and power function. These functions are treated as probability distribution functions in the range [0;1]. Nowadays methods apply mainly polynomial functions, for example Bernstein polynomials in Bezier curves, splines (Schumaker, 2007) and NURBS. But Bezier curves don't represent the interpolation method and cannot be used for example in signature and handwriting modeling with characteristic points (nodes). Numerical methods (Collins, 2003) for data interpolation are based on polynomial or trigonometric functions (Chapra, 2012), for example Lagrange, Newton, Aitken and Hermite methods (Ralston & Rabinowitz, 2001). These methods have some weak sides and are not sufficient for curve interpolation in the situations when the curve cannot be build by polynomials or trigonometric functions (Zhang & Lu, 2004).

This chapter aims at inverse problem to the curse of dimensionality: dimension N of feature space (i.e. number of features) is unchanged, but number of feature vectors (i.e. "points" in N-dimensional feature space) is reduced into the set of nodes. So the main problem is as follows: how to fix the set of feature vectors for the image and how to retrieve the features between the "nodes"? This chapter aims in giving the answer of this question.

Doxel Modeling: Color Image Retrieval via PFC Method

Color images in for example RGB color system (r,g,b) are the set of points (x,y,r,g,b) in a feature space of dimension $N = 5$. There can be more features, for example texture t, and then one pixel (x,y,r,g,b,t) exists in a feature space of dimension $N = 6$. But there are the sub-spaces of a feature space of dimension $N_1 < N$, for example (x,y,r), (x,y,g), (x,y,b) or (x,y,t) are points in a feature sub-space of dimension $N_1 = 3$. Reconstruction and interpolation of color coordinates or texture parameters is done like in chapter 3.1 for dimension $N = 3$. Appropriate combination of α_1 and α_2 leads to modeling of color r,g,b or texture t or another feature between the nodes. And for example (x,y,r,t), (x,y,g,t), $(x,y,b,t))$ are points in a feature sub-space of dimension $N_1=4$ called doxels. Appropriate combination of α_1, α_2 and α_3 leads to modeling of texture t or another feature between the nodes. For example color image, given as

Table 1. Color image with color and texture parameters (r,t) interpolated at each pixel

2,1	3,1	4,1	5,1	6,1	7,1	8,1	9,1	10,1
2,2	3,2	4,2	5,2	6,2	7,2	8,2	9,2	10,2
2,3	3,3	4,3	5,3	6,3	7,3	8,3	9,3	10,3
2,4	3,4	4,4	5,4	6,4	7,4	8,4	9,4	10,4
2,5	3,5	4,5	5,5	6,5	7,5	8,5	9,5	10,5
2,6	3,6	4,6	5,6	6,6	7,6	8,6	9,6	10,6
2,7	3,7	4,7	5,7	6,7	7,7	8,7	9,7	10,7
2,8	3,8	4,8	5,8	6,8	7,8	8,8	9,8	10,8
2,9	3,9	4,9	5,9	6,9	7,9	8,9	9,9	10,9

the set of doxels (x,y,r,t), is described for coordinates (x,y) via pairs (r,t) interpolated between nodes $(x_1,y_1,2,1)$ and $(x_2,y_2,10,9)$ as shown in Table 1.

So dealing with feature space of dimension N and using PFC method there is no problem called "the curse of dimensionality" and no problem called "feature selection" because each feature is important. There is no need to reduce the dimension N and no need to establish which feature is "more important" or "less important". Every feature that depends from N_1-1 other features can be interpolated (reconstructed) in the feature sub-space of dimension $N_1 < N$ via PFC method. But having a feature space of dimension N and using PFC method there is another problem: how to reduce the number of feature vectors and how to interpolate (retrieve) the features between the known vectors (called nodes).

Difference between two given approaches (the curse of dimensionality with feature selection and PFC interpolation) can be illustrated as follows. There is a feature matrix of dimension N x M: N means the number of features (dimension of feature space) and M is the number of feature vectors (interpolation nodes) – columns are feature vectors of dimension N. One approach: the curse of dimensionality with feature selection wants to eliminate some rows from the feature matrix and to reduce dimension N to $N_1 < N$. Second approach for PFC method wants to eliminate some columns from the feature matrix and to reduce dimension M to $M_1 < M$.

So after feature selection (Table 2) there are nine feature vectors (columns): $M = 9$ in a feature sub-space of dimension $N_1 = 6 < N$ (three features are fixed as less important and reduced). But feature elimination is a very unclear matter. And what to do if every feature is denoted as meaningful and then no feature is to be reduced? For PFC method (Table 3) there are seven feature

Table 2. The curse of dimensionality with feature selection wants to eliminate some rows from the feature matrix and to reduce dimension N

2	2	2	2	2	2	2	2	2
2	3	3	3	3	3	3	3	3
2	3	4	4	4	4	4	4	4
2	3	4	5	5	5	5	5	5
2	3	4	5	6	6	6	6	6
2	3	4	5	6	7	7	7	7
2	3	4	5	6	7	8	8	8
2	3	4	5	6	7	8	9	9
2	3	4	5	6	7	8	9	10

$\rightarrow$

2	2	2	2	2	2	2	2	2
2	3	3	3	3	3	3	3	3
2	3	4	4	4	4	4	4	4
2	3	4	5	5	5	5	5	5
2	3	4	5	6	6	6	6	6
2	3	4	5	6	7	7	7	7

Table 3. PFC method wants to eliminate some columns from the feature matrix and to reduce dimension M

2	2	2	2	2	2	2	2	2
2	3	3	3	3	3	3	3	3
2	3	4	4	4	4	4	4	4
2	3	4	5	5	5	5	5	5
2	3	4	5	6	6	6	6	6
2	3	4	5	6	7	7	7	7
2	3	4	5	6	7	8	8	8
2	3	4	5	6	7	8	9	9
2	3	4	5	6	7	8	9	10

$\rightarrow$

2	2	2	2	2	2	2
2	3	3	3	3	3	3
2	3	4	4	4	4	4
2	3	4	5	5	5	5
2	3	4	5	6	6	6
2	3	4	5	6	7	7
2	3	4	5	6	7	8
2	3	4	5	6	7	8
2	3	4	5	6	7	8

vectors (columns): $M_1 = 7 < M$ in a feature space of dimension $N = 9$. Then no feature is eliminated and the main problem is dealing with interpolation or extrapolation of feature values, like for example image retrieval (Table 1).

Recognition Tasks via High-Dimensional Feature Vectors' Interpolation

The process of biometric recognition and identification consists of three parts: pre-processing, image segmentation with feature extraction and recognition or verification. Pre-processing is a common stage for all methods with binarization, thinning, size standardization. Proposed approach is based on 2D curve modeling and multi-dimensional feature vectors' interpolation.

Feature extraction gives the key points (nodes as N-dimensional feature vectors) that are used in PFC curve reconstruction and identification. PFC method enables signature and handwriting recognition, which is used for biometric purposes, because human signature or handwriting consists of non-typical curves and irregular shapes (for example Fig.4-6). This process of recognition consists of three parts:

1. **Before Recognition – The Data Basis:** Patterns' modeling – choice of nodes combination, probabilistic distribution function (1) and values of features (pen pressure, speed, pen angle etc.) appearing in high dimensional feature vectors for known signature or handwritten letters of some persons in the basis;
2. **Feature Extraction:** Unknown author – fixing the values in feature vectors for unknown signature or handwritten words: N-dimensional feature vectors (x,y,p,s,a,t) with x,y-points' coordinates, p-pen pressure, s-speed of writing, a- pen angle or any other features t;
3. **The Result:** Recognition or identification-comparing the results of PFC interpolation for known patterns from the data basis with features of unknown object.

Information Retrieval and Multidimensional Recognition

Human signature or handwriting consists mainly of non-typical curves and irregular shapes. So how to model two-dimensional handwritten characters via PFC method? Each model has to be described (1) by the set of nodes, nodes combination h and a function $\gamma=F(\alpha)$ for each letter. Other features in multi-dimensional feature space are not visible but used in recognition process (for example p-pen pressure, s-speed of writing, a- pen angle). Less complicated models can take $h(p_1,p_2,...,p_m) = 0$ and then the formula of interpolation (1) looks as follows:

$$y(c) = \gamma \cdot y_i + (1 - \gamma)y_{i+1}. \tag{7}$$

Formula (7) represents the simplest linear interpolation for basic probability distribution if $\gamma=\alpha$. 2D curves are two-dimensional subspace of N-dimensional feature space, for example (x,y,p,s,a,t) when $N=6$. If the recognition process is working "offline" and features p-pen pressure, s-speed of writing, a- pen angle or another feature t are not given, the only information before recognition is situated in x,y-points' coordinates.

After pre-processing (binarization, thinning, size standarization), feature extraction is second part of biometric identification. If the recognition process is "online" and features p-pen pressure, s-speed of writing, a- pen angle or some feature t are given, then there is more information in the process of author recognition, identification or verification in a feature space (x,y,p,s,a,t) of dimension $N = 6$ or others. Some person may know how the signature of another man looks like, but other extremely important features p,s,a,t are not visible. Dimension N of a feature space may be very high, but this is no problem. As it is illustrated (Fig.10-11) the problem connected with the curse of dimensionality with feature selection does not matter. There is no need to fix which feature is less important and can be eliminated. Every feature is very important and each of them can be interpolated between the nodes using PFC high-dimensional interpolation. For example pressure of the pen p differs during the signature writing and p is changing for particular letters or fragments of the signature. Then feature vector (x,y,p) of dimension $N_1 = 3$ is dealing with p interpolation at the point (x,y) via modeling functions (4)-(6) or others. If angle of the pen a differs during the signature writing and a is changing for particular letters or fragments of the signature, then feature vector (x,y,a) of dimension $N_1 = 3$ is dealing with a interpolation at the point (x,y) via modeling functions (4)-(6) or others. If speed of the writing s differs during the signature writing and s is changing for particular letters or fragments of the signature, then feature vector (x,y,s) of dimension $N_1 = 3$ is dealing with s interpolation at the point (x,y) via modeling functions (4)-(6) or others. This PFC 3D interpolation is the same like in chapter 3.1 grey scale image retrieval but for selected pairs (α_1,α_2) – only for the points of signature between $(x_1,y_1,2)$ and $(x_2,y_2,10)$.

If a feature sub-space is dimension $N_1 = 4$ and feature vector is for example (x,y,p,s), then PFC 4D interpolation is the same like in chapter 3.2 color image retrieval but for selected pairs (α_1,α_2) – only for the points of signature between $(x_1,y_1,2,1)$ and $(x_2,y_2,10,9)$.

If a feature sub-space is dimension $N_1 = 5$ and feature vector is for example (x,y,p,s,a), then PFC 5D interpolation is the same like in chapter 3.2 color image retrieval but for selected pairs (α_1,α_2) – only for the points of signature between $(x_1,y_1,2,1,30)$ and $(x_2,y_2,10,9,60)$.

Tables 4-6 are the examples of denotation for the features that are not visible during the signing or handwriting but very important in the process of "online" recognition, identification or verification.

Table 4. Reconstructed speed of the writing s at the pixels of signature

2	3	0	0	0	0	0	0	0
0	0	4	5	0	0	0	0	0
0	0	0	0	6	0	0	0	0
0	0	0	0	0	7	0	0	0
0	0	0	0	0	0	8	0	0
0	0	0	0	0	0	0	9	0
0	0	0	0	0	0	0	0	10
0	0	0	0	0	0	0	0	10
0	0	0	0	0	0	0	0	10

Table 5. Reconstructed pen pressure p and speed of the writing s as (p,s) at the pixels of signature

2,1	3,1	0	0	0	0	0	0	0
0	0	4,2	5,2	0	0	0	0	0
0	0	0	0	6,3	0	0	0	0
0	0	0	0	0	7,4	0	0	0
0	0	0	0	0	0	8,5	0	0
0	0	0	0	0	0	0	9,6	0
0	0	0	0	0	0	0	0	10,7
0	0	0	0	0	0	0	0	10,8
0	0	0	0	0	0	0	0	10,9

Table 6. Reconstructed pen pressure p, speed of the writing s and angle a as (p,s,a) at the pixels of signature

2,1,30	3,1,30	0	0	0	0	0	0	0
0	0	4,2,32	5,2,34	0	0	0	0	0
0	0	0	0	6,3,37	0	0	0	0
0	0	0	0	0	7,4,43	0	0	0
0	0	0	0	0	0	8,5,45	0	0
0	0	0	0	0	0	0	9,6,46	0
0	0	0	0	0	0	0	0	10,7,53
0	0	0	0	0	0	0	0	10,8,56
0	0	0	0	0	0	0	0	10,9,60

Even if from technical reason or other reasons only some points of signature or handwriting (feature nodes) are given in the process of "online" recognition, identification or verification, the values of features between nodes are computed via multidimensional PFC interpolation like for example between $(x_1,y_1,2)$ and $(x_2,y_2,10)$ on Table 4, between $(x_1,y_1,2,1)$ and $(x_2,y_2,10,9)$ on Table 5 or between $(x_1,y_1,2,1,30)$ and $(x_2,y_2,10,9,60)$ on Table 6. Reconstructed features are compared with the features in the basis of patterns like parameter y in (8) and appropriate criterion gives the result.

So persons with the parameters of their signatures are allocated in the basis of patterns. Every letter or a part of signature is modeled by PFC via three factors: the set of high-dimensional feature nodes, probability distribution function $\gamma = F(\alpha)$ and nodes combination h. These three factors are chosen individually for each letter or a part of signature therefore this information about modeled curves seems to be enough for specific PFC multidimensional curve interpolation and handwriting identification. What is very important, PFC N-dimensional modeling is independent of the language or a kind of symbol (letters, numbers, characters or others).

SOLUTIONS AND RECOMMENDATIONS

Proposed method, called Probabilistic Features Combination (PFC), is the method of N-dimensional data interpolation and extrapolation using the set of key points (knots or nodes). Nodes can be treated as characteristic points of data for modeling and analyzing. The model of data can be built by choice of probability distribution function and nodes combination. PFC modeling via nodes combination and parameter γ as probability distribution function enables value anticipation in risk analysis and decision making. N-dimensional object is extrapolated and interpolated via nodes combination and different functions as discrete or continuous probability distribution functions: polynomial, sine, cosine, tangent, cotangent, logarithm, exponent, arc sin, arc cos, arc tan, arc cot or power function.

FUTURE RESEARCH DIRECTIONS

Future trends will go to various directions: how to fix the best probability distribution function for the nodes, how to calculate the most appropriate nodes combination and what extrapolation is the most valuable in decision making and risk analysis.

CONCLUSION

The method of Probabilistic Features Combination (PFC) enables interpolation and modeling of high-dimensional data using features' combinations and different coefficients γ as modeling function. Functions for γ calculations are chosen individually at each data modeling and it is treated as *N*-dimensional probability distribution function: γ depends on initial requirements and features' specifications. PFC method leads to data interpolation as handwriting or signature identification and image retrieval via discrete set of feature vectors in N-dimensional feature space. So PFC method makes possible the combination of two important problems: interpolation and modeling in a matter of image retrieval or writer identification. PFC interpolation develops a linear interpolation in multidimensional feature spaces into other functions as *N*-dimensional probability distribution functions. Future works are going to applications of PFC method in biometric recognition, computer vision and artificial intelligence.

What is the most important feature of MHR and PNC methods? Interpolation methods and curve fitting represent so huge problem that each individual interpolation is exceptional and requires specific solutions. PNC method is such a novel tool with its all pros and cons. The user has to decide which interpolation method is the best in a single situation. The choice is yours if you have any choice. Presented method is such a new possibility for curve fitting and interpolation when specific data (for example handwritten symbol or character) starts up with no rules for polynomial interpolation. The chapter consists of two generalizations: generalization of previous MHR method with various nodes combinations and generalization of linear interpolation with different (no basic) probability distribution functions and nodes combinations. The method of Probabilistic Nodes Combination (PNC) enables interpolation and modeling of two-dimensional curves using nodes combinations and different coefficients γ: polynomial, sinusoidal, cosinusoidal, tangent, cotangent, logarithmic, exponential, arc sin, arc cos, arc tan, arc cot or power function, also inverse functions. This probabilistic view is novel approach a problem of modeling and interpolation. Computer vision and pattern recognition are interested in appropriate methods of shape representation and curve modeling. PNC method represents the possibilities of shape reconstruction and curve interpolation via the choice of nodes combination and probability distribution function for interpolated points. It seems to be quite new look at the problem of contour representation and curve modeling in artificial intelligence and computer vision. Function for γ calculations is chosen individually at each curve modeling and it is treated as probability distribution function: γ depends on initial requirements and curve specifications. PNC method leads to curve interpolation as handwriting modeling via discrete set of fixed knots. So PNC makes possible the combination of two important problems: interpolation and modeling. The method of Probabilistic Features Combination (PFC) enables interpolation and modeling of high-dimensional N data using features' combinations and different coefficients γ: polynomial, sinusoidal, cosinusoidal, tangent, cotangent, logarithmic, exponential, arc sin, arc cos, arc tan, arc cot or power function. Functions for γ calculations are chosen individually at each data modeling and it is treated as N-dimensional probability distribution function: γ depends on initial requirements and features' specifications. PFC method leads to data interpolation as handwriting or signature identification and image retrieval via discrete set of feature vectors in N-dimensional feature space. So PFC method makes possible the combination of two important problems: interpolation and modeling in a matter of image retrieval or writer identification. Main features of PFC method are: PFC interpolation develops a linear interpolation in multidimensional feature spaces into other functions as N-dimensional probability distribution functions; PFC is a generalization of MHR method and PNC method via different nodes combinations; interpolation of L points is connected with the computational cost of rank $O(L)$ as in MHR and PNC method; nodes combination and coefficients γ are crucial in the process of data probabilistic parameterization and interpolation: they are computed individually for a single feature. Future works are going to applications of PFC method in signature and handwriting biometric recognition: choice and features of nodes combinations h and coefficients γ.

Proposed method, called Probabilistic Features Combination (PFC), is the method of N-dimensional data interpolation and extrapolation using the set of key points (knots or nodes). Nodes can be treated as characteristic points of data for modeling and analyzing. The model of data can be built by choice of probability distribution function and nodes combination. PFC modeling via nodes combination and parameter γ as probability distribution function enables value anticipation in risk analysis and decision making. N-dimensional object is extrapolated and interpolated via nodes combination and different functions as discrete or continuous probability distribution functions: polynomial, sine, cosine, tangent, cotangent, logarithm, exponent, arc sin, arc cos, arc tan, arc cot or power function. The method of Probabilistic Features Combination (PFC) enables interpolation and modeling of high-dimensional data using features' combinations and different coefficients γ as modeling function. Functions for γ calculations are chosen individually at each data modeling and it is treated as *N*-dimensional probability distribution function: γ depends on initial requirements and features' specifications. PFC method leads to data interpolation as handwriting or signature identification and image retrieval via discrete set of feature vectors in N-dimensional feature space. So PFC method makes possible the combination of two important problems: interpolation and modeling in a matter of image retrieval or writer identification. PFC interpolation develops a linear interpolation in multidimensional feature spaces into other functions as *N*-dimensional probability distribution functions. Future works are going to applications of PFC method in biometric recognition, computer vision and artificial intelligence. Nodes are treated as characteristic points of data for modeling and analyzing. The model of data can be built by choice of probability distribution function and nodes combination. PFC modeling via nodes combination and parameter γ as probability distribution function enables value anticipation in risk analysis and decision making. Two-dimensional object is extrapolated and interpolated via nodes combination and different functions as discrete or continuous probability distribution functions: polynomial, sine, cosine, tangent, cotangent, logarithm, exponent, arc sin, arc cos, arc tan, arc cot or power function. Functions for γ calculations are chosen individually at each data modeling and it is treated as 2-dimensional probability distribution function: γ depends on initial requirements and features' specifications. PFC method leads to data interpolation as handwriting or signature identification and image retrieval via discrete set of feature vectors in 2-dimensional feature space. So PFC method makes possible the combination of two important problems: interpolation and modeling in a matter of image retrieval or writer identification. PFC interpolation develops a linear interpolation in multidimensional feature spaces into other functions as two-dimensional probability distribution functions. Future works are going to applications of PFC method in biometric recognition, computer vision and artificial intelligence.

REFERENCES

Bulacu, M., & Schomaker, L. (2007). Text-independent writer identification and verification using textural and allographic features. *IEEE Transactions on Pattern Analysis and Machine Intelligence*, *29*(4), 701–717. doi:10.1109/TPAMI.2007.1009 PMID:17299226

Bulacu, M., Schomaker, L., & Brink, A. (2007). Text-independent writer identification and verification on off-line Arabic handwriting. *International Conference on Document Analysis and Recognition*, 769–773.

Chapra, S. C. (2012). *Applied Numerical Methods*. McGraw-Hill.

Chen, J., Cheng, W., & Lopresti, D. (2011). Using perturbed handwriting to support writer identification in the presence of severe data constraints. Document Recognition and Retrieval, 1–10. doi:10.1117/12.876497

Chen, J., Lopresti, D., & Kavallieratou, E. (2010). The impact of ruling lines on writer identification. *International Conference on Frontiers in Handwriting Recognition*, 439–444. doi:10.1109/ICFHR.2010.75

Collins, G. W. II. (2003). *Fundamental Numerical Methods and Data Analysis*. Case Western Reserve University.

Djeddi, C., & Souici-Meslati, L. (2010). A texture based approach for Arabic writer identification and verification. *International Conference on Machine and Web Intelligence*, 115–120.

Djeddi, C., & Souici-Meslati, L. (2011). Artificial immune recognition system for Arabic writer identification. *International Symposium on Innovation in Information and Communication Technology*, 159–165. doi:10.1109/ISIICT.2011.6149612

Galloway, M. M. (1975). Texture analysis using gray level run lengths. *Computer Graphics and Image Processing*, 4(2), 172–179. doi:10.1016/S0146-664X(75)80008-6

Garain, U., & Paquet, T. (2009). Off-line multi-script writer identification using AR coefficients. *International Conference on Document Analysis and Recognition*, 991–995. doi:10.1109/ICDAR.2009.222

Ghiasi, G., & Safabakhsh, R. (2013). Offline text-independent writer identification using codebook and efficient code extraction methods. *Image and Vision Computing*, 31(5), 379–391. doi:10.1016/j.imavis.2013.03.002

Jakóbczak, D. J. (2014). *2D Curve Modeling via the Method of Probabilistic Nodes Combination-Shape Representation, Object Modeling and Curve Interpolation-Extrapolation with the Applications*. Saarbrucken: LAP Lambert Academic Publishing.

Marti, U.-V., & Bunke, H. (2002). The IAM-database: An English sentence database for offline handwriting recognition. *Int. J. Doc. Anal. Recognit.*, *5*(1), 39–46. doi:10.1007/s100320200071

Nosary, A., Heutte, L., & Paquet, T. (2004). Unsupervised writer adaption applied to handwritten text recognition. *Pattern Recognition Letters*, *37*(2), 385–388. doi:10.1016/S0031-3203(03)00185-7

Ozaki, M., Adachi, Y., & Ishii, N. (2006). Examination of effects of character size on accuracy of writer recognition by new local arc method. *International Conference on Knowledge-Based Intelligent Information and Engineering Systems*, 1170–1175. doi:10.1007/11893004_148

Ralston, A., & Rabinowitz, P. (2001). *A First Course in Numerical Analysis* (2nd ed.). New York: Dover Publications.

Schlapbach, A., & Bunke, H. (2004). Using HMM based recognizers for writer identification and verification. *9th Int. Workshop on Frontiers in Handwriting Recognition*, 167–172. doi:10.1109/IWFHR.2004.107

Schlapbach, A., & Bunke, H. (2006). Off-line writer identification using Gaussian mixture models. *International Conference on Pattern Recognition*, 992–995.

Schlapbach, A., & Bunke, H. (2007). A writer identification and verification system using HMM based recognizers. *Pattern Analysis & Applications*, *10*(1), 33–43. doi:10.1007/s10044-006-0047-5

Schomaker, L., Franke, K., & Bulacu, M. (2007). Using codebooks of fragmented connected-component contours in forensic and historic writer identification. *Pattern Recognition Letters*, *28*(6), 719–727. doi:10.1016/j.patrec.2006.08.005

Schumaker, L. L. (2007). *Spline Functions: Basic Theory*. Cambridge Mathematical Library. doi:10.1017/CBO9780511618994

Shahabinejad, F., & Rahmati, M. (2007). A new method for writer identification and verification based on Farsi/Arabic handwritten texts. *Ninth International Conference on Document Analysis and Recognition (ICDAR 2007)*, 829–833.

Siddiqi, I., Cloppet, F., & Vincent, N. (2009). Contour based features for the classification of ancient manuscripts. Conference of the International Graphonomics Society, 226–229.

Siddiqi, I., & Vincent, N. (2010). Text independent writer recognition using redundant writing patterns with contour-based orientation and curvature features. *Pattern Recognition Letters*, *43*(11), 3853–3865. doi:10.1016/j.patcog.2010.05.019

Van, E. M., Vuurpijl, L., Franke, K., & Schomaker, L. (2005). The WANDA measurement tool for forensic document examination. *J. Forensic Doc. Exam.*, *16*, 103–118.

Zhang, D., & Lu, G. (2004). Review of Shape Representation and Description Techniques. *Pattern Recognition*, *1*(37), 1–19. doi:10.1016/j.patcog.2003.07.008

ADDITIONAL READING

Ballard, D. H. (1982). *Computer Vision*. New York, USA: Prentice Hall.

Basu, S., & Bresler, Y. (2000). $O(N^2 log_2 N)$ filtered backprojection reconstruction algorithm for tomography. *IEEE Transactions on Image Processing*, *9*(10), 1760–1773. doi:10.1109/83.869187 PMID:18262914

Brankov, J. G., Yang, Y., & Wernick, M. N. (2004). Tomographic image reconstruction based on a Content – Adaptive Mesh Model. *IEEE Transactions on Medical Imaging*, *2*(23), 202–212. doi:10.1109/TMI.2003.822822 PMID:14964565

Brasse, D., & Defrise, M. (2004). Fast fully 3-D image reconstruction in PET using planograms. *IEEE Transactions on Medical Imaging*, *4*(23), 413–425. doi:10.1109/TMI.2004.824231 PMID:15084067

Cetin, M., Karl, W. C., & Willsky, A. S. (2002, September). *Edge – preserving image reconstruction for coherent imaging application*. Paper presented at the IEEE International Conference on Image Processsing, Rochester, NY, USA. doi:10.1109/ICIP.2002.1039992

Chlebus, E., & Cholewa, M. (1999). Rapid prototyping – rapid tooling. *CADCAM Forum*, *11*, 23-28.

Choraś, R. S. (2005). *Computer Vision*. Warsaw, Poland: Exit.

Cocozza-Thivent, C., Eymard, R., Mercier, S., & Roussignol, M. (2006). Characterization of the Marginal Distributions of Markov Processes Used in Dynamic Reliability. *Journal of Applied Mathematics and Stochastic Analysis. Article ID*, *92156*, 1–18.

Cormen, T. H., Leiserson, C. E., & Rivest, R. L. (1996). *Introduction to algorithms*. Massachusetts, USA: the Massachusetts Institute of Technology Press and McGraw-Hill.

Dahlquist, G., & Bjoerck, A. (1974). *Numerical Methods*. New York, USA: Prentice Hall.

Defrise, M. (2001). A short readers guide to 3D tomographic reconstruction. *Computerized Medical Imaging and Graphics*, *25*(2), 113–116. doi:10.1016/S0895-6111(00)00061-6 PMID:11137787

Dejdumrong, N. (2007). A Shape Preserving Verification Techniques for Parametric Curves. *Computer Graphics, Imaging and Visualization. CGIV*, *2007*, 163–168.

Dryja, M., Jankowska, J., & Jankowski, M. (1982). *Survey of numerical methods and algorithms. Part II*. Warsaw, Poland: WNT.

Dyn, N., Levin, D., & Gregory, J. A. (1987). A 4-Point Interpolatory Subdivision Scheme for Curve Design. *Computer Aided Geometric Design*, *4*(4), 257–268. doi:10.1016/0167-8396(87)90001-X

Eldar, Y. C. (2001). *Quantum Signal Processing*. (Unpublished doctoral dissertation). Massachusetts Institute of Technology, USA.

Eldar, Y. C., & Oppenheim, A. V. (2002). Quantum Signal Processing. *IEEE Signal Processing Magazine*, *6*(19), 12–32. doi:10.1109/MSP.2002.1043298

Fortuna, Z., Macukow, B., & Wąsowski, J. (1982). *Numerical methods*. Warsaw, Poland: WNT.

Jakóbczak, D. (2005). Hurwitz-Radon matrices and their children. *Computer Science*, *5*(8), 29–38.

Jakóbczak, D. (2007). 2D and 3D Image Modeling Using Hurwitz-Radon Matrices. *Polish Journal of Environmental Studies*, *4A*(16), 104–107.

Jakóbczak, D. (2009). Curve Interpolation Using Hurwitz-Radon Matrices. *Polish Journal of Environmental Studies*, *3B*(18), 126–130.

Jakóbczak, D. (2010). Shape Representation and Shape Coefficients via Method of Hurwitz-Radon Matrices. *Lecture Notes in Computer Science*, *6374*, 411–419. doi:10.1007/978-3-642-15910-7_47

Jakóbczak, D. (2010). Object Modeling Using Method of Hurwitz-Radon Matrices of Rank k. In W. Wolski & M. Borawski (Eds.), *Computer Graphics: Selected Issues* (pp. 79–90). Szczecin, Poland: University of Szczecin Press.

Jakóbczak, D. (2011). Curve Parameterization and Curvature via Method of Hurwitz-Radon Matrices. *Image Processing & Communications-. International Journal (Toronto, Ont.)*, *1-2*(16), 49–56.

Jakóbczak, D. (2011). Data Extrapolation and Decision Making via Method of Hurwitz-Radon Matrices. *Lecture Notes in Computer Science*, *6922*, 173–182. doi:10.1007/978-3-642-23935-9_17

Jakóbczak, D. (2011). Curve Extrapolation and Data Analysis using the Method of Hurwitz-Radon Matrices. *Folia Oeconomica Stetinensia*. 9(17)/2010, 121-138.

Jakóbczak, D. (2013). Probabilistic Modeling of Signature using the Method of Hurwitz-Radon Matrices. *Global Perspectives on Artificial Intelligence*, *1*(1), 1–7.

Jankowska, J., & Jankowski, M. (1981). *Survey of numerical methods and algorithms. Part I*. Warsaw, Poland: WNT.

Kontaxakis, G., & Strauss, L. G. (1998). Maximum likelihood algorithms for image reconstruction in Positron Emission Tomography. *Radionuclides for Oncology – Current Status and Future Aspects, 1998,* 73-106.

Kowalczuk, Z., & Wiszniewski, B. (Eds.). (2007). *Intelligent data mining in diagnostic purposes: Automatics and informatics*. Gdansk, Poland: PWNT.

Kozera, R. (2004). *Curve Modeling via Interpolation Based on Multidimensional Reduced Data*. Gliwice, Poland: Silesian University of Technology Press.

Kundur, D., & Hatzinakos, D. (1998). A novel blind deconvolution scheme for image restoration using recursive filtering. *IEEE Transactions on Signal Processing*, *2*(46), 375–390. doi:10.1109/78.655423

Laine, A., & Zong, X. (1996). *Border identification of echocardiograms via multiscale edge detection and shape modeling.* Paper presented at the IEEE International Conference on Image Processsing, Lausanne, Switzerland. doi:10.1109/ICIP.1996.560486

Lang, S. (1970). *Algebra.* Reading, Massachusetts, USA: Addison-Wesley Publishing Company.

Le Buhan Jordan, C., Bossen, F., & Ebrahimi, T. (1997). *Scalable shape representation for content based visual data compression.* Paper presented at the International Conference on Image Processing, Santa Barbara, CA, USA. doi:10.1109/ICIP.1997.647962

Liu, T., & Geiger, D. (1999). Approximate tree matching and shape similarity. *Int. Conf. Computer Vision.* Corfu, Greece.

Lorton, A., Fouladirad, M., & Grall, A. (2013). A Methodology for Probabilistic Model-based Prognosis. *European Journal of Operational Research, 225*(3), 443–454. doi:10.1016/j.ejor.2012.10.025

Marker, J., Braude, I., Museth, K., & Breen, D. (2006). Contour-based surface reconstruction using implicit curve fitting, and distance field filtering and interpolation. *Volume Graphics, 2006,* 1–9.

Meyer, Y. (1993). *Wavelets: algorithms & applications.* Philadelphia, USA: Society for Industrial and Applied Mathematics.

Pergler, M., & Freeman, A. (2008). Probabilistic Modeling as an Exploratory Decision-Making Tool. *McKinsey Working Papers on Risk.* 6, 1-18.

Poggio, T., & Smale, S. (2003). The mathematics of learning: Dealing with data. *Notices of the American Mathematical Society, 5*(50), 537–544.

Przelaskowski, A. (2005). *Data compression.* Warsaw, Poland: BTC.

Rogers, D. F. (2001). *An Introduction to NURBS with Historical Perspective.* Morgan Kaufmann Publishers.

Rutkowski, L., Siekmann, J., Tadeusiewicz, R., & Zadeh, A. (Eds.). (2004). *Lecture notes on artificial intelligence: Artificial intelligence and soft computing.* Berlin-Heidelberg, Germany: Springer-Verlag.

Saber, E., Xu, Y., & Murat Tekalp, A. (2005). Partial shape recognition by sub-matrix matching for partial matching guided image labeling. *Pattern Recognition, 38*(10), 1560–1573. doi:10.1016/j.patcog.2005.03.027

Sebastian, T. B., Klein, P. N., & Kimia, B. B. (2003). On aligning curves. *IEEE Transactions on Pattern Analysis and Machine Intelligence*, 25(1), 116–124. doi:10.1109/TPAMI.2003.1159951

Tadeusiewicz, R., & Flasiński, M. (1991). *Image Recognition*. Warsaw, Poland: PWN.

Vakhania, N. (1993). Orthogonal random vectors and the Hurwitz – Radon-Eckmann theorem. *Proc. of the Georgian Academy of Sciences-Mathematics, 1(1)*, 109-125.

Willis, M. (2000). *Algebraic reconstruction algorithms for remote sensing image enhancement*. Unpublished doctoral dissertation, Department of Electrical and Computer Engineering, Brigham Young University.

Xu, Fang, & Mueller, K. (2005). Accelerating popular tomographic reconstruction algorithms on commodity PC graphics hardware. *IEEE Transactions on Nuclear Science*, 3(52), 654–661.

Zaletelj, J., & Tasic, J. F. (2003). *Optimization and tracking of polygon vertices for shape coding*. Berlin-Heidelberg, Germany: Springer-Verlag. doi:10.1007/978-3-540-45179-2_52

Zhang, J. K., Davidson, T., & Wong, K. M. (2004). Efficient design of orthonormal wavelet bases for signal representation. *IEEE Transactions on Signal Processing*, 7(52), 1983–1996. doi:10.1109/TSP.2004.828923

KEY TERMS AND DEFINITIONS

Contour Modeling: Calculation of unknown points of the object contour having information about some points of the object contour.

Curve Interpolation: Computing new and unknown points of a curve and creating a graph of a curve using existing data points – interpolation nodes.

Data Extrapolation: Calculation of unknown values for the points situated outside the ranges of nodes.

Hurwitz – Radon Matrices: A family of skew – symmetric and orthogonal matrices with columns and rows that create, together with identical matrix, the base in vector spaces of dimensions $N = 2$, 4 or 8.

MHR Method: The method of curve interpolation and extrapolation using linear (convex) combinations of OHR operators.

Object Interpolation: Computing new and unknown points of an object and creating a figure using existing data points – interpolation nodes.

OHR Operator: Matrix operator of Hurwitz – Radon built from coordinates of interpolation nodes.

Value Anticipation: Foreseeing next value when last value is known.

Chapter 7
Applications of PNC in Numerical Methods

ABSTRACT

Nodes are treated as characteristic points of data for modeling and analyzing. The model of data can be built by choice of probability distribution function and nodes combination. Two-dimensional object is extrapolated and interpolated via nodes combination and different functions as discrete or continuous probability distribution functions: polynomial, sine, cosine, tangent, cotangent, logarithm, exponent, arc sin, arc cos, arc tan, arc cot or power function. Curve interpolation represents one of the most important problems in mathematics and computer science: how to model the curve via discrete set of two-dimensional points? Also the matter of shape representation (as closed curve - contour) and curve parameterization is still opened. For example pattern recognition, signature verification or handwriting identification problems are based on curve modeling via the choice of key points. So interpolation is not only a pure mathematical problem but important task in computer vision and artificial intelligence.

INTRODUCTION

Numerical modeling is still developing branch of the computer science: operational research (for example probabilistic model-based prognosis) (Lorton, Fouladirad & Grall, 2013), decision making techniques and probabilistic modeling (Pergler & Freeman, 2008), artificial intelligence

DOI: 10.4018/978-1-5225-2531-8.ch007

and machine learning. There are used different aspects of probabilistic methods: stochastic processes and stochastic model-based techniques, Markov processes (Cocozza-Thivent, Eymard, Mercier & Roussignol, 2006), Poisson processes, Gamma processes, a Monte Carlo method, Bayes rule, conditional probability and many probability distributions. In this chapter the goal of probability distribution function is to describe the position of unknown points between given interpolation nodes. Two-dimensional curve (opened or closed) is used to represent the data points. So problem statement of this chapter is: how to reconstruct (interpolate) missing points of 2D curve having the set of interpolation nodes (key points) and using the information about probabilistic distribution of unknown points. For example the simplest basic distribution leads to the easiest interpolation – linear interpolation. Apart from probability distribution, additionally there is the second factor of proposed interpolation method: nodes combination. The simplest nodes combination is zero. Thus proposed curve modeling is based on two agents: probability distribution and nodes combination. Curve interpolation (Collins, 2003) represents one of the most important problems in mathematics and computer science: how to model the curve (Chapra, 2012) via discrete set of two-dimensional points (Ralston & Rabinowitz, 2001)? Also the matter of shape representation (as closed curve-contour) and curve parameterization is still opened (Zhang & Lu, 2004). For example pattern recognition, signature verification or handwriting identification problems are based on curve modeling via the choice of key points. So interpolation is not only a pure mathematical problem but important task in computer vision and artificial intelligence. The chapter wants to approach a problem of curve modeling by characteristic points. Proposed method relies on nodes combination and functional modeling of curve points situated between the basic set of key points. The functions that are used in calculations represent whole family of elementary functions with inverse functions: polynomials, trigonometric, cyclometric, logarithmic, exponential and power function. These functions are treated as probability distribution functions in the range [0;1]. Significant problem in machine vision and computer vision is that of appropriate 2D shape representation and reconstruction. Classical discussion about shape representation is based on the problem: contour versus skeleton. This monograph is voting for contour which forms boundary of the object. Contour of the object, represented by successive contour points, consists of information which allows us to describe many important features of the object as shape coefficients. 2D curve modeling and generation is a basic subject in many branches of industry and computer science, for example in the cad/

cam software. The representation of shape can have a great impact on the accuracy and effectiveness of object recognition. In the literature, shape has been represented by many options including curves, graph-based algorithms and medial axis to enable shape-based object recognition. Digital 2D curve (open or closed) can be represented by chain code (Freeman's code). Chain code depends on selection of the started point and transformations of the object. So Freeman's code is one of the method how to describe and to find contour of the object. Analog (continuous) version of Freeman's code is the curve α-s. Another contour representation and reconstruction is based on Fourier coefficients calculated in discrete Fourier transformation (DFT). These coefficients are used to fix similarity of the contours with different sizes or directions. If we assume that contour is built from segments of a line and fragments of circles or ellipses, hough transformation is applied to detect contour lines. Also geometrical moments of the object are used during the process of object shape representation. Contour is also applied in shape decomposition. Many branches of medicine, industry and manufacturing are looking for methods connected with geometry of the contour. Why and when should we use MHR and PNC methods? Interpolation methods and curve fitting represent so huge problem that each individual interpolation is exceptional and requires specific solutions. PNC method is such a novel tool with its all pros and cons. The user has to decide which interpolation method is the best in a single situation. The choice is yours if you have any choice. Presented method is such a new possibility for curve fitting and interpolation when specific data (for example handwritten symbol or character) starts up with no rules for polynomial interpolation. This book consists of two generalizations: generalization of previous MHR method with various nodes combinations and generalization of linear interpolation with different (no basic) probability distribution functions and nodes combinations.

BACKGROUND

An important problem in machine vision and computer vision (Ballard, 1982) is that of appropriate shape representation and reconstruction. Classical discussion about shape representation is based on the problem: contour versus skeleton. This chapter is voting for contour which forms boundary of the object. Contour of the object, represented by contour points, consists of information which allows us to describe many important features of the object as shape coefficients (Tadeusiewicz & Flasiński, 1991). In the chapter contour is dealing with a set of curves. Curve modeling and generation is a basic subject in many branches of industry and computer science, for example in the CAD/CAM software. The representation of shape has a great impact on the accuracy and effectiveness of object recognition (Saber, Yaowu & Murat Tekalp, 2005). In the literature, shape has been represented by many options including curves (Sebastian & Klein, 2003), graph-based algorithms and medial axis (Liu & Geiger, 1999) to enable shape-based object recognition. Digital curve (open or closed) can be represented by chain code (Freeman's code). Chain code depends on selection of the started point and transformations of the object. So Freeman's code is one of the method how to describe and to find contour of the object. An analog (continuous) version of Freeman's code is the curve α-s. Another contour representation and reconstruction is based on Fourier coefficients calculated in Discrete Fourier Transformation (DFT). These coefficients are used to fix similarity of the contours with different sizes or directions. If we assume that contour is built from segments of a line and fragments of circles or ellipses, Hough transformation is applied to detect contour lines. Also geometrical moments of the object are used during the process of object shape representation (Choraś, 2005). Nowadays methods apply mainly polynomial functions, for example Bernstein polynomials in Bezier curves, splines (Schumaker, 2007) and NURBS (Rogers, 2001). But Bezier curves don't represent the interpolation method and cannot be used for example in handwriting modeling with key points (interpolation nodes). In comparison PNC method with Bézier curves, Hermite curves and B-curves (*B-splines*) or NURBS one unpleasant feature of these curves has to be mentioned: small change of one characteristic point can result in unwanted change of whole reconstructed curve. Such a feature does not appear in proposed PNC method. Numerical methods for data interpolation are based on polynomial or trigonometric functions, for example Lagrange, Newton, Aitken and Hermite methods. These methods have many weak sides (Dahlquist & Bjoerck, 1974) and are not sufficient for curve interpolation in the situations when the curve cannot be build by polynomials or trigonometric functions. Also there exists several well established methods of curve modeling, for example shape-preserving techniques (Dejdumrong, 2007), subdivision algorithms (Dyn, Levin & Gregory, 1987) and others (Kozera, 2004) to overcome difficulties of polynomial interpolation, but probabilistic interpolation with nodes combination seems to be quite novel in the area of shape modeling. Proposed 2D curve interpolation is the functional modeling via any elementary functions and it helps us to fit the curve during the computations. The method of Probabilistic Nodes Combination (PNC) enables interpolation and modeling of two-dimensional curves using nodes combinations and different coefficients γ: polynomial, sinusoidal, cosinusoidal, tangent, cotangent, logarithmic, exponential, arc sin, arc cos, arc tan, arc cot or power function, also inverse functions. This probabilistic view is novel approach a problem of modeling and interpolation. Computer vision and pattern recognition are interested in appropriate methods of shape representation and curve modeling. PNC method represents the possibilities of shape reconstruction and curve interpolation via the choice of nodes combination and probability distribution function for interpolated points. It seems to be quite new look at the problem of contour representation and curve modeling in artificial intelligence and computer vision. Function for γ calculations is chosen individually at each curve modeling and it is treated as probability distribution function: γ depends on initial requirements and curve specifications. PNC method leads to curve interpolation as handwriting modeling via discrete set of fixed knots. So PNC makes possible the combination of two important problems: interpolation and modeling.

NUMERICAL METHODS: NUMERICAL ANALYSIS

Numerical Differentiation

Numerical calculations (Chapra, 2012) for derivative (Collins, 2003) are based on the definition of derivative in some points with known values (Ralston & Rabinowitz, 2001):

- Two-points ordinary difference:

$$f'\left(x_i\right) = \frac{f\left(x_{i+1}\right) - f\left(x_i\right)}{h} + O\left(h\right)$$

(1)

- Three-points ordinary difference:

$$f'\left(x_i\right) = \frac{-3f\left(x_i\right) + 4f\left(x_{i+1}\right) - f\left(x_{i+2}\right)}{2h} + O\left(h^2\right),$$

(2)

- Two-points back difference:

$$f'\left(x_i\right) = \frac{f\left(x_i\right) - f\left(x_{i-1}\right)}{h} + O\left(h\right), \tag{3}$$

- Three-points back difference:

$$f'\left(x_i\right) = \frac{f\left(x_{i-2}\right) - 4f\left(x_{i-1}\right) + 3f\left(x_i\right)}{2h} + O\left(h^2\right), \tag{4}$$

- Two-points central difference:

$$f'\left(x_i\right) = \frac{f\left(x_{i+1}\right) - f\left(x_{i-1}\right)}{2h} + O\left(h^2\right), \tag{5}$$

for first coordinates $x_{i-2}, x_{i-1}, x_i, x_{i+1}, x_{i+2}$ with distance h (Dahlquist & Bjoerck, 1974).

Example 1: Values of function $f\left(x\right)$ are in the Table 1.

Then there are approximations from formulas (1) – (5):

$$\rightarrow f'\left(x_0\right) = \frac{2,42 - 2,39}{1,51 - 1,5} = \frac{0,03}{0,01} = 3, \tag{1}$$

$$\rightarrow f'\left(x_0\right) = \frac{-3 \cdot 2,39 + 4 \cdot 2,42 - 2,45}{1,52 - 1,5} = \frac{0,06}{0,02} = 3, \tag{2}$$

Table 1. Function $f\left(x\right)$

i	-2	-1	0	1	2
x_i	$1,48$	$1,49$	$1,5$	$1,51$	$1,52$
$f\left(x_i\right)$	$2,34$	$2,36$	$2,39$	$2,42$	$2,45$

$$\rightarrow f'\left(x_0\right) = \frac{2,39 - 2,36}{1,5 - 1,49} = \frac{0,03}{0,01} = 3, \tag{3}$$

$$\rightarrow f'\left(x_0\right) = \frac{2,34 - 4 \cdot 2,36 + 3 \cdot 2,39}{1,5 - 1,48} = \frac{0,07}{0,02} = 3,5, \tag{4}$$

$$\left(5\right) \rightarrow f'\left(x_0\right) = \frac{2,42 - 2,36}{1,51 - 1,49} = \frac{0,06}{0,02} = 3. \tag{5}$$

Example 2: Values of function $f\left(x\right)$ are in the Table 2.

Then there are approximations from formulas (1) – (5):

$$\rightarrow f'\left(x_0\right) = \frac{1,25 - 1,43}{0,8 - 0,7} = \frac{-0,18}{0,1} = -1,8, \tag{1}$$

$$\rightarrow f'\left(x_0\right) = \frac{-3 \cdot 1,43 + 4 \cdot 1,25 - 1,11}{0,9 - 0,7} = \frac{-0,4}{0,2} = -2, \tag{2}$$

$$\rightarrow f'\left(x_0\right) = \frac{1,43 - 1,67}{0,7 - 0,6} = \frac{-0,24}{0,1} = -2,4, \tag{3}$$

Table 2. Function $f\left(x\right)$

i	-2	-1	0	1	2
x_i	$0,5$	$0,6$	$0,7$	$0,8$	$0,9$
$f\left(x_i\right)$	2	$1,67$	$1,43$	$1,25$	$1,11$

$$\rightarrow f'\left(x_0\right) = \frac{2 - 4 \cdot 1,67 + 3 \cdot 1,43}{0,7 - 0,5} = \frac{-0,39}{0,2} = -1,95, \tag{4}$$

$$\rightarrow f'\left(x_0\right) = \frac{1,25 - 1,67}{0,8 - 0,6} = \frac{-0,42}{0,2} = -2,1. \tag{5}$$

Now there are calculations for function $f\left(x\right) = 2^x$ interpolated by PNC (Jakóbczak, 2014) method with parameters:

$$\gamma = \log_2\left(\alpha^s + 1\right),$$

$$s = 1,$$

$$h = 0$$

and seven nodes, as shown in Figures 1 and 2.

Numerical values of derivative (Bhat Rama & Chakraverty, 2003) for function $f\left(x\right) = 2^x$ in $x_0 = 0.7$ and points interpolated via PNC method (Figures 1-2) are as follows:

- Two-points ordinary difference:

$$f'\left(0.7\right) = 1.2$$

- Three-points ordinary difference:

$$f'\left(0.7\right) = 1.25$$

- Two-points back difference:

$$f'\left(0.7\right) = 1.1$$

- Three-points back difference:

Figure 2. PNC interpolation of function y = 2ˣ

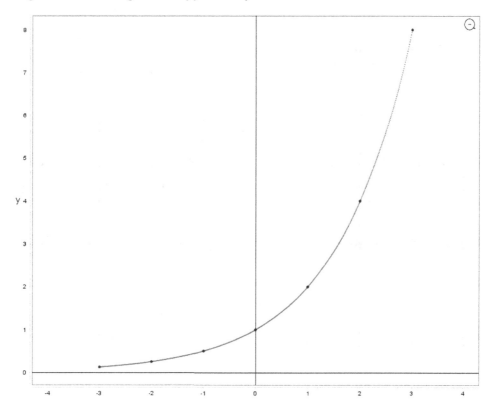

Figure 1. Nodes of function before PNC interpolation and modeling

Lp.	x	y
1	-3.0	0.125
2	-2.0	0.25
3	-1.0	0.5
4	0.0	1.0
5	1.0	2.0
6	2.0	4.0
7	3.0	8.0

$f'(0.7) = 1.1$

- Two-points central difference:

$f'(0.7) = 1.15$

Precise value of derivative for function $f(x) = 2^x$ in the point $x = 0.7$ is $f'(x) = 1.126$. Of course numerical formulas even for very accurate table function do not guarantee exact values (Zhang & Lu, 2004), but PNC modeling of function enables quite good interpolation and numerical calculations.

Numerical Integration

There are three basic methods of quadratures, which are described in this chapter: rectangle formula, trapezium formula and Simpson formula.

1. Rectangle formula:

$$I \approx h \sum_{i=1}^{n} f\left(\frac{x_{i-1} + x_i}{2}\right) \tag{6}$$

Figure 3. Graphic for rectangle formula

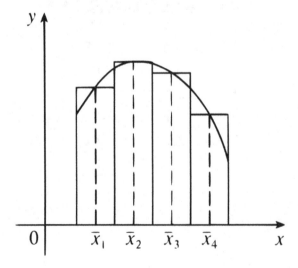

Here is an example of rectangle formula for $n = 4$ (four nodes):

$$\int\limits_{2}^{4} \frac{x}{x-1}\,dx,$$

$$h = \frac{4-2}{4} = \frac{1}{2}.$$

Rectangle formula:

$$\frac{1}{2} * \left[\frac{9}{5} + \frac{11}{7} + \frac{13}{9} + \frac{15}{11} \right] \cong 3.089.$$

Precise value:

$$\int\limits_{2}^{4} \frac{x}{x-1}\,dx \approx 3.098.$$

Second example of rectangle formula:

$$\int\limits_{1}^{3} x^2 dx, \ h_1 = \frac{1}{2}, \ h_2 = \frac{3}{2}.$$

Rectangle formula:

Table 3. Values of integrated function

	x_1	x_2	x_3	x_4
x	2.25	2.75	3.25	3.75
$f(x)$	$\dfrac{2.25}{1.25} = \dfrac{9}{5}$	$\dfrac{2.75}{1.75} = \dfrac{11}{7}$	$\dfrac{3.25}{2.25} = \dfrac{13}{9}$	$\dfrac{3.75}{2.75} = \dfrac{15}{11}$

Table 4. Values of integrated function

	x_1	x_2
x	$\dfrac{5}{4}$	$\dfrac{9}{4}$
$f(x)$	$\dfrac{25}{16}$	$\dfrac{81}{16}$

$$\left(\frac{1}{2} * \frac{25}{16}\right) + \left(\frac{3}{2} * \frac{81}{16}\right) \cong 8,375.$$

Precise value:

$$\int\limits_1^3 x^2 dx \approx 8,667 .$$

1.   Trapezium formula:

$$I \approx \sum_{i=0}^{n} \frac{1}{2} h \left(f_{i-1} + f_i\right) = h\left(\frac{1}{2} f_0 + f_1 + \ldots + f_n + \frac{1}{2} f_n\right) \qquad (7)$$

Example of trapezium formula for:

$$\int\limits_0^1 \sqrt{1 + x}\, dx ,$$

$$h = \frac{1 - 0}{3} = \frac{1}{3} .$$

Quadrature of trapezium method:

Figure 4. Graphic for trapezium formula

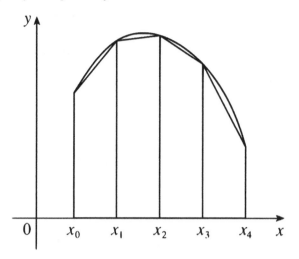

Table 5. Values for trapezium formula

	x_0	x_1	x_2	x_3
x	0	$\dfrac{1}{3}$	$\dfrac{2}{3}$	1
$f(x)$	1	$\sqrt{1+\dfrac{1}{3}}$	$\sqrt{1+\dfrac{2}{3}}$	$\sqrt{2}$

$$\frac{1}{3}\left(\frac{1}{2}*1+\sqrt{1+\frac{1}{3}}+\sqrt{1+\frac{2}{3}}+\frac{1}{2}*\sqrt{2}\right)\cong 1.217\,.$$

Precise integral:

$$\int_0^1 \sqrt{1+x}\,dx \approx 1.218\,.$$

Second example of trapezium formula:

Table 6. Values for trapezium formula

	x_0	x_1	x_2
x	1	$\dfrac{5}{2}$	3
$f\left(x\right)$	1	$\dfrac{2}{5}$	$\dfrac{1}{3}$

$$\int_{1}^{3} \frac{1}{x}\,dx\,,\ h_1 = \frac{3}{2}, h_1 = \frac{1}{2}.$$

Quadrature of trapezium method:

$$\left(\frac{\left(1+\dfrac{2}{5}\right)}{2} * \frac{3}{2}\right) + \left(\frac{\left(\dfrac{2}{5}+\dfrac{1}{3}\right)}{2} * \frac{1}{2}\right) \cong 1.233.$$

Precise integral:

$$\int_{1}^{3} \frac{1}{x}\,dx \approx 1.098.$$

1. Simpson formula:

$$I = h * \left[f\left(x_0\right) + 4f\left(x_1\right) + 2f\left(x_2\right) + 4f\left(x_3\right) + \ldots + 2f\left(x_{n-2}\right) + 4f\left(x_{n-1}\right) + f\left(x_n\right)\right]$$

(8)

Example of Simpson formula:

$$\int_{2}^{4} \frac{x}{x-1}\,dx\,,$$

Figure 5. Graphic for Simpson formula

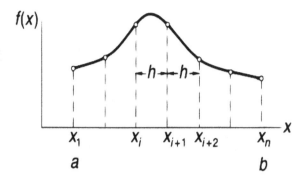

$$h = \frac{1}{12}.$$

Quadrature of Simpson method:

$$\frac{1}{12} * 2 + \frac{36}{5} + \frac{10}{7} + \frac{44}{9} + 3 + \frac{52}{9} + \frac{14}{5} + \frac{60}{11} + \frac{4}{3} \cong 3.098.$$

Precise integral:

$$\int_{2}^{4} \frac{x}{x-1} dx \approx 3.098.$$

Second example of Simpson formula:

$$\int_{1}^{3} \frac{1}{x+1} dx, h_1 = \frac{1}{6}, \ h_2 = \frac{1}{2}$$

Table 7. Values for Simpson method

	x_0	x_1	x_2	x_3	x_4	x_5	x_6	x_7	x_8
x	2	2.25	2.5	2.75	3	3.25	3.5	3.75	4
$f(x)$	2	$\frac{9}{5}$	$\frac{5}{3}$	$\frac{11}{7}$	$\frac{3}{2}$	$\frac{13}{9}$	$\frac{7}{5}$	$\frac{15}{11}$	$\frac{4}{3}$

Table 8. Values for Simpson method

	x_0	x_1	x_2	x_3	x_4
x	1	$\dfrac{5}{4}$	$\dfrac{3}{2}$	$\dfrac{9}{4}$	3
$f(x)$	$\dfrac{1}{2}$	$\dfrac{4}{9}$	$\dfrac{2}{5}$	$\dfrac{4}{13}$	$\dfrac{1}{4}$

Quadrature of Simpson method:

$$\left(\frac{3}{2}-1*\frac{\left(\frac{1}{2}+\frac{2}{5}\right)+4*\frac{4}{9}}{6}\right)+\left(3-\frac{3}{2}*\frac{\left(\frac{2}{5}+\frac{1}{4}\right)+4*\frac{4}{13}}{6}\right)\cong 0.916.$$

Precise integral:

$$\int\limits_{1}^{3}\frac{1}{x+1}\,dx \approx 0.693.$$

Now the example of function is interpolated using PNC method and then taken to numerical calculations. PNC modeling of function $f(x)=\dfrac{x}{x^2-1}$ is done with five nodes:

$$(-0.9;4.736),(-0.5;0.666),(0;0),(0.5;-0.666),(0.9;-4.736).$$

Precise graph of function $f(x)=\dfrac{x}{x^2-1}$ in the range [-1;1] is shown in Figure 6.

PNC modeling with parameters $\gamma=\left(2^\alpha-1\right)^s$, $s=1.2$, $h=0$ are shown in Figure 7.

PNC modeling with parameters: $\gamma = \log_2\left(\alpha^s + 1\right)$, $s = 0.945$, $h = 0$ are shown in Figure 8.

PNC modeling for $\gamma = \left(2^\alpha - 1\right)^s$, $s = 1.2$ and $h = 0$ gives very good approximation in the range $\left(-1;0\right)$ for function $f\left(x\right) = \dfrac{x}{x^2 - 1}$ (Table 9).

One can compare with exact values of function $f\left(x\right) = \dfrac{x}{x^2 - 1}$. See Table 10.

Figure 6. Graph of function $f\left(x\right) = \dfrac{x}{x^2 - 1}$

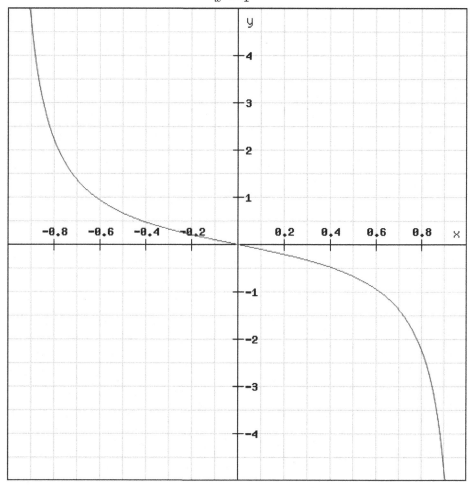

Figure 7. PNC modeling with exponential parameter

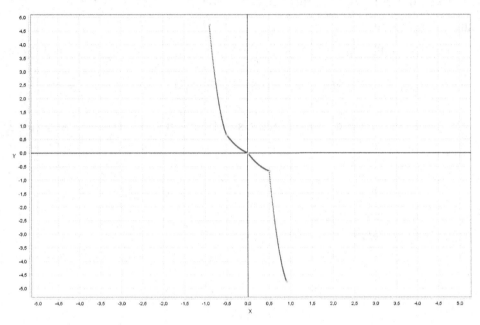

Figure 8. PNC modeling with logarithmic parameter

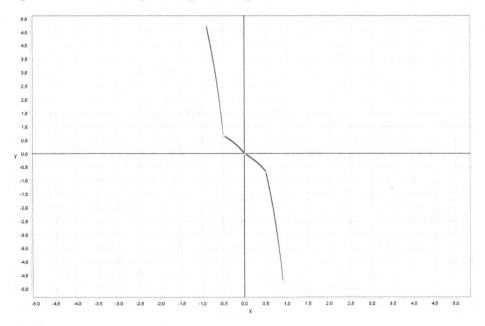

Table 9. Interpolated values f(x) via PNC method

x	−0.495	−0.49	−0.485	−0.48	−0.475	−0.47	−0.465	−0.46	−0.455
$f(x)$	0.655	0.644	0.633	0.623	0.612	0.601	0.591	0.581	0.571

In the range (0;1) quite good interpolation of function $f(x) = \dfrac{x}{x^2 - 1}$ is given for parameters: $\gamma = \log_2\left(\alpha^s + 1\right)$, $s = 0.945$ and $h = 0$. See Table 11.

One can compare with exact values of function $f(x) = \dfrac{x}{x^2 - 1}$ as shown in Table 12.

Precise integral of function $f(x) = \dfrac{x}{x^2 - 1}$ in the range $\left(-0.495; -0.02\right)$ is equal 0.14. In the range $\left(0.01; 0.475\right)$ integral of function $f(x) = \dfrac{x}{x^2 - 1}$ equals -0.128. For more accurate approximation in the range $\left(0; 0.9\right)$ PNC interpolation is done for parameters $\gamma = \log_2\left(\alpha^s + 1\right)$, $s = 0.945$ and $h = 0$. Here are numerical values of quadratures for values interpolated using PNC method.

Table 10. Precise values of function $f(x) = \dfrac{x}{x^2 - 1}$

x	−0.495	−0.49	−0.485	−0.48	−0.475	−0.47	−0.465	−0.46	−0.455
$f(x)$	0.656	0.645	0.634	0.624	0.613	0.603	0.593	0.583	0.574

Table 11. Interpolated values f(x) via PNC method

x	0.005	0.01	0.015	0.02	0.025	0.46	0.465	0.47	0.475
$f(x)$	−0.005	−0.009	−0.014	−0.018	−0.023	−0.582	−0.591	−0.601	−0.611

Table 12. Precise values of function $f(x) = \dfrac{x}{x^2 - 1}$

x	0.005	0.01	0.015	0.02	0.025	0.46	0.465	0.47	0.475
$f(x)$	-0.005	-0.010	-0.015	-0.02	-0.025	-0.583	-0.593	-0.603	-0.613

Figure 9. Area of integraf for PNC interpolation

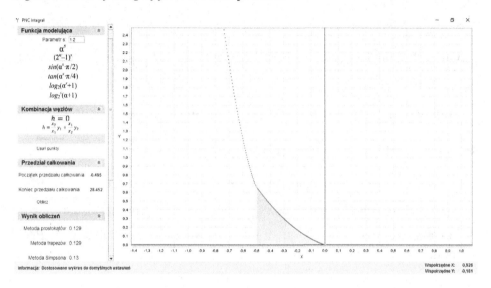

Numerical quadratures for function $f(x) = \dfrac{x}{x^2 - 1}$ interpolated via PNC method in the range $(-0.495; -0.02)$ are as follow:

- **Rectangle Method:** 0.129
- **Trapezium Method:** 0.129
- **Simpson's Method:** 0.13

Numerical quadratures for function $f(x) = \dfrac{x}{x^2 - 1}$ interpolated via PNC method in the range $(0.01; 0.475)$ are as follow:

- **Rectangle Method:** -0.127
- **Trapezium Method:** -0.127

Figure 10. PNC interpolation and a graph of inverse function

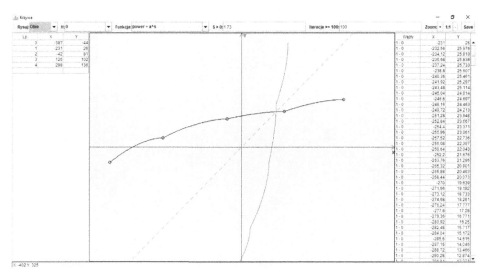

- **Simpson's Method:** -0.124

This examples show that any function can be modeled using PNC method for numerical calculations. Precise interpolation depends on the range and parameters γ, s, h. Interpolated values are used in other numerical methods in such a problem: solving non-linear equations (roots of function), searching values of inverse function or any applications for modeled curves.

Inverse Function

Searching for the inverse function is a big computational challenge. It is possible to achieve a graph of inverse function and values of points after PNC interpolation (Figure 10).

Root of the Function: Solution of Nonlinear Equations

Solving a nonlinear equations and searching for the root of function is also a huge numerical challenge (Gerald & Wheatley, 2003). It is possible to have a reconstructed point (Schumaker, 2007) with second coordinate $y = 0$ or very close to zero after PNC interpolation – point on axis OX (Figure 11-12).

Figure 11. PNC interpolation and a graph with the root of function

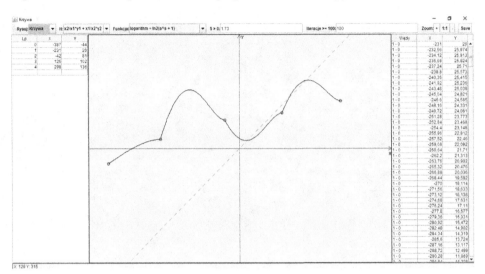

Figure 12. PNC interpolation and a graph with the root of function

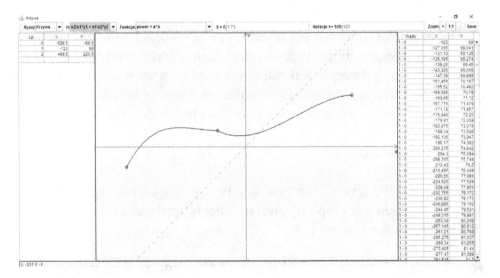

Geometrical Operations

PNC modeling enables geometrical operations (Chakraverty Snehashish, 2008) of the figure with low computational costs because of PNC interpolation for new nodes (Figures 13-16).

Figure 13. PNC interpolation of the object and geometrical translation

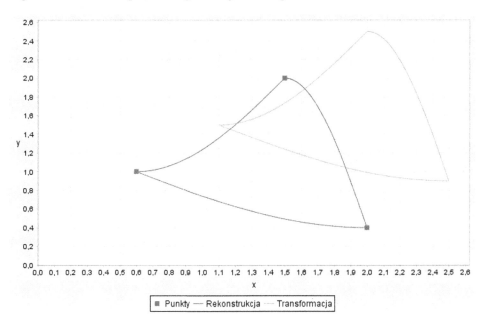

Figure 14. PNC interpolation of the object and geometrical operation

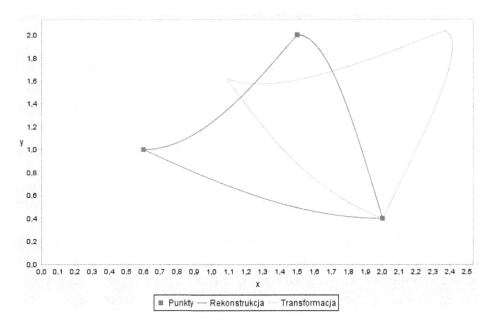

Figure 15. PNC modeling of the object and geometrical operation

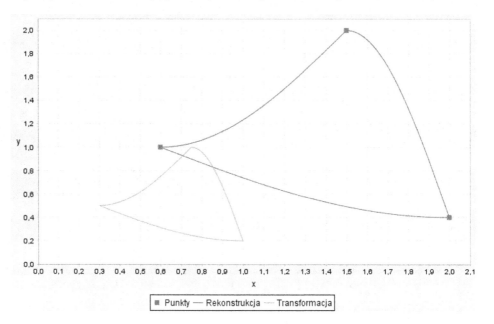

Proposed method, called Probabilistic Nodes Combination (PNC), is the method of 2D curve interpolation and extrapolation using the set of key points (knots or nodes). Nodes can be treated as characteristic points of data for modeling and analyzing. The model of data can be built by choice of probability distribution function and nodes combination. PNC modeling via nodes combination and parameter γ as probability distribution function enables value anticipation in risk analysis and decision making. Two-dimensional curve is extrapolated and interpolated via nodes combination and different functions as discrete or continuous probability distribution functions: polynomial, sine, cosine, tangent, cotangent, logarithm, exponent, arc sin, arc cos, arc tan, arc cot or power function. Novelty of this book consists of two generalizations: generalization of previous MHR method with various nodes combinations and generalization of linear interpolation with different (no basic) probability distribution functions and nodes combinations. Computer vision needs suitable methods of shape representation and contour reconstruction. One of them, invented by the author and called method of Hurwitz-Radon Matrices (MHR), can be used in representation and reconstruction of shapes of the objects in the plane. Proposed method is based on a family of Hurwitz-Radon (HR)

Figure 16. PNC interpolation of the figure and geometrical operation

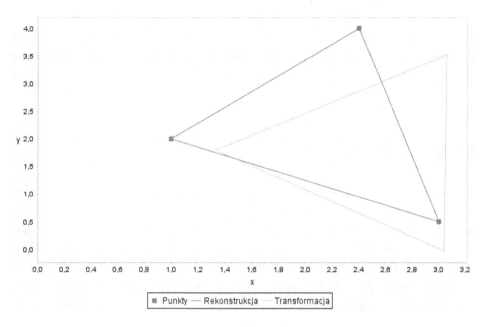

matrices. The matrices are skew-symmetric and possess columns composed of orthogonal vectors. 2D shape is represented by the set of successive nodes. It is shown how to create the orthogonal and discrete OHR operator and how to use it in a process of shape representation and reconstruction. Then MHR method is generalized to Probabilistic Nodes Combination (PNC) method.

SOLUTIONS AND RECOMMENDATIONS

Nodes are treated as characteristic points of data for modeling and analyzing. The model of data can be built by choice of probability distribution function and nodes combination. PFC modeling via nodes combination and parameter γ as probability distribution function enables value anticipation in risk analysis and decision making. Two-dimensional object is extrapolated and interpolated via nodes combination and different functions as discrete or continuous probability distribution functions: polynomial, sine, cosine, tangent, cotangent, logarithm, exponent, arc sin, arc cos, arc tan, arc cot or power function.

FUTURE RESEARCH DIRECTIONS

Future trends will go to various directions: how to fix the best probability distribution function for the nodes, how to calculate the most appropriate nodes combination and what extrapolation is the most valuable in decision making and risk analysis.

CONCLUSION

Functions for γ calculations are chosen individually at each data modeling and it is treated as 2-dimensional probability distribution function: γ depends on initial requirements and features' specifications. PFC method leads to data interpolation as handwriting or signature identification and image retrieval via discrete set of feature vectors in 2-dimensional feature space. So PFC method makes possible the combination of two important problems: interpolation and modeling in a matter of image retrieval or writer identification. PFC interpolation develops a linear interpolation in multidimensional feature spaces into other functions as two-dimensional probability distribution functions. Future works are going to applications of PFC method in biometric recognition, computer vision and artificial intelligence.

REFERENCES

Ballard, D. H. (1982). *Computer Vision*. New York: Prentice Hall.

Bhat, Rama, & Chakraverty, S. (2003). *Numerical Analysis in Engineering*. Alpha Science International Ltd.

Chakraverty, S. (2008). *Vibration of Plates*. CRC Press. doi:10.1201/9781420053968

Chapra, S. C. (2012). *Applied Numerical Methods*. McGraw-Hill.

Choraś, R. S. (2005). *Computer Vision*. Warsaw, Poland: Exit.

Cocozza-Thivent, C., Eymard, R., Mercier, S., & Roussignol, M. (2006). Characterization of the Marginal Distributions of Markov Processes Used in Dynamic Reliability. *Journal of Applied Mathematics and Stochastic Analysis*, 1–18.

Collins, G. W. II. (2003). *Fundamental Numerical Methods and Data Analysis*. Case Western Reserve University.

Dahlquist, G., & Bjoerck, A. (1974). *Numerical Methods*. New York: Prentice Hall.

Dejdumrong, N. (2007). A Shape Preserving Verification Techniques for Parametric Curves. *Computer Graphics, Imaging and Visualization*, 163–168.

Dyn, N., Levin, D., & Gregory, J. A. (1987). A 4-Point Interpolatory Subdivision Scheme for Curve Design. *Computer Aided Geometric Design*, *4*(4), 257–268. doi:10.1016/0167-8396(87)90001-X

Gerald, C. F., & Wheatley, P. O. (2003). *Applied Numerical Analysis* (7th ed.). Pearson.

Jakóbczak, D. (2007). 2D and 3D Image Modeling Using Hurwitz-Radon Matrices. *Polish Journal of Environmental Studies*, *4A*(16), 104–107.

Jakóbczak, D. (2009). Curve Interpolation Using Hurwitz-Radon Matrices. *Polish Journal of Environmental Studies*, *3B*(18), 126–130.

Jakóbczak, D. (2010a). Shape Representation and Shape Coefficients via Method of Hurwitz-Radon Matrices. *Lecture Notes in Computer Science*, *6374*, 411–419. doi:10.1007/978-3-642-15910-7_47

Jakóbczak, D. (2010b). Object Modeling Using Method of Hurwitz-Radon Matrices of Rank k. In W. Wolski & M. Borawski (Eds.), *Computer Graphics: Selected Issues* (pp. 79–90). Szczecin, Poland: University of Szczecin Press.

Jakóbczak, D. (2011a). Curve Parameterization and Curvature via Method of Hurwitz-Radon Matrices. *Image Processing & Communications- International Journal (Toronto, Ont.)*, *1-2*(16), 49–56.

Jakóbczak, D. (2011b). Data Extrapolation and Decision Making via Method of Hurwitz-Radon Matrices. *Lecture Notes in Computer Science*, *6922*, 173–182. doi:10.1007/978-3-642-23935-9_17

Jakóbczak, D. (2011c). Curve Extrapolation and Data Analysis using the Method of Hurwitz-Radon Matrices. *Folia Oeconomica Stetinensia, 9*(17), 121-138.

Jakóbczak, D. (2013). Probabilistic Modeling of Signature using the Method of Hurwitz-Radon Matrices. *Global Perspectives on Artificial Intelligence*, *1*(1), 1–7.

Kozera, R. (2004). *Curve Modeling via Interpolation Based on Multidimensional Reduced Data*. Gliwice, Poland: Silesian University of Technology Press.

Liu, T., & Geiger, D. (1999). Approximate tree matching and shape similarity. *Int. Conf. Computer Vision,* Corfu, Greece.

Lorton, A., Fouladirad, M., & Grall, A. (2013). A Methodology for Probabilistic Model-based Prognosis. *European Journal of Operational Research*, *225*(3), 443–454. doi:10.1016/j.ejor.2012.10.025

Pergler, M., & Freeman, A. (2008). Probabilistic Modeling as an Exploratory Decision-Making Tool. *McKinsey Working Papers on Risk, 6*, 1-18.

Ralston, A., & Rabinowitz, P. (2001). *A First Course in Numerical Analysis* (2nd ed.). New York: Dover Publications.

Rogers, D. F. (2001). *An Introduction to NURBS with Historical Perspective*. Morgan Kaufmann Publishers.

Saber, E., Xu, Y., & Murat Tekalp, A. (2005). Partial shape recognition by sub-matrix matching for partial matching guided image labeling. *Pattern Recognition*, *38*(10), 1560–1573. doi:10.1016/j.patcog.2005.03.027

Schumaker, L. L. (2007). *Spline Functions: Basic Theory*. Cambridge Mathematical Library. doi:10.1017/CBO9780511618994

Sebastian, T. B., Klein, P. N., & Kimia, B. B. (2003). On aligning curves. *IEEE Transactions on Pattern Analysis and Machine Intelligence*, *25*(1), 116–124. doi:10.1109/TPAMI.2003.1159951

Tadeusiewicz, R., & Flasiński, M. (1991). *Image Recognition*. Warsaw, Poland: PWN.

Zhang, D., & Lu, G. (2004). Review of Shape Representation and Description Techniques. *Pattern Recognition*, *1*(37), 1–19. doi:10.1016/j. patcog.2003.07.008

ADDITIONAL READING

Basu, S., & Bresler, Y. (2000). $O(N^2\log_2 N)$ filtered backprojection reconstruction algorithm for tomography. *IEEE Transactions on Image Processing*, 9(10), 1760–1773. doi:10.1109/83.869187 PMID:18262914

Brankov, J. G., Yang, Y., & Wernick, M. N. (2004). Tomographic image reconstruction based on a Content – Adaptive Mesh Model. *IEEE Transactions on Medical Imaging*, 2(23), 202–212. doi:10.1109/TMI.2003.822822 PMID:14964565

Brasse, D., & Defrise, M. (2004). Fast fully 3-D image reconstruction in PET using planograms. *IEEE Transactions on Medical Imaging*, 4(23), 413–425. doi:10.1109/TMI.2004.824231 PMID:15084067

Bulacu, M., & Schomaker, L. (2007). Text-independent writer identification and verification using textural and allographic features. *IEEE Transactions on Pattern Analysis and Machine Intelligence*, 29(4), 701–717. doi:10.1109/TPAMI.2007.1009 PMID:17299226

Bulacu, M., Schomaker, L., & Brink, A. (2007). *Text-independent writer identification and verification on off-line Arabic handwriting.* In: *International Conference on Document Analysis and Recognition.* 769–773.

Cetin, M., Karl, W. C., & Willsky, A. S. (2002, September). *Edge – preserving image reconstruction for coherent imaging application.* Paper presented at the IEEE International Conference on Image Processsing, Rochester, NY, USA. doi:10.1109/ICIP.2002.1039992

Chen, J., Cheng, W., & Lopresti, D. (2011). Using perturbed handwriting to support writer identification in the presence of severe data constraints. In: Document Recognition and Retrieval. 1–10. doi:10.1117/12.876497

Chen, J., Lopresti, D., & Kavallieratou, E. (2010). *The impact of ruling lines on writer identification.* In: *International Conference on Frontiers in Handwriting Recognition.* 439–444. doi:10.1109/ICFHR.2010.75

Chlebus, E., & Cholewa, M. (1999). Rapid prototyping – rapid tooling. *CADCAM Forum, 11*, 23-28.

Cormen, T. H., Leiserson, C. E., & Rivest, R. L. (1996). *Introduction to algorithms*. Massachusetts, USA: the Massachusetts Institute of Technology Press and McGraw-Hill.

Defrise, M. (2001). A short readers guide to 3D tomographic reconstruction. *Computerized Medical Imaging and Graphics, 25*(2), 113–116. doi:10.1016/S0895-6111(00)00061-6 PMID:11137787

Djeddi, C., & Souici-Meslati, L. (2010). *A texture based approach for Arabic writer identification and verification*. In: *International Conference on Machine and Web Intelligence*. 115–120.

Djeddi, C., & Souici-Meslati, L. (2011). *Artificial immune recognition system for Arabic writer identification*. In: *International Symposium on Innovation in Information and Communication Technology*. 159–165. doi:10.1109/ISIICT.2011.6149612

Dryja, M., Jankowska, J., & Jankowski, M. (1982). *Survey of numerical methods and algorithms. Part II*. Warsaw, Poland: WNT.

Eldar, Y. C. (2001). *Quantum Signal Processing*. (Unpublished doctoral dissertation). Massachusetts Institute of Technology, USA.

Eldar, Y. C., & Oppenheim, A. V. (2002). Quantum Signal Processing. *IEEE Signal Processing Magazine, 6*(19), 12–32. doi:10.1109/MSP.2002.1043298

Fortuna, Z., Macukow, B., & Wąsowski, J. (1982). *Numerical methods*. Warsaw, Poland: WNT.

Galloway, M. M. (1975). Texture analysis using gray level run lengths. *Computer Graphics and Image Processing, 4*(2), 172–179. doi:10.1016/S0146-664X(75)80008-6

Garain, U., & Paquet, T. (2009). *Off-line multi-script writer identification using AR coefficients*. In: *International Conference on Document Analysis and Recognition*. 991–995. doi:10.1109/ICDAR.2009.222

Ghiasi, G., & Safabakhsh, R. (2013). Offline text-independent writer identification using codebook and efficient code extraction methods. *Image and Vision Computing, 31*(5), 379–391. doi:10.1016/j.imavis.2013.03.002

Jakóbczak, D. (2005). Hurwitz-Radon matrices and their children. *Computer Science, 5*(8), 29–38.

Jakóbczak, D. J. (2014). *2D Curve Modeling via the Method of Probabilistic Nodes Combination-Shape Representation, Object Modeling and Curve Interpolation-Extrapolation with the Applications.* Saarbrucken: LAP Lambert Academic Publishing.

Jankowska, J., & Jankowski, M. (1981). *Survey of numerical methods and algorithms. Part I.* Warsaw, Poland: WNT.

Kontaxakis, G., & Strauss, L. G. (1998). Maximum likelihood algorithms for image reconstruction in Positron Emission Tomography. *Radionuclides for Oncology – Current Status and Future Aspects, 1998,* 73-106.

Kowalczuk, Z., & Wiszniewski, B. (Eds.). (2007). *Intelligent data mining in diagnostic purposes: Automatics and informatics.* Gdansk, Poland: PWNT.

Kundur, D., & Hatzinakos, D. (1998). A novel blind deconvolution scheme for image restoration using recursive filtering. *IEEE Transactions on Signal Processing, 2*(46), 375–390. doi:10.1109/78.655423

Laine, A., & Zong, X. (1996). *Border identification of echocardiograms via multiscale edge detection and shape modeling.* Paper presented at the IEEE International Conference on Image Processsing, Lausanne, Switzerland. doi:10.1109/ICIP.1996.560486

Lang, S. (1970). *Algebra.* Reading, Massachusetts, USA: Addison-Wesley Publishing Company.

Le Buhan Jordan, C., Bossen, F., & Ebrahimi, T. (1997). *Scalable shape representation for content based visual data compression.* Paper presented at the International Conference on Image Processing, Santa Barbara, CA, USA. doi:10.1109/ICIP.1997.647962

Marker, J., Braude, I., Museth, K., & Breen, D. (2006). Contour-based surface reconstruction using implicit curve fitting, and distance field filtering and interpolation. *Volume Graphics, 2006,* 1–9.

Marti, U.-V., & Bunke, H. (2002). The IAM-database: An English sentence database for offline handwriting recognition. *Int. J. Doc. Anal. Recognit., 5*(1), 39–46. doi:10.1007/s100320200071

Meyer, Y. (1993). *Wavelets: algorithms & applications.* Philadelphia, USA: Society for Industrial and Applied Mathematics.

Nosary, A., Heutte, L., & Paquet, T. (2004). Unsupervised writer adaption applied to handwritten text recognition. *Pattern Recognition Letters, 37*(2), 385–388. doi:10.1016/S0031-3203(03)00185-7

Ozaki, M., Adachi, Y., & Ishii, N. (2006). *Examination of effects of character size on accuracy of writer recognition by new local arc method.* In: International Conference on Knowledge- Based Intelligent Information and Engineering Systems. 1170–1175. doi:10.1007/11893004_148

Poggio, T., & Smale, S. (2003). The mathematics of learning: Dealing with data. *Notices of the American Mathematical Society, 5*(50), 537–544.

Przelaskowski, A. (2005). *Data compression.* Warsaw, Poland: BTC.

Rutkowski, L., Siekmann, J., Tadeusiewicz, R., & Zadeh, A. (Eds.). (2004). *Lecture notes on artificial intelligence: Artificial intelligence and soft computing.* Berlin-Heidelberg, Germany: Springer-Verlag.

Schlapbach, A., & Bunke, H. (2004). *Using HMM based recognizers for writer identification and verification. 9th Int. Workshop on Frontiers in Handwriting Recognition.* 167–172. doi:10.1109/IWFHR.2004.107

Schlapbach, A., & Bunke, H. (2006). *Off-line writer identification using Gaussian mixture models.* In: *International Conference on Pattern Recognition.* 992–995.

Schlapbach, A., & Bunke, H. (2007). A writer identification and verification system using HMM based recognizers. *Pattern Analysis & Applications, 10*(1), 33–43. doi:10.1007/s10044-006-0047-5

Schomaker, L., Franke, K., & Bulacu, M. (2007). Using codebooks of fragmented connected- component contours in forensic and historic writer identification. *Pattern Recognition Letters, 28*(6), 719–727. doi:10.1016/j.patrec.2006.08.005

Shahabinejad, F., & Rahmati, M. (2007). A new method for writer identification and verification based on Farsi/Arabic handwritten texts, *Ninth International Conference on Document Analysis and Recognition (ICDAR 2007).* 829–833.

Siddiqi, I., Cloppet, F., & Vincent, N. (2009). Contour based features for the classification of ancient manuscripts. In: Conference of the International Graphonomics Society. 226–229.

Siddiqi, I., & Vincent, N. (2010). Text independent writer recognition using redundant writing patterns with contour-based orientation and curvature features. *Pattern Recognition Letters*, *43*(11), 3853–3865. doi:10.1016/j.patcog.2010.05.019

Vakhania, N. (1993). Orthogonal random vectors and the Hurwitz – Radon-Eckmann theorem. *Proc. of the Georgian Academy of Sciences-Mathematics, 1(1)*, 109-125.

Van, E. M., Vuurpijl, L., Franke, K., & Schomaker, L. (2005). The WANDA measurement tool for forensic document examination. *J. Forensic Doc. Exam.*, *16*, 103–118.

Willis, M. (2000). *Algebraic reconstruction algorithms for remote sensing image enhancement*. Unpublished doctoral dissertation, Department of Electrical and Computer Engineering, Brigham Young University.

Xu, Fang, & Mueller, K. (2005). Accelerating popular tomographic reconstruction algorithms on commodity PC graphics hardware. *IEEE Transactions on Nuclear Science*, *3*(52), 654–661.

Zaletelj, J., & Tasic, J. F. (2003). *Optimization and tracking of polygon vertices for shape coding*. Berlin-Heidelberg, Germany: Springer-Verlag. doi:10.1007/978-3-540-45179-2_52

Zhang, J. K., Davidson, T., & Wong, K. M. (2004). Efficient design of orthonormal wavelet bases for signal representation. *IEEE Transactions on Signal Processing*, *7*(52), 1983–1996. doi:10.1109/TSP.2004.828923

KEY TERMS AND DEFINITIONS

Contour Modeling: Calculation of unknown points of the object contour having information about some points of the object contour.

Data Extrapolation: Calculation of unknown values for the points situated outside the ranges of nodes.

Function Interpolation: Computing new and unknown points of a function and creating a graph using existing data points – interpolation nodes.

Hurwitz – Radon Matrices: A family of skew – symmetric and orthogonal matrices with columns and rows that create, together with identical matrix, the base in vector spaces of dimensions N = 2, 4 or 8.

Methods of Quadratures: Rectangle Formula, Trapezium Formula and Simpson Formula.

MHR Method: The method of curve interpolation and extrapolation using linear (convex) combinations of OHR operators.

Numerical Calculations for Derivative: Definition of derivative in some points.

OHR Operator: Matrix operator of Hurwitz – Radon built from coordinates of interpolation nodes.

Root of the Function: Solution of nonlinear equations.

Chapter 8
Applications of PNC in Artificial Intelligence

ABSTRACT

Interpolation methods and curve fitting represent so huge problem that each individual interpolation is exceptional and requires specific solutions. Presented method is such a new possibility for curve fitting and interpolation when specific data (for example handwritten symbol or character) starts up with no rules for polynomial interpolation. The method of Probabilistic Nodes Combination (PNC) enables interpolation and modeling of two-dimensional curves using nodes combinations and different coefficients γ. This probabilistic view is novel approach a problem of modeling and interpolation. Computer vision and pattern recognition are interested in appropriate methods of shape representation and curve modeling. PNC method represents the possibilities of shape reconstruction and curve interpolation via the choice of nodes combination and probability distribution function for interpolated points. It seems to be quite new look at the problem of contour representation and curve modeling in artificial intelligence and computer vision.

INTRODUCTION

Probabilistic modeling is still developing branch of the computer science: operational research (for example probabilistic model-based prognosis) (Lorton, Fouladirad & Grall, 2013), decision making techniques and probabilistic modeling (Pergler & Freeman, 2008), artificial intelligence

DOI: 10.4018/978-1-5225-2531-8.ch008

and machine learning. There are used different aspects of probabilistic methods: stochastic processes and stochastic model-based techniques, Markov processes (Cocozza-Thivent, Eymard, Mercier & Roussignol, 2006), Poisson processes, Gamma processes, a Monte Carlo method, Bayes rule, conditional probability and many probability distributions. In this chapter the goal of probability distribution function is to describe the position of unknown points between given interpolation nodes. Two-dimensional curve (opened or closed) is used to represent the data points. So problem statement of this chapter is: how to reconstruct (interpolate) missing points of 2D curve having the set of interpolation nodes (key points) and using the information about probabilistic distribution of unknown points. For example the simplest basic distribution leads to the easiest interpolation – linear interpolation. Apart from probability distribution, additionally there is the second factor of proposed interpolation method: nodes combination. The simplest nodes combination is zero. Thus proposed curve modeling is based on two agents: probability distribution and nodes combination. Curve interpolation (Collins, 2003) represents one of the most important problems in mathematics and computer science: how to model the curve (Chapra, 2012) via discrete set of two-dimensional points (Ralston & Rabinowitz, 2001)? Also the matter of shape representation (as closed curve-contour) and curve parameterization is still opened (Zhang & Lu, 2004). For example pattern recognition, signature verification or handwriting identification problems are based on curve modeling via the choice of key points. So interpolation is not only a pure mathematical problem but important task in computer vision and artificial intelligence. The chapter wants to approach a problem of curve modeling by characteristic points. Proposed method relies on nodes combination and functional modeling of curve points situated between the basic set of key points. The functions that are used in calculations represent whole family of elementary functions with inverse functions: polynomials, trigonometric, cyclometric, logarithmic, exponential and power function. These functions are treated as probability distribution functions in the range [0;1]. Probabilistic modeling represents a subject arising in many branches of mathematics, economics and computer science. Such modeling connects pure mathematics with applied sciences. Operations research similarly is situated on the border between pure mathematics and applied sciences. So when probabilistic modeling meets operations research, it is very interesting occasion. Our life and work are impossible without planning, time-tabling, scheduling, decision making, optimization, simulation, data analysis, risk analysis and process modeling. Thus, it is a part of management science or decision science. This comprehensive and timely publication aims to be an essential reference source, building on the available literature in the field of probabilistic modeling, operational research, planning and scheduling, data extrapolation in decision making, probabilistic interpolation and extrapolation in simulation, stochastic processes, and decision analysis. It is hoped that this text will provide the resources necessary for economics and management sciences, also for mathematics and computer sciences. Decision makers, academicians, researchers, advanced-level students, technology developers, and government officials will find this text useful in furthering their research exposure to pertinent topics in operations research and assisting in furthering their own research efforts in this field. Proposed method, called Probabilistic Features Combination (PFC), is the method of 2D curve interpolation and extrapolation using the set of key points (knots or nodes). Nodes can be treated as characteristic points of data for modeling and analyzing. The model of data can be built by choice of probability distribution function and nodes combination.

PFC modeling via nodes combination and parameter γ as probability distribution function enables value anticipation in risk analysis and decision making. Two-dimensional curve is extrapolated and interpolated via nodes combination and different functions as discrete or continuous probability distribution functions: polynomial, sine, cosine, tangent, cotangent, logarithm, exponent, arc sin, arc cos, arc tan, arc cot or power function.

BACKGROUND

An important problem in machine vision and computer vision (Ballard, 1982) is that of appropriate shape representation and reconstruction. Classical discussion about shape representation is based on the problem: contour versus skeleton. This chapter is voting for contour which forms boundary of the object. Contour of the object, represented by contour points, consists of information which allows us to describe many important features of the object as shape coefficients (Tadeusiewicz & Flasiński, 1991). In the chapter contour is dealing with a set of curves. Curve modeling and generation is a basic subject in many branches of industry and computer science, for example in the CAD/CAM software. The representation of shape has a great impact on the accuracy and effectiveness of object recognition (Saber, Yaowu & Murat Tekalp, 2005). In the literature, shape has been represented by many options including curves (Sebastian & Klein, 2003), graph-based algorithms and medial axis (Liu & Geiger, 1999) to enable shape-based object recognition. Digital curve (open or closed) can be represented by chain code (Freeman's code). Chain code depends on selection of the started point and transformations of the object. So Freeman's code is one of the method how to describe and to find contour of the object. An analog (continuous) version of Freeman's code is the curve α-s. Another contour representation and reconstruction is based on Fourier coefficients calculated in Discrete Fourier Transformation (DFT). These coefficients are used to fix similarity of the contours with different sizes or directions. If we assume that contour is built from segments of a line and fragments of circles or ellipses, Hough transformation is applied to detect contour lines. Also geometrical moments of the object are used during the process of object shape representation (Choraś, 2005).

Nowadays methods apply mainly polynomial functions, for example Bernstein polynomials in Bezier curves, splines (Schumaker, 2007) and NURBS (Rogers, 2001). But Bezier curves don't represent the interpolation method and cannot be used for example in handwriting modeling with key points (interpolation nodes). In comparison PNC method with Bézier curves, Hermite curves and B-curves (*B-splines*) or NURBS one unpleasant feature of these curves has to be mentioned: small change of one characteristic point can result in unwanted change of whole reconstructed curve. Such a feature does not appear in proposed PNC method. Numerical methods for data interpolation are based on polynomial or trigonometric functions, for example Lagrange, Newton, Aitken and Hermite methods. These methods have many weak sides (Dahlquist & Bjoerck, 1974) and are not sufficient for curve interpolation in the situations when the curve cannot be build by polynomials or trigonometric functions. Also there exists several well established methods of curve modeling, for example shape-preserving techniques (Dejdumrong, 2007), subdivision algorithms (Dyn, Levin & Gregory, 1987) and others (Kozera, 2004) to overcome difficulties of polynomial interpolation, but probabilistic interpolation with nodes combination seems to be quite novel in the area of shape modeling. Proposed 2D curve interpolation is the functional modeling via any elementary functions and it helps us to fit the curve during the computations. The method of Probabilistic Nodes Combination (PNC) enables interpolation and modeling of two-dimensional curves using nodes combinations and different coefficients γ: polynomial, sinusoidal, cosinusoidal, tangent, cotangent, logarithmic, exponential, arc sin, arc cos, arc tan, arc cot or power function, also inverse functions. This probabilistic view is novel approach a problem of modeling and interpolation. Computer vision and pattern recognition are interested in appropriate methods of shape representation and curve modeling. PNC method represents the possibilities of shape reconstruction and curve interpolation via the choice of nodes combination and probability distribution function for interpolated points. It seems to be quite new look at the problem of contour representation and curve modeling in artificial intelligence and computer vision. Function for γ calculations is chosen individually at each curve modeling and it is treated as probability distribution function: γ depends on initial requirements and curve specifications. PNC method leads to curve interpolation as handwriting modeling via discrete set of fixed knots. So PNC makes possible the combination of two important problems: interpolation and modeling. The method of Probabilistic Features Combination (PFC) enables interpolation and modeling of high-dimensional N data using features' combinations and different coefficients γ: polynomial, sinusoidal, cosinusoidal, tangent, cotangent, logarithmic, exponential, arc sin, arc cos, arc tan, arc cot or power function. Functions for γ calculations are chosen individually at each data modeling and it is treated as N-dimensional probability distribution function: γ depends on initial requirements and features' specifications. PFC method leads to data interpolation as handwriting or signature identification and image retrieval via discrete set of feature vectors in N-dimensional feature space. So PFC method makes possible the combination of two important problems: interpolation and modeling in a matter of image retrieval or writer identification. Main features of PFC method are: PFC interpolation develops a linear interpolation in multidimensional feature spaces into other functions as N-dimensional probability distribution functions; PFC is a generalization of MHR method and PNC method via different nodes combinations; interpolation of L points is connected with the computational cost of rank $O(L)$ as in MHR and PNC method; nodes combination and coefficients γ are crucial in the process of data probabilistic parameterization and interpolation: they are computed individually for a single feature. Proposed method, called Probabilistic Features Combination (PFC), is the method of N-dimensional data interpolation and extrapolation using the set of key points (knots or nodes). Nodes can be treated as characteristic points of data for modeling and analyzing. The model of data can be built by choice of probability distribution function and nodes combination. PFC modeling via nodes combination and parameter γ as probability distribution function enables value anticipation in risk analysis and decision making. N-dimensional object is extrapolated and interpolated via nodes combination and different functions as discrete or continuous probability distribution functions: polynomial, sine, cosine, tangent, cotangent, logarithm, exponent, arc sin, arc cos, arc tan, arc cot or power function.

PNC IN OBJECT RECOGNITION

This chapter consists of some examples with PNC applications in Artificial Intelligence (Zhang & Lu, 2004). First example is dealing with PNC method in MHR version.

Object Recognition via Contour Reconstruction

The Example: Models

Assume that one part of *OBJECT1* contour is described by the set of points S_1 = $\{(x_0, y_0^{(1)}), (x_1, y_1^{(1)}), ..., (x_M, y_M^{(1)})\}$ for $x_j < x_{j+1}$. Also one part of *OBJECT2* contour is described by the set of points $S_2 = \{(x_0, y_0^{(2)}), (x_1, y_1^{(2)}), ..., (x_M, y_M^{(2)})\}$. Additionally exists $k = 0, 1, ..., M$ that $y_k^{(1)} = y_k^{(2)}$ (at least one common point of models). These sets of nodes S_1 and S_2 are models of contour fragment for *OBJECT1* and *OBJECT2*. For example $M = 4$: $S_1 = \{(0;1), (1;1), (2;1), (3;1), (4;1)\}$ and $S_2 = \{(0;0), (1;0.5), (2;1), (3;0.5), (4;0)\}$. Of course it is possible to deal with more models S_i: let there is given the set $S_3 = \{(0;0), (1;0.75), (2;1), (3;0.75), (4;0)\}$ for *OBJECT3*.

The nodes from Figure 1 are monotonic in coordinates x_i. MHR method is also working with nodes monotonic in coordinates y_i. For example here are three other models of three other objects: $S_1' = \{(1;0), (1;1), (1;2), (1;3), (1;4)\}$, $S_2' = \{(3;0), (2;1), (1;2), (2;3), (3;4)\}$, $S_3' = \{(2;0), (1.1;1), (1;2), (1.1;3), (2;4)\}$.

Figure 1. The sets of nodes S_1, S_2, S_3 and contour fragments of three objects

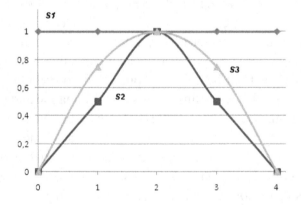

Figure 2. The set of nodes S_3 and contour fragment of the object

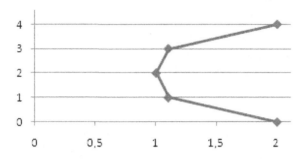

Five nodes is the minimum number for MHR method to find points between the nodes. Curves of the contour are smooth (Figure 1) or not smooth (Figure 2). The number of nodes influences precise reconstruction of the curve.

Detection

The unknown object (one part of its contour) is described by detected interpolation nodes according to MHR method: $S = \{(x_0',y_0'), (x_1',y_1'),\ldots, (x_m',y_m')\}$ for $x_j' < x_{j+1}'$. Also assume: exists $i = 0, 1, \ldots, m$ that $(x_i',y_i') \in S_1$, $(x_i',y_i') \in S_2$ (common point of models and recognized object) and $x_0' \leq x_0$, $x_m' \geq x_M$ because of using all nodes of S_1 and S_2 to recognition. Another part of the contour could be described by detected interpolation nodes monotonic in coordinates y_i: $S' = \{(x_0',y_0'), (x_1',y_1'),\ldots, (x_l',y_l')\}$ for $y_j' < y_{j+1}'$. Number

Figure 3. The set of nodes S and contour fragment of unknown object

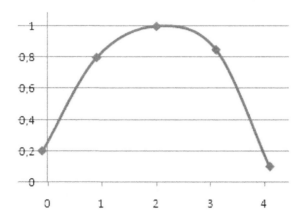

of models S_i is determined for $i = 1, 2, 3, 4...$ Let there is given the set $S=$ {(-0.1;0.2), (0.9;0.8), (2;1), (3.1;0.85), (4.1;0.1)} for unknown object.

How the unknown object from Figure 3 can be recognized as *OBJECT1*, *OBJECT2* or *OBJECT3* from Figure 1?

Recognition

Contour points of unknown object have to be calculated by MHR method: (x_0,y_0), (x_1,y_1),..., (x_M,y_M). The criterion of object recognition for models S_j, $j = 1,2,3...$ is:

$$\sum_{i=0}^{M} \left| y_i - y_i^{(j)} \right| \to \min.$$

How does this criterion work for models S_1, S_2, S_3 and for the set of contour points S? According to characteristic points (x_i,y_i) of unknown object from Figure 3 have to be computed for $x_i = 0, 1, 3, 4$. MHR calculations are done as follows:

For nodes (-0.1;0.2), (2;1) OHR operator (1)

$$M_0 = \begin{bmatrix} 0.494 & 0.125 \\ -0.125 & 0.494 \end{bmatrix},$$

for nodes (0.9;0.8), (3.1;0.85) OHR operator

$$M_1 = \begin{bmatrix} 0.322 & 0.165 \\ -0.165 & 0.322 \end{bmatrix},$$

for $c_1 = 0$:

$$\alpha = \frac{0.9 - 0}{0.9 - (-0.1)} = 0.9,$$

$$c_2 = \alpha \cdot 2 + (1 - \alpha) \cdot 3.1 = 2.11,$$

$$M_2 = \alpha \cdot M_0 + (1 - \alpha) \cdot M_1 = \begin{bmatrix} 0.477 & 0.129 \\ -0.129 & 0.477 \end{bmatrix},$$

$$M_2 \cdot \begin{bmatrix} 0 \\ 2.11 \end{bmatrix} = \begin{bmatrix} 0.272 \\ 1.006 \end{bmatrix},$$

for $c_2 = 3$:

$$\alpha = \frac{3.1 - 3}{3.1 - 2} = 0.091,$$

$$c_1 = \alpha \cdot (-0.1) + (1 - \alpha) \cdot 0.9 = 0.809,$$

$$M_2 = \alpha \cdot M_0 + (1 - \alpha) \cdot M_1 = \begin{bmatrix} 0.338 & 0.161 \\ -0.161 & 0.338 \end{bmatrix},$$

$$M_2 \cdot \begin{bmatrix} 0.809 \\ 3 \end{bmatrix} = \begin{bmatrix} 0.756 \\ 0.883 \end{bmatrix};$$

For nodes (0.9;0.8), (3.1;0.85) OHR operator

$$M_0 = \begin{bmatrix} 0.322 & 0.165 \\ -0.165 & 0.322 \end{bmatrix},$$

for nodes (2;1), (4.1;0.1) OHR operator

$$M_1 = \begin{bmatrix} 0.116 & 0.187 \\ -0.187 & 0.116 \end{bmatrix},$$

for $c_1 = 1$:

$$\alpha = \frac{2-1}{2-0.9} = 0.909 \,,$$

$$c_2 = \alpha \cdot 3.1 + (1-\alpha) \cdot 4.1 = 3.191 \,,$$

$$M_2 = \alpha \cdot M_0 + (1-\alpha) \cdot M_1 = \begin{bmatrix} 0.303 & 0.167 \\ -0.167 & 0.303 \end{bmatrix},$$

$$M_2 \cdot \begin{bmatrix} 1 \\ 3.191 \end{bmatrix} = \begin{bmatrix} 0.835 \\ 0.801 \end{bmatrix},$$

for $c_2 = 4$:

$$\alpha = \frac{4.1-4}{4.1-3.1} = 0.1 \,,$$

$$c_1 = \alpha \cdot 0.9 + (1-\alpha) \cdot 2 = 1.89 \,,$$

$$M_2 = \alpha \cdot M_0 + (1-\alpha) \cdot M_1 = \begin{bmatrix} 0.136 & 0.185 \\ -0.185 & 0.136 \end{bmatrix},$$

$$M_2 \cdot \begin{bmatrix} 1.89 \\ 4 \end{bmatrix} = \begin{bmatrix} 0.998 \\ 0.196 \end{bmatrix}.$$

Figure 4. The set of nodes **S** *and four calculated points used in the criterion*

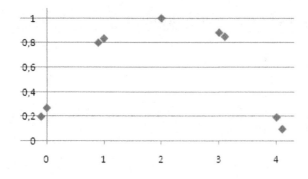

So here are computed points to use in criterion: (0;0.272), (1;0.835), (3;0.883), (4;0.196).

The criterion gives the results:

1. For *OBJECT1* and set S_1: $\sum_{i=0}^{4} \left| y_i - y_i^{(1)} \right| = 1.814$;

2. For *OBJECT2* and set S_2: $\sum_{i=0}^{4} \left| y_i - y_i^{(2)} \right| = 1.186$;

3. For *OBJECT3* and set S_3: $\sum_{i=0}^{4} \left| y_i - y_i^{(3)} \right| = 0.686 = \text{minimum}$.

It means that unknown object from Figure 3 with the set of nodes S is recognized as *OBJECT3* from Figure 3 with the model S_3.

Discussion of the Example

This example is very simple and this chapter goes to first step of application MHR method in object recognition (Ballard, 1982). Models of known objects possess special features: appropriate contour points with characteristic (identical) one coordinate. Also unknown object must have the same one coordinate. And geometrical transformations ought to be considered (translations, rotations, scaling): if unknown object is transformed, then models of the object (points) have to be also transformed and then MHR recognition is possible.

OFFLINE TEXT-INEPENDENT HANDWRITING IDENTIFICATION AND SHAPE MODELING VIA PROBABILISTIC NODES COMBINATION

Handwriting identification and writer verification are still the open questions in artificial intelligence (Choraś, 2005) and computer vision (Tadeusiewicz & Flasiński, 1991). Handwriting based author recognition offers a huge number of significant implementations which make it an important research area in pattern recognition (Lorton, Fouladirad & Grall, 2013). There are so many possibilities and applications of the recognition algorithms that implemented methods have to be concerned on a single problem. Handwriting and signature identification represents such a significant problem. In the case of writer recognition, described in this chapter, each person is represented by the set of modeled letters or symbols. The sketch of proposed method consists of three steps: first handwritten letter or symbol must be modeled by a curve (Sebastian & Klein, 2003), then compared with unknown letter and finally there is a decision of identification (Liu & Geiger, 1999). Author recognition of handwriting and signature is based on the choice of key points and curve modeling. Reconstructed curve does not have to be smooth in the nodes because a writer does not think about smoothing during the handwriting. Curve interpolation in handwriting identification is not only a pure mathematical problem but important task in pattern recognition and artificial intelligence (Saber, Yaowu & Murat Tekalp, 2005) such as: biometric recognition (Pergler & Freeman, 2008), personalized handwriting recognition, automatic forensic document examination, classification of ancient manuscripts. Also writer recognition in monolingual handwritten texts is an extensive area of study and the methods independent from the language are well-seen. Proposed method represents language-independent and text-independent approach because it identifies the author via a single letter or symbol from the sample. This novel method is also applicable to short handwritten text.

Writer recognition methods in the recent years are going to various directions: writer recognition using multi-script handwritten texts, introduction of new features, combining different types of features, studying the sensitivity of character size on writer identification, investigating writer identification in multi-script environments, impact of ruling lines on writer identification, model perturbed handwriting, methods based on run-length features, the edge-direction and edge-hinge features, a combination of codebook and visual features extracted from chain code and polygonized representation of contours, the autoregressive coefficients, codebook and efficient code extraction methods, texture analysis with Gabor filters and extracting features, using Hidden Markov Model (Cocozza-Thivent, Eymard, Mercier & Roussignol, 2006) or Gaussian Mixture Model. But no method is dealing with writer identification via curve modeling (Dyn, Levin & Gregory, 1987) or interpolation (Kozera, 2004) and points comparing as it is presented in this chapter.

Handwriting Modeling and Author Identification

PNC method enables signature and handwriting recognition. This process of recognition consists of three parts:

1. **Modeling:** Choice of nodes combination and probabilistic distribution function for known signature or handwritten letters;
2. **Unknown Writer:** Choice of characteristic points (nodes) for unknown signature or handwritten word and the coefficients of points between nodes;
3. **Decision of Recognition:** Comparing the results of PNC interpolation for known models with coordinates of unknown text.

Modeling: The Basis of Patterns

Known letters or symbols ought to be modeled by the choice of nodes, determining specific nodes combination and characteristic probabilistic distribution function. For example a handwritten word or signature "*rw*" may look different for persons A, B or others (Dejdumrong, 2007). How to model "*rw*" for some persons via PNC method? Each model has to be described by the set of nodes for letters "*r*" and "*w*", nodes combination h and a function $\gamma = F(\alpha)$ for each letter. Less complicated models can take $h(p_1, p_2, \ldots, p_m) = 0$ and then the formula of interpolation looks as follows:

$$y(c) = \gamma \cdot y_i + (1 - \gamma)y_{i+1}.$$

It is linear interpolation for basic probability distribution ($\gamma = \alpha$). How first letter "*r*" is modeled in three versions for nodes combination $h = 0$ and $\alpha = 0.1, 0.2 \ldots 0.9$? Of course α is a random variable and $\alpha \in [0;1]$.

Person A: Nodes (1;3), (3;1), (5;3), (7;3) and $\gamma = F(\alpha) = \alpha^2$ (see Figure 5).
Person B: Nodes (1;3), (3;1), (5;3), (7;2) and $\gamma = F(\alpha) = \alpha^2$: (see Figure 6)
Person C: Nodes (1;3), (3;1), (5;3), (7;4) and $\gamma = F(\alpha) = \alpha^3$: (see Figure 7)

These three versions of letter "*r*" (Figures 5-7) with nodes combination $h = 0$ differ at fourth node and probability distribution functions $\gamma = F(\alpha)$. Much more possibilities of modeling are connected with a choice of nodes combination $h(p_1, p_2, \ldots, p_m)$. MHR method (Jakóbczak, 2007) uses the combination h with good features because of orthogonal rows and columns at Hurwitz-Radon family of matrices (Jakóbczak, 2010):

Figure 5. PNC modeling for nine reconstructed points between nodes

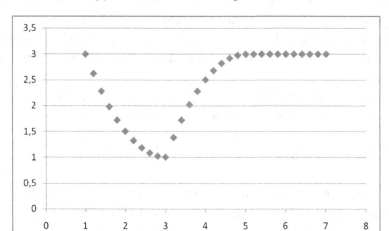

Figure 6. PNC modeling of letter "r" with four nodes

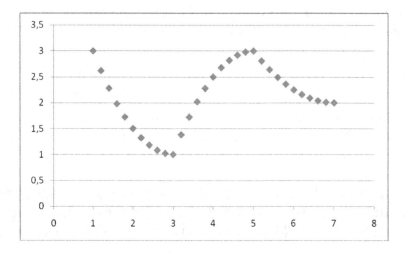

$$h(p_i, p_{i+1}) = \frac{y_i}{x_i} x_{i+1} + \frac{y_{i+1}}{x_{i+1}} x_i$$

and then

$$y(c) = \gamma \cdot y_i + (1 - \gamma)y_{i+1} + \gamma(1 - \gamma) \cdot h(p_i, p_{i+1},).$$

Figure 7. PNC modeling of handwritten letter "r"

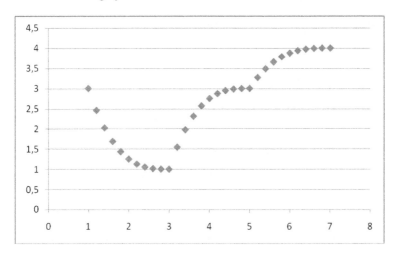

Here are two examples of PNC modeling (Jakóbczak, 2011) with MHR combination.

Person D: Nodes (1;3), (3;1), (5;3) and $\gamma = F(\alpha) = \alpha^2$: (see Figure 8)
Person E: Nodes (1;3), (3;1), (5;3) and $\gamma = F(\alpha) = \alpha^{1.5}$: (see Figure 9)

Figures 5- 9 show modeling of letter "r". Now let us consider a letter "w" with nodes combination $h = 0$.

Figure 8. PNC modeling of letter "r" with three nodes

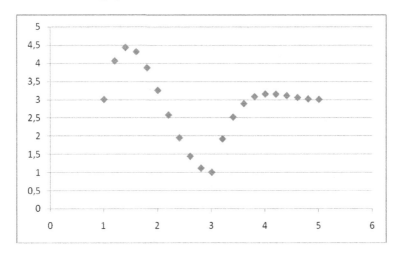

Figure 9. PNC modeling of handwritten letter "r"

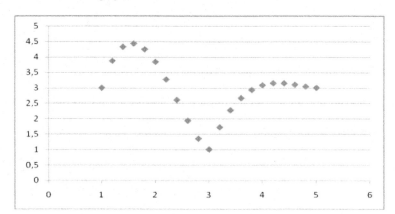

Person A: Nodes (2;2), (3;1), (4;2), (5;1), (6;2) and $\gamma = F(\alpha) = (5^{\alpha}-1)/4$:
(see Figure 10)
Person B: Nodes (2;2), (3;1), (4;2), (5;1), (6;2) and $\gamma = F(\alpha) = sin(\alpha \cdot \pi/2)$:
(see Figure 11)
Person C: Nodes (2;2), (3;1), (4;2), (5;1), (6;2) and $\gamma = F(\alpha) = sin^{3.5}(\alpha \cdot \pi/2)$:
(see Figure 12)

These three versions of letter "*w*" (Figures 10-12) with nodes combination $h = 0$ and the same nodes differ only at probability distribution functions

Figure 10. PNC modeling for nine reconstructed points between nodes

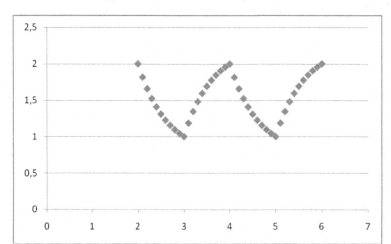

Figure 11. PNC modeling of letter "w" with five nodes

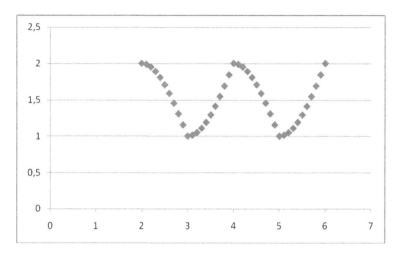

Figure 12. PNC modeling of handwritten letter "w"

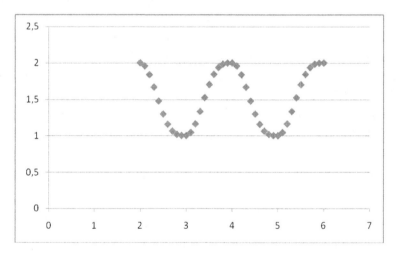

$\gamma = F(\alpha)$. Figure 13 is the example of nodes combination h formula from MHR method.

Person D: Nodes (2;2), (3;1), (4;1), (5;1), (6;2) and $\gamma = F(\alpha) = 2^{\alpha}-1$: (see Figure 13)

Examples above have one function $\gamma = F(\alpha)$ and one combination h for all ranges between nodes. But it is possible to create a model with functions $\gamma_i =$

Figure 13. PNC modeling for nine reconstructed points between nodes

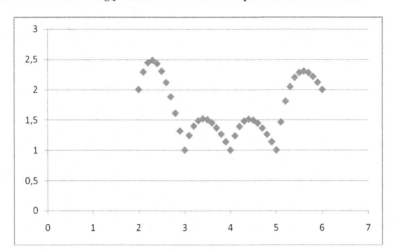

$F_i(\alpha)$ and combinations h_i individually for a range of nodes $(p_i;p_{i+1})$. It enables very precise modeling of handwritten symbol between each successive pair of nodes. Each person has its own characteristic and individual handwritten letters, numbers or other marks. The range of coefficients x has to be the same for all models because of comparing appropriate coordinates y. Every letter is modeled by PNC via three factors: the set of nodes, probability distribution function $\gamma = F(\alpha)$ and nodes combination h. These three factors are chosen individually for each letter, therefore this information about modeled letters seems to be enough for specific PNC curve interpolation, comparing and handwriting identification. Function γ is selected via the analysis of points between nodes and we may assume $h = 0$ at the beginning. What is very important-PNC modeling is independent of the language or a kind of symbol (letters, numbers or others). One person may have several patterns for one handwritten letter. Summarize: every person has the basis of patterns for each handwritten letter or symbol, described by the set of nodes, probability distribution function $\gamma = F(\alpha)$ and nodes combination h. Whole basis of patterns consists of models S_j for $j = 0,1,2,3...K$.

Unknown Writer: Points of Handwritten Symbol

Choice of characteristic points (nodes) for unknown letter or handwritten symbol is a crucial factor in object recognition. The range of coefficients

x has to be the same like the x range in the basis of patterns. Knots of the curve (opened or closed) ought to be settled at key points (Schumaker, 2007), for example local minimum or maximum (the highest point of the curve in a particular orientation), convexity changing or curvature maximum and at least one node between two successive key points (Rogers, 2001). When the nodes are fixed, each coordinate of every chosen point on the curve (x_0^c, y_0^c), $(x_1^c, y_1^c), \ldots, (x_M^c, y_M^c)$ is accessible to be used for comparing with the models. Then probability distribution function $\gamma = F(\alpha)$ and nodes combination h have to be taken from the basis of modeled letters to calculate appropriate second coordinates $y_i^{(j)}$ of the pattern S_j for first coordinates x_i^c, $i = 0,1,\ldots,M$.

Figures 14-16 present a reconstructed signature or a handwritten symbol of unknown writer for 17 nodes (red dots). These three interpolations (Figures 14-16) are calculated for PNC method in MHR version where probability distribution function is $\gamma = F(\alpha) = \alpha^2$. Figure 14 is computed for Hurwitz-Radon matrices of dimension $N = 2$ (MHR-2) and nodes combination h with four ($2N$) points:

Figure 14. MHR-2 curve modeling for 99 reconstructed points between nodes

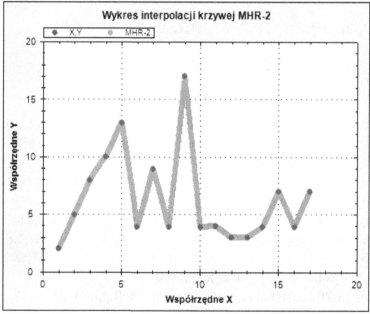

287

Figure 15. MHR-4 interpolation with 99 reconstructed points between nodes

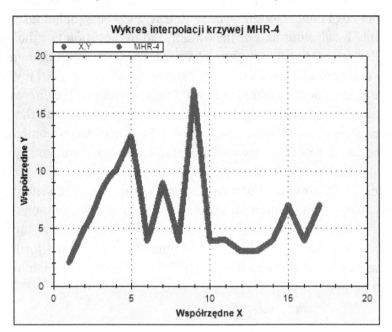

$$h(p_1, p_2, p_3, p_4) = \frac{1}{x_1^2 + x_3^2}(x_1 x_2 y_1 + x_2 x_3 y_3 + x_3 x_4 y_1 - x_1 x_4 y_3)$$
$$+ \frac{1}{x_2^2 + x_4^2}(x_1 x_2 y_2 + x_1 x_4 y_4 + x_3 x_4 y_2 - x_2 x_3 y_4)$$

Figure 15 is reconstructed for unknown author with $h(p_1, p_2, \ldots, p_8)$ build similarly for Hurwitz-Radon matrices of dimension $N = 4$ (MHR-4) and eight ($2N$) successive nodes.

Figure 16 is reconstructed with $h(p_1, p_2, \ldots, p_{16})$ build similarly for Hurwitz-Radon matrices of dimension $N=8$ (MHR-8) and sixteen ($2N$) successive nodes.

Figure 17 represents the comparison of three curves from Figures 14-16. There are minimal differences between MHR-2, MHR-4 and MHR-8 because of orthogonal Hurwitz-Radon matrices. Important feature of MHR and then PNC method is the stability of calculations.

Figures 18-20 consist of Lagrange (Ralston & Rabinowitz, 2001) classical polynomial interpolations (Collins, 2003) for the same 17 nodes as Figures 14-17. Figure 18 represents four splined polynomials (Chapra, 2012) of degree 4, each polynomial is built for five successive nodes.

Figure 16. MHR-8 method for 99 reconstructed points between nodes

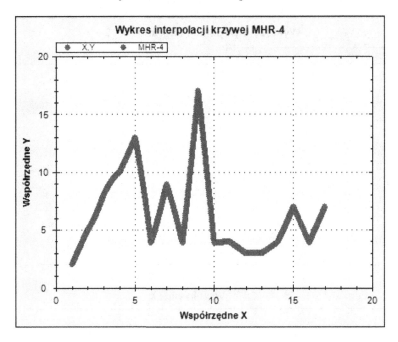

Figure 17. Three versions of MHR method for the same nodes are almost identical

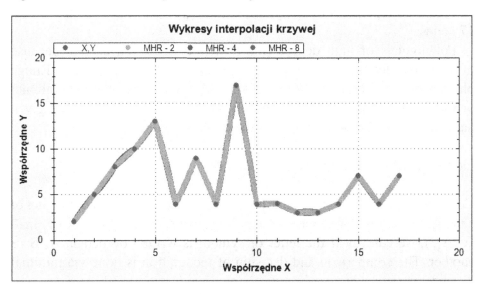

Figure 18. Four splined interpolation polynomials of degree 4

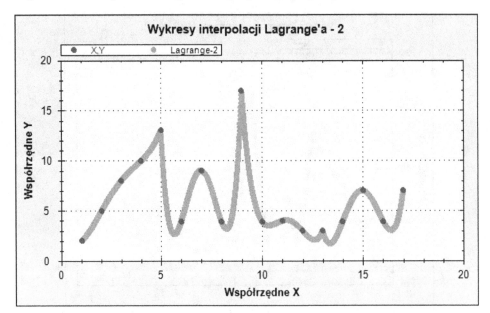

Figure 19 represents two splined polynomials of degree 8, each polynomial is built for nine successive nodes.

Figure 20 represents the polynomial of degree 16, which is built for all 17 nodes.

Polynomials of high degree (more then 4) are often useless because of some bad features (Dahlquist & Bjoerck, 1974): roots (zeros), Runge phenomenon and others. PNC modeling is more accurate then polynomial or spline interpolations. After interpolation it is possible to compare given handwritten symbol with a letter in the basis of patterns.

Decision of Recognition: The Author

Comparing the results of PNC interpolation for required second coordinates of a model in the basis of patterns with points on the curve (x_0^c, y_0^c), (x_1^c, y_1^c),…, (x_M^c, y_M^c), we can say if the letter or symbol is written by person A, B or another. The comparison and decision of recognition is done via minimal distance criterion. Curve points of unknown handwritten symbol are: (x_0^c, y_0^c), (x_1^c, y_1^c),…, (x_M^c, y_M^c). The criterion of recognition for models $S_j = \{(x_0^c, y_0^{(j)})$, $(x_1^c, y_1^{(j)})$,…, $(x_M^c, y_M^{(j)})\}$, $j=0,1,2,3…K$ is given as:

Figure 19. Two splined interpolation polynomials of degree 8

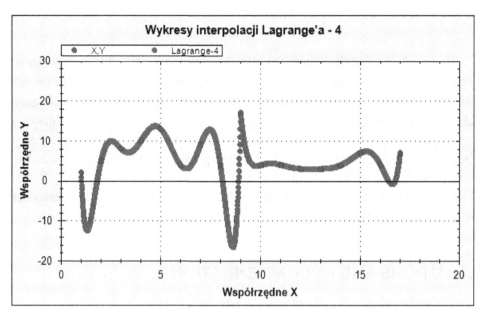

Figure 20. Interpolation polynomial of degree 16

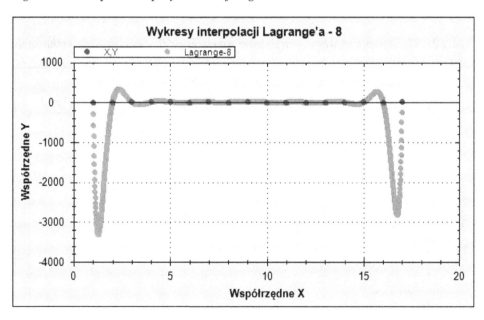

$$\sum_{i=0}^{M} \left| y_i^{\,c} - y_i^{\,(j)} \right| \to \min .$$

Figures 21 and 22 show how the criterion is used for $M = 1600$ (number of reconstructed points together with nodes in Figure 14-16 is 1601) and $j = 0,1$ (an easy example with two persons S_0 and S_1 in the basis of patterns). Figure 21 with the model S_0 presents less differences between graphs (or between coordinates) then Figure 22 with the model S_1. So using two persons from the basis of patterns, our unknown writer (pink curve) is recognized as the pattern S_0 from Figure 21 (orange curve).

Minimal distance criterion helps us to fix a candidate for unknown writer as a person from the model S_0 .

SOLUTIONS AND RECOMMENDATIONS

Proposed method, called Probabilistic Features Combination (PFC), is the method of 2D curve interpolation and extrapolation using the set of key points (knots or nodes). Nodes can be treated as characteristic points of data

Figure 21. The comparison between unknown writer and first person S_0 from the basis

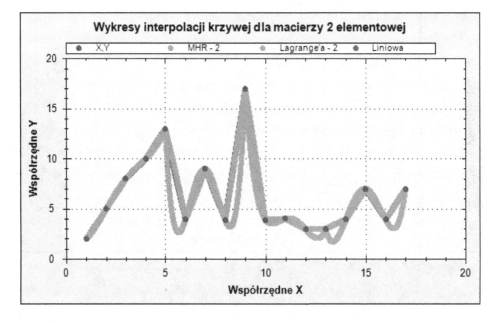

Figure 22. The comparison between unknown writer and second person S_1 from the basis

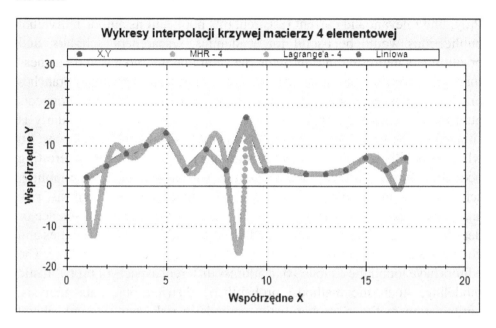

for modeling and analyzing. The model of data can be built by choice of probability distribution function and nodes combination. PFC modeling via nodes combination and parameter γ as probability distribution function enables value anticipation in risk analysis and decision making. Two-dimensional curve is extrapolated and interpolated via nodes combination and different functions as discrete or continuous probability distribution functions: polynomial, sine, cosine, tangent, cotangent, logarithm, exponent, arc sin, arc cos, arc tan, arc cot or power function.

FUTURE RESEARCH DIRECTIONS

Future trends will go to various directions: how to fix the best probability distribution function for the nodes, how to calculate the most appropriate nodes combination and what extrapolation is the most valuable in decision making and risk analysis.

FINAL CONCLUSION

Providing relevant and current research, this book and its author'individual publications would be useful for academics, researchers, scholars, and practitioners interested in improving decision making models and business functions. Probabilistic modeling represents a subject arising in many branches of mathematics, economics and computer science. Such modeling connects pure mathematics with applied sciences. Operations research similarly is situated on the border between pure mathematics and applied sciences. So when probabilistic modeling meets operations research, it is very interesting occasion. Our life and work are impossible without planning, time-tabling, scheduling, decision making, optimization, simulation, data analysis, risk analysis and process modeling. Thus, it is a part of management science or decision science. This book looks to discuss and address the difficulties and challenges that occur during the process of planning or decision making. The editors have found the chapters that address different aspects of probabilistic modeling, stochastic methods, probabilistic distributions, data analysis, optimization methods, probabilistic methods in risk analysis, and related topics. Additionally, the book explores the impact of such probabilistic modeling with other approaches.

This comprehensive and timely publication aims to be an essential reference source, building on the available literature in the field of probabilistic modeling, operational research, planning and scheduling, data extrapolation in decision making, probabilistic interpolation and extrapolation in simulation, stochastic processes, and decision analysis. It is hoped that this text will provide the resources necessary for economics and management sciences, also for mathematics and computer sciences. Decision makers, academicians, researchers, advanced-level students, technology developers, and government officials will find this text useful in furthering their research exposure to pertinent topics in operations research and assisting in furthering their own research efforts in this field. Proposed method, called Probabilistic Features Combination (PFC), is the method of 2D curve interpolation and extrapolation using the set of key points (knots or nodes). Nodes can be treated as characteristic points of data for modeling and analyzing. The model of data can be built by choice of probability distribution function and nodes combination. PFC modeling via nodes combination and parameter γ as probability distribution function enables value anticipation in risk analysis and decision making. Two-dimensional curve is extrapolated and interpolated via nodes combination and different functions as discrete or continuous probability distribution functions: polynomial, sine, cosine, tangent, cotangent, logarithm, exponent, arc sin, arc cos, arc tan, arc cot or power function.

Risk analysis needs suitable methods of data extrapolation and decision making. Proposed method of Hurwitz-Radon Matrices (MHR) can be used in extrapolation and interpolation of curves in the plane. For example quotations from the Stock Exchange, the market prices or rate of a currency form a curve. This chapter contains the way of data anticipation and extrapolation via MHR method and decision making: to buy or not, to sell or not. Proposed method is based on a family of Hurwitz-Radon (HR) matrices. The matrices are skew-symmetric and possess columns composed of orthogonal vectors. The operator of Hurwitz-Radon (OHR), built from these matrices, is described. Two-dimensional data are represented by the set of curve points. It is shown how to create the orthogonal and discrete OHR and how to use it in a process of data foreseeing and extrapolation. MHR method is interpolating and extrapolating the curve point by point without using any formula or function.

Proposed method, called Probabilistic Nodes Combination (PNC), is the method of 2D curve interpolation and extrapolation using the set of key points (knots or nodes). Nodes can be treated as characteristic points of data for modeling and analyzing. The model of data can be built by choice of probability distribution function and nodes combination. PNC modeling via nodes combination and parameter γ as probability distribution function enables value anticipation in risk analysis and decision making. Two-dimensional curve is extrapolated and interpolated via nodes combination and different functions as discrete or continuous probability distribution functions: polynomial, sine, cosine, tangent, cotangent, logarithm, exponent, arc sin, arc cos, arc tan, arc cot or power function. Novelty of this book consists of two generalizations: generalization of previous MHR method with various nodes combinations and generalization of linear interpolation with different (no basic) probability distribution functions and nodes combinations. Computer vision needs suitable methods of shape representation and contour reconstruction. One of them, invented by the author and called method of Hurwitz-Radon Matrices (MHR), can be used in representation and reconstruction of shapes of the objects in the plane. Proposed method is based on a family of Hurwitz-Radon (HR) matrices. The matrices are skew-symmetric and possess columns composed of orthogonal vectors. 2D shape is represented by the set of successive nodes. It is shown how to create the orthogonal and discrete OHR operator and how to use it in a process of shape representation and reconstruction. Then MHR method is generalized to Probabilistic Nodes Combination (PNC) method.

This work clarifies the significance and novelty of the proposed method compared to existing methods (for example polynomial interpolations and Bézier curves). Previous published papers of the author were dealing with the method of Hurwitz-Radon Matrices (MHR method). Novelty of this monograph and proposed method consists in the fact that calculations are free from the family of Hurwitz-Radon Matrices. Problem statement of this book is: how to reconstruct (interpolate) missing points of 2D curve having the set of interpolation nodes (key points) and using the information about probabilistic distribution of unknown points. For example the simplest basic distribution leads to the easiest interpolation – linear interpolation. Apart from probability distribution, additionally there is the second factor of proposed interpolation method: nodes combination. The simplest nodes combination is zero. Thus proposed curve modeling is based on two agents: probability distribution and nodes combination. Significance of this chapter consists in generalization for MHR method: the computations are done without matrices in curve fitting and shape modeling, with clear point interpolation formula based on probability distribution function (continuous or discrete) and nodes combination. This book also consists of generalization for linear interpolation with different (no basic) probability distribution functions and nodes combinations. So this chapter answers the question: "Why and when should we use PNC method?".

Curve interpolation represents one of the most important problems in mathematics and computer science: how to model the curve via discrete set of two-dimensional points? Also the matter of shape representation (as closed curve-contour) and curve parameterization is still opened. For example pattern recognition, signature verification or handwriting identification problems are based on curve modeling via the choice of key points. So interpolation is not only a pure mathematical problem but important task in computer vision and artificial intelligence. The book wants to approach a problem of curve modeling by characteristic points. Proposed method relies on nodes combination and functional modeling of curve points situated between the basic set of key points. The functions that are used in calculations represent whole family of elementary functions with inverse functions: polynomials, trigonometric, cyclometric, logarithmic, exponential and power function. These functions are treated as probability distribution functions in the range [0;1]. Significant problem in machine vision and computer vision is that of appropriate 2D shape representation and reconstruction. Classical discussion about shape representation is based on the problem: contour versus skeleton. This monograph is voting for contour which forms boundary of the object.

Contour of the object, represented by successive contour points, consists of information which allows us to describe many important features of the object as shape coefficients. 2D curve modeling and generation is a basic subject in many branches of industry and computer science, for example in the cad/cam software. The representation of shape can have a great impact on the accuracy and effectiveness of object recognition. In the literature, shape has been represented by many options including curves, graph-based algorithms and medial axis to enable shape-based object recognition. Digital 2D curve (open or closed) can be represented by chain code (Freeman's code). Chain code depends on selection of the started point and transformations of the object. So Freeman's code is one of the method how to describe and to find contour of the object. Analog (continuous) version of Freeman's code is the curve α-*s*. Another contour representation and reconstruction is based on Fourier coefficients calculated in discrete Fourier transformation (DFT). These coefficients are used to fix similarity of the contours with different sizes or directions. If we assume that contour is built from segments of a line and fragments of circles or ellipses, hough transformation is applied to detect contour lines. Also geometrical moments of the object are used during the process of object shape representation. Contour is also applied in shape decomposition. Many branches of medicine, industry and manufacturing are looking for methods connected with geometry of the contour.

Why and when should we use MHR and PNC methods? Interpolation methods and curve fitting represent so huge problem that each individual interpolation is exceptional and requires specific solutions. PNC method is such a novel tool with its all pros and cons. The user has to decide which interpolation method is the best in a single situation. The choice is yours if you have any choice. Presented method is such a new possibility for curve fitting and interpolation when specific data (for example handwritten symbol or character) starts up with no rules for polynomial interpolation. This chapter consists of two generalizations: generalization of previous MHR method with various nodes combinations and generalization of linear interpolation with different (no basic) probability distribution functions and nodes combinations. The method of Probabilistic Nodes Combination (PNC) enables interpolation and modeling of two-dimensional curves using nodes combinations and different coefficients γ: polynomial, sinusoidal, cosinusoidal, tangent, cotangent, logarithmic, exponential, arc sin, arc cos, arc tan, arc cot or power function, also inverse functions. This probabilistic view is novel approach a problem of modeling and interpolation. Computer vision and pattern recognition are interested in appropriate methods of shape representation and curve modeling. PNC method represents the possibilities of shape reconstruction and curve interpolation via the choice of nodes combination and probability distribution function for interpolated points. It seems to be quite new look at the problem of contour representation and curve modeling in artificial intelligence and computer vision.

Function for γ calculations is chosen individually at each curve modeling and it is treated as probability distribution function: γ depends on initial requirements and curve specifications. PNC method leads to curve interpolation as handwriting modeling via discrete set of fixed knots. So PNC makes possible the combination of two important problems: interpolation and modeling. Main features of PNC method are:

1. The smaller distance between knots the better;
2. Calculations for coordinates close to zero and near by extremum require more attention because of importance of these points;
3. PNC interpolation develops a linear interpolation into other functions as probability distribution functions;
4. PNC is a generalization of MHR method via different nodes combinations;
5. Interpolation of L points is connected with the computational cost of rank $O(L)$ as in MHR method;
6. Nodes combination and coefficient γ are crucial in the process of curve probabilistic parameterization and interpolation: they are computed individually for a single curve.

What is the most important feature of MHR and PNC methods? Interpolation methods and curve fitting represent so huge problem that each individual interpolation is exceptional and requires specific solutions. PNC method is such a novel tool with its all pros and cons. The user has to decide which interpolation method is the best in a single situation. The choice is yours if you have any choice. Presented method is such a new possibility for curve fitting and interpolation when specific data (for example handwritten symbol or character) starts up with no rules for polynomial interpolation. This chapter consists of two generalizations: generalization of previous MHR method with various nodes combinations and generalization of linear interpolation with different (no basic) probability distribution functions and nodes combinations. The method of Probabilistic Nodes Combination (PNC) enables interpolation and modeling of two-dimensional curves using nodes combinations and different coefficients γ: polynomial, sinusoidal, cosinusoidal, tangent, cotangent, logarithmic, exponential, arc sin, arc cos, arc tan, arc cot or power function, also inverse functions. This probabilistic view is novel approach a problem of modeling and interpolation. Computer vision and pattern recognition are interested in appropriate methods of shape representation and curve modeling. PNC method represents the possibilities of shape reconstruction and curve interpolation via the choice of nodes combination and probability distribution function for interpolated points. It seems to be quite new look at the problem of contour representation and curve modeling in artificial intelligence and computer vision. Function for γ calculations is chosen individually at each curve modeling and it is treated as probability distribution function: γ depends on initial requirements and curve specifications. PNC method leads to curve interpolation as handwriting modeling via discrete set of fixed knots. So PNC makes possible the combination of two important problems: interpolation and modeling. The method of Probabilistic Features Combination (PFC) enables interpolation and modeling of high-dimensional N data using features' combinations and different coefficients γ: polynomial, sinusoidal, cosinusoidal, tangent, cotangent, logarithmic, exponential, arc sin, arc cos, arc tan, arc cot or power function. Functions for γ calculations are chosen individually at each data modeling and it is treated as N-dimensional probability distribution function: γ depends on initial requirements and features' specifications. PFC method leads to data interpolation as handwriting or signature identification and image retrieval via discrete set of feature vectors in N-dimensional feature space. So PFC method makes possible the combination of two important problems: interpolation and modeling in a matter of image retrieval or writer identification. Main features of PFC method are: PFC interpolation develops a linear interpolation in multidimensional feature spaces into other functions as N-dimensional probability distribution functions; PFC is a generalization of MHR method and PNC method via different nodes combinations; interpolation of L points is connected with the computational cost of rank $O(L)$ as in MHR and PNC method; nodes combination and coefficients γ are crucial in the process of data probabilistic parameterization and interpolation: they are computed individually for a single feature. Future works are going to applications of PFC method in signature and handwriting biometric recognition: choice and features of nodes combinations h and coefficients γ.

Proposed method, called Probabilistic Features Combination (PFC), is the method of N-dimensional data interpolation and extrapolation using the set of key points (knots or nodes). Nodes can be treated as characteristic points of data for modeling and analyzing. The model of data can be built by choice of probability distribution function and nodes combination. PFC modeling via nodes combination and parameter γ as probability distribution function enables value anticipation in risk analysis and decision making. *N*-dimensional object is extrapolated and interpolated via nodes combination and different functions as discrete or continuous probability distribution functions: polynomial, sine, cosine, tangent, cotangent, logarithm, exponent, arc sin, arc cos, arc tan, arc cot or power function. The method of Probabilistic Features Combination (PFC) enables interpolation and modeling of high-dimensional data using features' combinations and different coefficients γ as modeling function. Functions for γ calculations are chosen individually at each data modeling and it is treated as *N*-dimensional probability distribution function: γ depends on initial requirements and features' specifications. PFC method leads to data interpolation as handwriting or signature identification and image retrieval via discrete set of feature vectors in N-dimensional feature space. So PFC method makes possible the combination of two important problems: interpolation and modeling in a matter of image retrieval or writer identification. PFC interpolation develops a linear interpolation in multidimensional feature spaces into other functions as *N*-dimensional probability distribution functions. Future works are going to applications of PFC method in biometric recognition, computer vision and artificial intelligence. Nodes are treated as characteristic points of data for modeling and analyzing. The model of data can be built by choice of probability distribution function and nodes combination. PFC modeling via nodes combination and parameter γ as probability distribution function enables value anticipation in risk analysis and decision making. Two-dimensional object is extrapolated and interpolated via nodes combination and different functions as discrete or continuous probability distribution functions: polynomial, sine, cosine, tangent, cotangent, logarithm, exponent, arc sin, arc cos, arc tan, arc cot or power function. Functions for γ calculations are chosen individually at each data modeling and it is treated as 2-dimensional probability distribution function: γ depends on initial requirements and features' specifications. PFC method leads to data interpolation as handwriting or signature identification and image retrieval via discrete set of feature vectors in 2-dimensional feature space. So PFC method makes possible the combination of two important problems: interpolation and modeling in a matter of image retrieval or writer identification. PFC interpolation develops a linear interpolation in multidimensional feature spaces into other functions as two-dimensional probability distribution functions. Future works are going to applications of PFC method in biometric recognition, computer vision and artificial intelligence.

Future works are going to: application of PNC method in signature and handwriting recognition, choice and features of nodes combinations and coefficient γ, implementation of PNC in computer vision and artificial intelligence: shape geometry, contour modelling, object recognition and curve parameterization.

REFERENCES

Ballard, D. H. (1982). *Computer Vision*. New York: Prentice Hall.

Chapra, S. C. (2012). *Applied Numerical Methods*. McGraw-Hill.

Choraś, R. S. (2005). *Computer Vision*. Warsaw, Poland: Exit.

Cocozza-Thivent, C., Eymard, R., Mercier, S., & Roussignol, M. (2006). Characterization of the Marginal Distributions of Markov Processes Used in Dynamic Reliability. *Journal of Applied Mathematics and Stochastic Analysis*, 1–18.

Collins, G. W. II. (2003). *Fundamental Numerical Methods and Data Analysis*. Case Western Reserve University.

Dahlquist, G., & Bjoerck, A. (1974). *Numerical Methods*. New York: Prentice Hall.

Dejdumrong, N. (2007). A Shape Preserving Verification Techniques for Parametric Curves. *Computer Graphics, Imaging and Visualization*, 163–168.

Dyn, N., Levin, D., & Gregory, J. A. (1987). A 4-Point Interpolatory Subdivision Scheme for Curve Design. *Computer Aided Geometric Design*, *4*(4), 257–268. doi:10.1016/0167-8396(87)90001-X

Jakóbczak, D. (2007). 2D and 3D Image Modeling Using Hurwitz-Radon Matrices. *Polish Journal of Environmental Studies*, *4A*(16), 104–107.

Jakóbczak, D. (2009). Curve Interpolation Using Hurwitz-Radon Matrices. *Polish Journal of Environmental Studies*, *3B*(18), 126–130.

Jakóbczak, D. (2010a). Shape Representation and Shape Coefficients via Method of Hurwitz-Radon Matrices. *Lecture Notes in Computer Science*, *6374*, 411–419. doi:10.1007/978-3-642-15910-7_47

Jakóbczak, D. (2010b). Object Modeling Using Method of Hurwitz-Radon Matrices of Rank k. In W. Wolski & M. Borawski (Eds.), *Computer Graphics: Selected Issues* (pp. 79–90). Szczecin, Poland: University of Szczecin Press.

Jakóbczak, D. (2011a). Curve Parameterization and Curvature via Method of Hurwitz-Radon Matrices. *Image Processing & Communications- International Journal (Toronto, Ont.)*, *1-2*(16), 49–56.

Jakóbczak, D. (2011b). Data Extrapolation and Decision Making via Method of Hurwitz-Radon Matrices. *Lecture Notes in Computer Science*, *6922*, 173–182. doi:10.1007/978-3-642-23935-9_17

Jakóbczak, D. (2011c). Curve Extrapolation and Data Analysis using the Method of Hurwitz-Radon Matrices. *Folia Oeconomica Stetinensia*, *9*(17), 121-138.

Jakóbczak, D. (2013). Probabilistic Modeling of Signature using the Method of Hurwitz-Radon Matrices. *Global Perspectives on Artificial Intelligence*, *1*(1), 1–7.

Kozera, R. (2004). *Curve Modeling via Interpolation Based on Multidimensional Reduced Data*. Gliwice, Poland: Silesian University of Technology Press.

Liu, T., & Geiger, D. (1999). Approximate tree matching and shape similarity. *Int. Conf. Computer Vision,* Corfu, Greece.

Lorton, A., Fouladirad, M., & Grall, A. (2013). A Methodology for Probabilistic Model-based Prognosis. *European Journal of Operational Research*, *225*(3), 443–454. doi:10.1016/j.ejor.2012.10.025

Pergler, M., & Freeman, A. (2008). Probabilistic Modeling as an Exploratory Decision-Making Tool. *McKinsey Working Papers on Risk, 6*, 1-18.

Ralston, A., & Rabinowitz, P. (2001). *A First Course in Numerical Analysis* (2nd ed.). New York: Dover Publications.

Rogers, D. F. (2001). *An Introduction to NURBS with Historical Perspective*. Morgan Kaufmann Publishers.

Saber, E., Xu, Y., & Murat Tekalp, A. (2005). Partial shape recognition by sub-matrix matching for partial matching guided image labeling. *Pattern Recognition*, *38*(10), 1560–1573. doi:10.1016/j.patcog.2005.03.027

Schumaker, L. L. (2007). *Spline Functions: Basic Theory*. Cambridge Mathematical Library. doi:10.1017/CBO9780511618994

Sebastian, T. B., Klein, P. N., & Kimia, B. B. (2003). On aligning curves. *IEEE Transactions on Pattern Analysis and Machine Intelligence*, 25(1), 116–124. doi:10.1109/TPAMI.2003.1159951

Tadeusiewicz, R., & Flasiński, M. (1991). *Image Recognition*. Warsaw, Poland: PWN.

Zhang, D., & Lu, G. (2004). Review of Shape Representation and Description Techniques. *Pattern Recognition*, 1(37), 1–19. doi:10.1016/j.patcog.2003.07.008

ADDITIONAL READING

Basu, S., & Bresler, Y. (2000). O($N^2\log_2 N$) filtered backprojection reconstruction algorithm for tomography. *IEEE Transactions on Image Processing*, 9(10), 1760–1773. doi:10.1109/83.869187 PMID:18262914

Brankov, J. G., Yang, Y., & Wernick, M. N. (2004). Tomographic image reconstruction based on a Content – Adaptive Mesh Model. *IEEE Transactions on Medical Imaging*, 2(23), 202–212. doi:10.1109/TMI.2003.822822 PMID:14964565

Brasse, D., & Defrise, M. (2004). Fast fully 3-D image reconstruction in PET using planograms. *IEEE Transactions on Medical Imaging*, 4(23), 413–425. doi:10.1109/TMI.2004.824231 PMID:15084067

Bulacu, M., & Schomaker, L. (2007). Text-independent writer identification and verification using textural and allographic features. *IEEE Transactions on Pattern Analysis and Machine Intelligence*, 29(4), 701–717. doi:10.1109/TPAMI.2007.1009 PMID:17299226

Bulacu, M., Schomaker, L., & Brink, A. (2007). *Text-independent writer identification and verification on off-line Arabic handwriting*. In: *International Conference on Document Analysis and Recognition*. 769–773.

Cetin, M., Karl, W. C., & Willsky, A. S. (2002, September). *Edge – preserving image reconstruction for coherent imaging application.* Paper presented at the IEEE International Conference on Image Processsing, Rochester, NY, USA. doi:10.1109/ICIP.2002.1039992

Chen, J., Cheng, W., & Lopresti, D. (2011). Using perturbed handwriting to support writer identification in the presence of severe data constraints. In: Document Recognition and Retrieval. 1–10. doi:10.1117/12.876497

Chen, J., Lopresti, D., & Kavallieratou, E. (2010). *The impact of ruling lines on writer identification.* In: *International Conference on Frontiers in Handwriting Recognition.* 439–444. doi:10.1109/ICFHR.2010.75

Chlebus, E., & Cholewa, M. (1999). Rapid prototyping – rapid tooling. *CADCAM Forum, 11*, 23-28.

Cormen, T. H., Leiserson, C. E., & Rivest, R. L. (1996). *Introduction to algorithms.* Massachusetts, USA: the Massachusetts Institute of Technology Press and McGraw-Hill.

Defrise, M. (2001). A short readers guide to 3D tomographic reconstruction. *Computerized Medical Imaging and Graphics, 25*(2), 113–116. doi:10.1016/S0895-6111(00)00061-6 PMID:11137787

Djeddi, C., & Souici-Meslati, L. (2010). *A texture based approach for Arabic writer identification and verification.* In: *International Conference on Machine and Web Intelligence.* 115–120.

Djeddi, C., & Souici-Meslati, L. (2011). *Artificial immune recognition system for Arabic writer identification.* In: *International Symposium on Innovation in Information and Communication Technology.* 159–165. doi:10.1109/ISIICT.2011.6149612

Dryja, M., Jankowska, J., & Jankowski, M. (1982). *Survey of numerical methods and algorithms. Part II.* Warsaw, Poland: WNT.

Eldar, Y. C. (2001). *Quantum Signal Processing.* (Unpublished doctoral dissertation). Massachusetts Institute of Technology, USA.

Eldar, Y. C., & Oppenheim, A. V. (2002). Quantum Signal Processing. *IEEE Signal Processing Magazine, 6*(19), 12–32. doi:10.1109/MSP.2002.1043298

Fortuna, Z., Macukow, B., & Wąsowski, J. (1982). *Numerical methods.* Warsaw, Poland: WNT.

Galloway, M. M. (1975). Texture analysis using gray level run lengths. *Computer Graphics and Image Processing, 4*(2), 172–179. doi:10.1016/S0146-664X(75)80008-6

Garain, U., & Paquet, T. (2009). *Off-line multi-script writer identification using AR coefficients*. In: *International Conference on Document Analysis and Recognition*. 991–995. doi:10.1109/ICDAR.2009.222

Ghiasi, G., & Safabakhsh, R. (2013). Offline text-independent writer identification using codebook and efficient code extraction methods. *Image and Vision Computing, 31*(5), 379–391. doi:10.1016/j.imavis.2013.03.002

Jakóbczak, D. (2005). Hurwitz-Radon matrices and their children. *Computer Science, 5*(8), 29–38.

Jakóbczak, D. J. (2014). *2D Curve Modeling via the Method of Probabilistic Nodes Combination-Shape Representation, Object Modeling and Curve Interpolation-Extrapolation with the Applications*. Saarbrucken: LAP Lambert Academic Publishing.

Jankowska, J., & Jankowski, M. (1981). *Survey of numerical methods and algorithms. Part I*. Warsaw, Poland: WNT.

Kontaxakis, G., & Strauss, L. G. (1998). Maximum likelihood algorithms for image reconstruction in Positron Emission Tomography. *Radionuclides for Oncology – Current Status and Future Aspects, 1998,* 73-106.

Kowalczuk, Z., & Wiszniewski, B. (Eds.). (2007). *Intelligent data mining in diagnostic purposes: Automatics and informatics*. Gdansk, Poland: PWNT.

Kundur, D., & Hatzinakos, D. (1998). A novel blind deconvolution scheme for image restoration using recursive filtering. *IEEE Transactions on Signal Processing, 2*(46), 375–390. doi:10.1109/78.655423

Laine, A., & Zong, X. (1996). *Border identification of echocardiograms via multiscale edge detection and shape modeling*. Paper presented at the IEEE International Conference on Image Processsing, Lausanne, Switzerland. doi:10.1109/ICIP.1996.560486

Lang, S. (1970). *Algebra*. Reading, Massachusetts, USA: Addison-Wesley Publishing Company.

Le Buhan Jordan, C., Bossen, F., & Ebrahimi, T. (1997). *Scalable shape representation for content based visual data compression.* Paper presented at the International Conference on Image Processing, Santa Barbara, CA, USA. doi:10.1109/ICIP.1997.647962

Marker, J., Braude, I., Museth, K., & Breen, D. (2006). Contour-based surface reconstruction using implicit curve fitting, and distance field filtering and interpolation. *Volume Graphics, 2006,* 1–9.

Marti, U.-V., & Bunke, H. (2002). The IAM-database: An English sentence database for offline handwriting recognition. *Int. J. Doc. Anal. Recognit., 5*(1), 39–46. doi:10.1007/s100320200071

Meyer, Y. (1993). *Wavelets: algorithms & applications.* Philadelphia, USA: Society for Industrial and Applied Mathematics.

Nosary, A., Heutte, L., & Paquet, T. (2004). Unsupervised writer adaption applied to handwritten text recognition. *Pattern Recognition Letters, 37*(2), 385–388. doi:10.1016/S0031-3203(03)00185-7

Ozaki, M., Adachi, Y., & Ishii, N. (2006). *Examination of effects of character size on accuracy of writer recognition by new local arc method.* In: International Conference on Knowledge- Based Intelligent Information and Engineering Systems. 1170–1175. doi:10.1007/11893004_148

Poggio, T., & Smale, S. (2003). The mathematics of learning: Dealing with data. *Notices of the American Mathematical Society, 5*(50), 537–544.

Przelaskowski, A. (2005). *Data compression.* Warsaw, Poland: BTC.

Rutkowski, L., Siekmann, J., Tadeusiewicz, R., & Zadeh, A. (Eds.). (2004). *Lecture notes on artificial intelligence: Artificial intelligence and soft computing.* Berlin-Heidelberg, Germany: Springer-Verlag.

Schlapbach, A., & Bunke, H. (2004). *Using HMM based recognizers for writer identification and verification. 9th Int. Workshop on Frontiers in Handwriting Recognition.* 167–172. doi:10.1109/IWFHR.2004.107

Schlapbach, A., & Bunke, H. (2006). *Off-line writer identification using Gaussian mixture models.* In: International Conference on Pattern Recognition. 992–995.

Schlapbach, A., & Bunke, H. (2007). A writer identification and verification system using HMM based recognizers. *Pattern Analysis & Applications*, *10*(1), 33–43. doi:10.1007/s10044-006-0047-5

Schomaker, L., Franke, K., & Bulacu, M. (2007). Using codebooks of fragmented connected- component contours in forensic and historic writer identification. *Pattern Recognition Letters*, *28*(6), 719–727. doi:10.1016/j.patrec.2006.08.005

Shahabinejad, F., & Rahmati, M. (2007). A new method for writer identification and verification based on Farsi/Arabic handwritten texts, *Ninth International Conference on Document Analysis and Recognition (ICDAR 2007)*. 829–833.

Siddiqi, I., Cloppet, F., & Vincent, N. (2009). Contour based features for the classification of ancient manuscripts. In: Conference of the International Graphonomics Society. 226–229.

Siddiqi, I., & Vincent, N. (2010). Text independent writer recognition using redundant writing patterns with contour-based orientation and curvature features. *Pattern Recognition Letters*, *43*(11), 3853–3865. doi:10.1016/j.patcog.2010.05.019

Vakhania, N. (1993). Orthogonal random vectors and the Hurwitz – Radon-Eckmann theorem. *Proc. of the Georgian Academy of Sciences-Mathematics*, *1(1)*, 109-125.

Van, E. M., Vuurpijl, L., Franke, K., & Schomaker, L. (2005). The WANDA measurement tool for forensic document examination. *J. Forensic Doc. Exam.*, *16*, 103–118.

Willis, M. (2000). *Algebraic reconstruction algorithms for remote sensing image enhancement*. Unpublished doctoral dissertation, Department of Electrical and Computer Engineering, Brigham Young University.

Xu, Fang, & Mueller, K. (2005). Accelerating popular tomographic reconstruction algorithms on commodity PC graphics hardware. *IEEE Transactions on Nuclear Science*, *3*(52), 654–661.

Zaletelj, J., & Tasic, J. F. (2003). *Optimization and tracking of polygon vertices for shape coding*. Berlin-Heidelberg, Germany: Springer-Verlag. doi:10.1007/978-3-540-45179-2_52

Zhang, J. K., Davidson, T., & Wong, K. M. (2004). Efficient design of orthonormal wavelet bases for signal representation. *IEEE Transactions on Signal Processing*, 7(52), 1983–1996. doi:10.1109/TSP.2004.828923

KEY TERMS AND DEFINITIONS

Artificial Intelligence: Intelligence of machines and computers, as a connection of algorithms and hardware, which makes that a man – human being can be simulated by the machines in analyzing risk, decision making, reasoning, knowledge, planning, learning, communication, perception and the ability to move and manipulate objects.

Contour Modeling: Calculation of unknown points of the object contour having information about some points of the object contour.

Curve Interpolation: Computing new and unknown points of a curve and creating a graph of a curve using existing data points – interpolation nodes.

Data Extrapolation: Calculation of unknown values for the points situated outside the ranges of nodes.

Hurwitz – Radon Matrices: A family of skew – symmetric and orthogonal matrices with columns and rows that create, together with identical matrix, the base in vector spaces of dimensions $N = 2$, 4 or 8.

MHR Method: The method of curve interpolation and extrapolation using linear (convex) combinations of OHR operators.

OHR Operator: Matrix operator of Hurwitz – Radon built from coordinates of interpolation nodes.

About the Author

Dariusz Jacek Jakóbczak was born in Koszalin, Poland, on December 30, 1965. He graduated in mathematics (numerical methods and programming) from the University of Gdansk, Poland in 1990. He received the Ph.D. degree in 2007 in computer science from the Polish-Japanese Institute of Information Technology, Warsaw, Poland. From 1991 to 1994 he was a civilian programmer in the High Military School in Koszalin. He was a teacher of mathematics and computer science in the Private Economic School in Koszalin from 1995 to 1999. Since March 1998 he has worked in the Department of Electronics and Computer Science, Koszalin University of Technology, Poland and since October 2007 he has been an Assistant Professor in the Chair of Computer Science and Management in this department. His research interests connect mathematics with computer science and include computer vision, artificial intelligence, shape representation, curve interpolation, contour reconstruction and geometric modeling, numerical methods, probabilistic methods, game theory, operational research and discrete mathematics.

Index

2D curve 1-4, 7, 16, 34-35, 45, 47, 50, 75-78, 87, 89, 120, 133-134, 137, 141, 149-150, 154, 166, 186, 190, 219, 236-238, 258, 270-272, 292, 294-297

3D Visualization 194, 207

3-dimensional probability 179, 181, 185, 200

A

Artificial Intelligence 3, 42, 46-47, 77-78, 85, 99, 120, 123, 133-134, 136, 144, 169, 179, 181, 196, 200-201, 211, 224, 226, 235-236, 260, 269-270, 274, 279-280, 296, 300-301, 308

B

Bézier curves 3, 6, 35, 45, 49-50, 77, 137, 238, 272, 296

biometric recognition 88, 99, 120, 122-124, 136, 168-169, 179, 181, 189, 196, 199-201, 210-211, 219, 224-226, 260, 280, 299-300

C

Classical discussion 4, 46, 78, 134, 136, 149, 154, 236-237, 271, 296

computational cost 2, 5, 7, 21, 32, 34, 122-123, 168, 199, 225, 273, 299

computer vision 1-4, 34, 44, 47-48, 76-78, 87-89, 99, 120-121, 123, 133-136, 141, 144, 149, 154, 166-169, 179, 181, 189, 196, 198, 200-201, 209, 211, 216, 224, 226, 235-237, 239, 258, 260, 269-273, 279, 295-301

Contour 1-2, 4, 33-34, 42, 44, 46-48, 51, 64, 76, 78, 89, 121, 132, 134-136, 141, 145, 149-150, 154-157, 159-160, 162-164, 167-169, 176, 189, 198, 208, 216, 224, 233, 235-236, 238-239, 258, 267, 269, 271-276, 279, 295, 297-299, 301, 308

Contour Modeling 42, 64, 145, 156, 162, 208, 233, 267, 308

Curve Interpolation 2-3, 5, 33-34, 43-44, 46-48, 50, 53, 58, 60, 62, 64, 75-77, 85-86, 88-90, 120-121, 131, 133, 135, 137-138, 141-143, 145, 149, 154, 166-168, 176-177, 179-180, 194, 198-199, 208, 216-217, 223-225, 233, 235-236, 238-239, 258, 268-273, 280, 286, 292, 294-296, 298-299, 308

D

Data Extrapolation 2, 6-7, 24, 34, 43, 53, 85, 104, 107, 116, 131, 176, 186-187, 208, 233, 267, 271, 294-295, 308

data modeling 2, 46, 58, 87, 89-90, 98-99, 116, 122-123, 132, 135, 154, 166, 168-169, 178-181, 196, 199-200, 209-211, 216, 224-226, 260, 273, 299-300

decision making 2, 5-6, 24-25, 29, 31, 33-34, 42, 45-47, 68, 75-76, 78, 85, 89, 99, 116, 120-123, 132, 135, 141, 149, 154, 166, 168-169, 178, 181, 196, 198-200, 211, 223, 225-226, 235, 258-260, 269-271, 273, 293-295, 300, 308

F

fixed knots 76, 121, 135, 154, 167-168, 199, 225, 239, 273, 298-299
Freeman's code 4, 46, 78, 134, 136, 237-238, 272, 297
Function Interpolation 186, 267

H

Handwriting 3, 47, 49, 64, 77, 88-90, 98-99, 103, 116, 121-124, 132-133, 135-136, 144-145, 154, 160, 167-169, 178-181, 188, 190-192, 194, 196, 199-200, 209-211, 216-217, 220-221, 223-226, 235-236, 238-239, 260, 270, 272-273, 279-280, 286, 296, 298-301
handwriting identification 3, 47, 77, 88-89, 133, 144, 179-180, 194, 210, 217, 223, 235-236, 270, 279-280, 286, 296
handwritten letter 51, 57, 64, 67, 88, 90, 96, 145, 148, 179, 181, 186, 194, 210-211, 215, 280, 283-286
Hurwitz-Radon Matrices 1-3, 5-7, 9, 17, 19-20, 33-35, 43, 45, 50, 76-77, 86, 131, 137, 141, 177, 208, 233, 258, 267, 287-288, 295-296, 308

I

image retrieval 87-88, 90, 98-99, 116, 122-123, 132, 135, 160, 168-169, 178-179, 181, 188-189, 192, 196, 199-200, 209-211, 215, 217, 219, 221, 224-226, 260, 273, 299-300
initial requirements 44, 53, 76, 93, 98-99, 116, 121-123, 132, 135, 154, 167-169, 178-179, 181, 183, 196, 199-200, 209, 211, 213, 224-226, 239, 260, 273, 298-300

M

market prices 2, 5, 16, 34, 295
Methods of Quadratures 244, 268

MHR Method 1-7, 9, 16-17, 19-21, 23-28, 30-35, 43, 45, 47, 50, 52-53, 70, 73, 75-77, 86-87, 89, 91, 93, 121-123, 131, 135, 137, 141-142, 149, 167-168, 177, 182-183, 198-199, 208, 212, 224-225, 233, 237, 258-259, 268, 273-276, 279, 281, 285, 289, 295-299, 308
multidimensional data 87, 90, 181, 209-210

N

N-dimensional data 88-89, 98, 122, 168, 179-180, 196, 199, 209-211, 216, 223, 225, 273, 299
N-dimensional probability 88, 92, 94, 98, 122-123, 132, 168-169, 178-179, 196, 199-200, 209-211, 213-214, 224-226, 273, 299-300
Numerical Calculations for Derivative 268

O

Object Interpolation 163, 195, 234
OHR Operator 1, 3, 17, 26, 35, 43, 77, 86, 131, 142, 177, 208, 234, 259, 268, 276-277, 295, 308

P

pattern recognition 3, 44, 47-48, 77, 87-88, 121, 133, 135, 143, 154, 166-167, 178-179, 198, 209-210, 224, 235-236, 239, 269-270, 272, 279-280, 296-297, 299
polynomial interpolations 3, 5, 33, 35, 45, 77, 288, 296
Probabilistic Features 88, 90, 98, 120-123, 132, 166, 168-169, 178-179, 181, 196, 199-200, 209-211, 223-225, 271, 273, 292, 294, 299-300
probabilistic nodes 3, 34-35, 44, 46-47, 50, 75-77, 88-89, 121, 135, 137, 141-142, 149-150, 166-167, 198, 224, 238, 258-259, 269, 272, 279, 295, 297-298
Probabilistic Nodes Combination (PNC) 3, 34-35, 44, 46-47, 50, 75-77, 88-

89, 121, 135, 137, 141-142, 149-150, 166-167, 198, 224, 238, 258-259, 269, 272, 295, 297-298

probability distribution function 3, 34-35, 44-45, 47-48, 50, 57, 64-65, 68, 75-77, 88-89, 94, 98-99, 116, 120-123, 132-133, 135, 137, 141, 145-146, 148-149, 154, 166-169, 178-181, 185-186, 194, 196, 198-200, 209-211, 214, 223-226, 235-236, 239, 258-260, 269-271, 273, 286-287, 293-296, 298-300

R

risk analysis 2, 5-6, 24, 31, 33-34, 46-47, 75-76, 89, 99, 116, 120-123, 135, 141, 149, 154, 166, 168-169, 178, 181, 196, 198-200, 211, 223, 225-226, 258-260, 270-271, 273, 293-295, 300

Root of the Function 255, 268

S

Shape Representation 1-4, 34-35, 44, 46-48, 76-78, 87-88, 121, 133-136, 141-143, 149, 154, 166-167, 177, 198, 224, 235-239, 258-259, 269-272, 295-297, 299

soft computing 89-90, 180-181, 210-211, 216

Surface Interpolation 208

V

Value Anticipation 2, 34, 43, 47, 75-76, 86, 89, 99, 116, 120, 122-123, 131, 135, 141, 149, 154, 166, 168-169, 177-178, 181, 196, 199-200, 208, 211, 223, 225-226, 234, 258-259, 271, 273, 293-295, 300

W

writer identification 89, 98-99, 116, 122-123, 132, 135, 160, 168-169, 179-181, 196, 199-200, 209, 211, 216, 224-226, 260, 273, 280, 299-300

Stay Current on the Latest Emerging Research Developments

Become an IGI Global Reviewer for Authored Book Projects

Premier Reference Source

Solutions for High-Touch Communications in a High-Tech World

Premier Reference Source

Advanced Research on Biologically Inspired Cognitive Architectures

Premier Reference Source

Workforce Development Theory and Practice in the Mental Health Sector

Premier Reference Source

Resource Management and Efficiency in Cloud Computing Environments

The overall success of an authored book project is dependent on quality and timely reviews.

In this competitive age of scholarly publishing, constructive and timely feedback significantly decreases the turnaround time of manuscripts from submission to acceptance, allowing the publication and discovery of progressive research at a much more expeditious rate. Several IGI Global authored book projects are currently seeking highly qualified experts in the field to fill vacancies on their respective editorial review boards:

Applications may be sent to:
development@igi-global.com

Applicants must have a doctorate (or an equivalent degree) as well as publishing and reviewing experience. Reviewers are asked to write reviews in a timely, collegial, and constructive manner. All reviewers will begin their role on an ad-hoc basis for a period of one year, and upon successful completion of this term can be considered for full editorial review board status, with the potential for a subsequent promotion to Associate Editor.

If you have a colleague that may be interested in this opportunity, we encourage you to share this information with them.

Printed in the United States
By Bookmasters